The Eighteenth-Century
English Stage

Essays on

The Eighteenth-Century English Stage

Edited by Kenneth Richards
and Peter Thomson

*The Proceedings of a Symposium
sponsored by the Manchester University
Department of Drama*

Methuen & Co Ltd
11 New Fetter Lane London EC4P 4EE

First published in 1972
by Methuen & Co Ltd
11 New Fetter Lane, London EC4P 4EE
© 1972 Methuen
Set in Press Roman by
Santype Ltd, (Coldtype Division)
Salisbury, Wiltshire,
England
and printed in Great Britain by
Redwood Press Limited
Trowbridge, Wiltshire

SBN 416 75640 9

Distributed in the USA by
HARPER & ROW PUBLISHERS, INC.
BARNES & NOBLE IMPORT DIVISION

Contents

Introduction

The eleven papers published here are a partial record of the second Manchester Symposium on Theatre, held at St Anselm Hall from 16—18 July 1971. Some things, inevitably, are missing from these pages. We cannot easily explain the contribution made to the proceedings by the general tone of generous interest, nor the pleasure of making and renewing friendships, and certain things that happened cannot be made to happen again: Graham Barlow's detailed use of slides, Lucylle Hook's questions (and answers) from the floor, the quality of Edgar Roberts' sung illustrations to his account of Fielding, and the exchange between Arnold Hare and Cecil Price that might have become the *subject* of a paper on drama rather than the *consequence* of one. But in one respect the book has clearly gained over the Symposium. Kenneth Robinson was taken ill at the last minute, and his paper reached us a day too late to be read, so that only now does it find its rightful place.

It has been the intention of the editors, both of this volume and of the earlier *Nineteenth-Century British Theatre*, to give due weight to aspects of theatre that are not often the concern of the literary scholar. We are firm allies of the admirable Society for Theatre Research, and still surprised by those who believe that university Drama Departments are simply the pampered pets of English Departments given a special bone to worry. We would have liked to include a further paper on a playwright (Arthur Murphy perhaps), and some socio-political approach to the theatre of the period, but the balance of the volume is otherwise as we would have it. The actor should have pride of place in a century flanked by Betterton and Kemble, and the developing importance of designers and managers is proportionately represented. It is of no comfort to readers to learn that the papers were finely spoken when they were first delivered, but the writers' enthusiasm for their subjects is, we believe, discernible. Theatre studies are still, emphatically, the consequence and the cause of delight.

We should like, in conclusion, to record various debts. To Manchester colleagues, to Arthur Colby Sprague (again) who is so fine to be with, to the representatives of the Society for Theatre Research who are the best of audiences when they can spare time from being the best of speakers, to our graduate assistants Richard Wright and George Wewiora, and to Gillian Robson of Methuen.

Kenneth Richards
Peter Thomson

Members of the Symposium

James Arnott	University of Glasgow
Kathleen Barker	Society for Theatre Research
Graham Barlow	University of Glasgow
Christopher Baugh	University of Manchester
Philip Cook	University of Manchester
Eileen Cottis	Society for Theatre Research
Robin Estill	University of Manchester
Harvey Goodman	U.C.L.A.
Arnold Hare	University of Bristol
Nicholas Hern	University of Hull
Lucylle Hook	Barnard College, Columbia University
Anthony Jackson	University of Manchester
Malcolm Kelsall	University of Reading
Helene Koon	California State College
Jan McDonald	University of Glasgow
Cecil Price	University College, Swansea
Jack Reading	Society for Theatre Research
Kenneth Richards	University of Manchester
Edgar Roberts	City University of New York
Philip Roberts	University of Newcastle
Kenneth Robinson	University College, Cardiff
Sybil Rosenfeld	Editor, *Theatre Notebook*
David Rostron	Northern Counties College of Education
Donald Roy	University of Hull
Paul Sawyer	Bradley University, Illinois
Claude Schumacher	University of Manchester
A. J. Smith	University College, Swansea
Arthur Colby Sprague	Bryn Mawr College
George Taylor	University of Manchester
Peter Thomson	University of Manchester
Graham Woodruff	University of Birmingham

Graduate Assistants:
Richard Wright
George Wewiora

Publishers' Representatives:
Gillian Robson
Geoffrey Strachan

1 MALCOLM KELSALL

Terence and Steele

My theme is the *humanitas* of Terence and Steele. They are united for comparison not only because the last of Steele's plays, *The Conscious Lovers*, is an imitation of *Andria*, but also because both dramatists throughout their lives show a common concern in exploring the relation of compassionate humane love to mere sexuality.

The importance of Terence in shaping neo-classic dramatic theory and sensibility needs no emphasis. Among the many influences coming to bear upon Steele's reformative dramatic endeavour, an especial place must be granted to a writer whom it was generally agreed was pre-eminent in the 'new comedy' for his moral insight into human nature, who was a model not only of form and style, but of that purity of sentiment in his characters which, Laurence Echard wrote, teaches that '*Obscenities* and *Debaucheries* are no ways necessary to make a good *Comedy*', leaving modern poets 'ready to blush when they see *Heathens* so plainly out-do us *Christians* in their *Morals*' [1]. Steele's opposition to the promiscuity of Restoration mores, and his compassionate morality have been readily associated with Jeremy Collier, or the growth of English sentimentalism, but the ethos of his plays is classic in its origins, however tempered by local circumstance, and if, like Aeneas, one should follow the command *antiquam exquirite matrem*, the journey leads to Italic soil.

Terence is a sentimentalist of classic theatre. Tears are the mark of his men of good feeling. In *Andria* when Simo first sees his son Pamphilus and his son's mistress Glycerium, both are weeping as she casts herself into her lover's arms: *Reiecit se in eum flens quam familiariter* (136) [2]. In *The Self-Tormentor* (*Heautontimorumenos*) Chremes twice sheds tears in the first scene at the loss of his son's affection. Aeschinus, reconciled to Micio in *The Brothers* (*Adelphi*), weeps. The dialogue would do credit to the sentimental theatre:

Micio: abeamus. quid est?
                    quid lacrumas?
Aeschinus: pater, obsecro, ausculta.
Micio: Aeschine, audivi omnia
                    et scio; nam te amo: quo magis quae agis curae sunt mihi.
Aeschinus: ita velim me promerentem ames, dum vivas, mi pater,
                    ut me hoc delictum admisisse in me, id mihi vehementer dolet
                    et me tui pudet.   (678–83)

Micio: Let us go. But what is this? Why are you weeping? *Aeschinus*: Father, I beg you, listen to me. *Micio*: Aeschinus, I have heard everything, and understand: for I love you, thus all the more I am concerned with all you do. *Aeschinus*: May I never deserve your love as long as you live, father, if my fault does not bitterly grieve me, and shame me before you.

To this element in Terence, Steele readily responded. Defending his own moral and tearful plays by the example of the ancients, he wrote, in the *Spectator* 521, of the 'most excellent Comedy' *The Self-Tormentor*, that there are in it 'several Incidents which would draw Tears from any Man of Sense, and not one which would move his Laughter.' Terence's power to touch the heart was praised likewise by Madame Dacier [3]. He was a dramatist sometimes 'grave, sententious, and even sorrowful' — so Joseph Trapp claimed [4]. Traditionally acknowledged, since Julius Caesar's criticism, as lacking the *vis comica*, he was valued rather for his moral insight into men and manners, *in ethesin* as Varro had written. Avoiding the *detorta* and *depravata* which raise vulgar laughter, he came home instead to the bosoms of the wise and philosophical who found their pleasure and utility in comedy's truth to nature, its *imitationem vitae, speculum consuetudinis, imaginem veritatis* [5]. Terentian comedy, wrote Daniel Heinsius, was *perfectior utiliorque, ita minus ridicula* [6]. It was from Terence's truth to essential nature that moral utility might be derived: *velut admoniti, prudentius judicemus de rebus humanis* — so Philip Melanchthon [7]. From his portraits of virtue, from that characteristic tendency to heighten the goodness of human nature which Euanthius and Vossius touch upon [8], men might learn with delight rather than bitterness what path they should pursue. Moral (as far as paganism permitted), gentle, truthful, chaste (for one who wrote of adolescent love), Terence's pleasantry reached beyond the fancy and imagination 'even to the Heart and Soul of the Audience' [9]. When Steele, moving 'a joy too exquisite for laughter', sought to touch with delight the moral sense of the wise rather than to draw laughter by ridiculing folly and vice, he was, in *The Conscious Lovers*, emulating the spirit and not merely following the plot of Terence's *Andria*. 'It is not the lively Jest, the smart Repartee, or the witty Conceit; but the natural Views of Life, the moral Painting, the Manners, ... it is the Human Heart in all its odd Variety, pleasantly represented, that makes up the elegant Entertainment of Comedy' — so it was claimed in the ninth number of *The Lay Monastery*, where the 'fine touches of Humanity' of *The Funeral* were likened to Terence and Plautus. Thus it is that good men may be made better. When Steele recruited the sentiments of humanity in the cause of moral idealism, of faithful love, of filial duty, he was following in an honourable tradition.

What is it, in this tradition, to be human? What is it to possess *humanitas*?

Homo sum: humani nil a me alienum puto.

'I am a man: I consider all human affairs concern me' — so Chremes in the most famous of Terentian commonplaces — and hence he is moved to comfort the unhappy and lonely Menedemus. 'I am a Man, and cannot help feeling any Sorrow that can arrive at Man' is Steele's version in *Spectator* 502. It is, however, with more than sorrow that Terence's humanity is concerned. Human affairs in the plays are often by any standard corrupt, or corrupting. Pamphilus in *The Mother-in-Law (Hecyra)* has raped a woman. In *The Eunuch* Chaerea seduces and savages a virgin; Phaedria at the end of *Phormio* departs in triumph to carouse with his bought mistress. In *Andria* we hear the shrieks of Glycerium as she brings forth Pamphilus' bastard. It is matters of this kind which demand, and receive, pardon. *Persuasit nox amor vinum, adulescentia:/Humanumst*, 'Night, love, wine, youth swayed him: that's human nature', so Hegio excuses the sexual freedom of Aeschinus in *The Brothers* (470–71). It is the way of the world. Thus Thais pardons Chaerea in *The Eunuch*:

scio,

et pol propterea magis nunc ignosco tibi.
non adeo inhumano ingenio sum, Chaerea,
neque ita inperita, ut quid amor valeat nesciam.

(878–81)

I know that you loved her, truly that makes me readier to forgive you. I am not so inhuman, Chaerea, or so inexperienced that I do not know the power of love.

Consider the component elements of these lines. They are spoken by a courtesan. It is important that experience should speak, for she is, as she says, not unpractised in the ways of love, not without knowledge of its power. She knows all, and because she knows, all the more she pardons Chaerea's passion. Not to do so would show an inhuman spirit, and like Bacchis, the generous-spirited prostitute of *The Mother-in-Law*, she is a compassionate being.

But this is the world of comic theatre, which makes it easier to forgive. If one rapes a woman, later she becomes one's wife. If one seduces a virgin, it is because of love; later she is discovered to be of the right class and a marriage is arranged. If one goes with a courtesan, she has a noble spirit, she may even, like Bacchis, praise one's eventual choice of a wife.

The liberty of youth, and of the theatre, should not be confused, however, with the permissiveness of a promiscuous and selfish society. *Homo sum: humani nil a me alienum puto* Chremes began, but he continues his speech to Menedemus:

> vel me monere hoc vel percontari puta:
> rectumst, ego ut faciam; non est, te ut deterream.

> Think, as you like, that I am offering you advice, or asking a question: if you are right, I will do likewise, if you are wrong, I may be able to dissuade you.

He is a moral empiricist. He studies human nature in all its aspects so that he may learn good from evil, that he may follow the good, and seek to preserve others from going astray. This is similar to the practical morality taught Horace by his father, so he claimed, and Horace's *sermones* are often Terentian.

The just discrimination of right from wrong in Terence's plays is outside the scope of this discussion. But humanity without justice is mere flabby carelessness, and tolerant in the extreme though these comedies are, permissive in that sense they are not. Comic justice is not harsh, sometimes it may reside even in irony, as at the end of *Phormio* where both father and son having done wrong, the two ills are allowed to cancel each other out, and the characters, as in *Bartholomew Fair*, depart to what one hopes is a feast of reconciliation. Yet wrong does not thereby go uncensured, and there is profound truth in the just lament of the ageing and deceived wife (which Heinsius much admired):

> an mea forma atque aetas magis nunc expetendast, Demipho?
> quid mi hic adfers, quam ob rem exspectem aut sperem porro non fore?
>   (1024–5)

Is my youth or my beauty now more desirable than it was when he was
unfaithful to me, Demipho? Can you suggest on the evidence that I can
expect or hope any amendment in the future?

We must not only admit that Nausistrata has been wronged, we pity her
also. There is ironic justice too in the conclusion of that highly
permissive play, *The Eunuch*. Will the young lover wish for long to
share his mistress with a sot like Thraso, who is necessary to pay her
bills? More direct is the ending of *The Brothers*. Ctesipho is allowed to
bring home his mistress, but with the warning *in instac finem faciat* —
let this be the last time. His brother, meantime, is to be married.
Marriage, indeed, is the norm to which Terentian comedy is directed,
and to flee from just social responsibility is to invite just reproach. It is
the task of finding a wife which unites both fathers and sons with a
common bond of duty, and if youth is wild in the plays, it is often the
final fling which we see. Granted, affairs, if discreet, may be tolerated:
*nonne ea dissimulare nos/magis humanumst quam dare operam id scire,
qui nos oderit*?, 'isn't it kinder for us to turn a blind eye than pry into
things and make ourselves hated? , so runs Phidippus' argument in *The
Mother-in-Law* (552–3); and has not age itself been young once? But to
tolerate is not to approve. As Horace likewise argues, there comes a
time when it is necessary to order one's life maturely, and there is, even
in Terence, a mark which, if overstepped, may condemn a man. Hence
the difficulty of finding a wife for Pamphilus in *Andria*. Chremes will
not marry his daughter to a notorious keeper.

If one turns specifically to *Andria*, the union of humanity with
justice and responsibility is clearly apparent. When Simo sees Pamphilus
weeping at the funeral of Chrysis he rejoices, for how well would the
young man behave if he had been in love, how lament the death of a
father?

> haec ego putabam esse omnia humani ingeni
> mansuetique animi officia. (113–14)

> I thought all this the dutiful acts of a humane mind and gentle spirit.

The good man performs those services which are due to his fellow
creatures, and he performs them not as mere duties, nor from merely
rational benevolence, but because he is kind, because of his *humanitas*.
Hence Pamphilus' outburst (which impressed Joseph Trapp) on his first
entry, after his father had passed him in the forum, and casually informed him to prepare for marriage that day. The son rightly complains

> Hocinest humanum factu aut inceptu? hocinest officium patris? (236)

> Was this the deed or the plan of a human being? Was this the duty of a father?

There has been a failure of responsibility on the part of Simo. Pamphilus does not wilfully wish to fly in his face, but Simo has not acted with due care, with proper consideration, but rather, *inhumane*, as is not proper for a man.

Pamphilus returns again to the theme of the duty and affection proper to a man shortly after when Mysis, in alarm for Glycerium, wonders if her lover has the strength of mind to remain constant. In a powerful speech Pamphilus exclaims

> adeon me ignavom putas,
> adeon porro ingratum aut inhumanum aut ferum,
> ut neque me consuetudo neque amor neque pudor
> commoveat neque commoneat ut servem fidem?   (277–80)

> Do you think me so spineless, so ungrateful, so inhuman, so brutish that neither sex, nor love, nor decency can move me or urge me to keep faith?

Here is the fundamental and classic distinction between human being and beast – *me putas inhumanum aut ferum*? – but it is not expressed in the traditional terms of rationality as opposed to instinct. On the contrary, Pamphilus, true to the character of his first speech, and true also to the character of a young man who has become the lover of a waif, is emotional and passionate. There are certain feelings which distinguish humanity from bestiality: in a man, courage, gratitude, love, honour, fidelity. These are the qualities which lead him to bind himself to Glycerium against the duty which he owes to his father. He speaks with a sincere simplicity which does not shrink from the whole truth about their physical relationship. He speaks not only of *amor* but of *consuetudo*. There is no smutty innuendo in the reference, nor any of the self-conscious assertiveness of a Lawrence or an Orton, but rather a firm and balanced awareness of the whole nature of his relationship, sexual, moral, social, so much so that with a favoured device Terence is able to undercut his sentiments almost at once with a certain brutal directness. 'But where are you going?' Pamphilus asks Mysis. 'To fetch the midwife', is the terse reply.

There is no lover in Terence with more humane sentiment than Pamphilus. Yet if his is romantic love, it is not romanticized, nor is the *humanitas* of his loyal affection allowed to obscure the darker aspects of the human condition. It was at the house of a woman forced by

want to prostitution where he first met Glycerium. The very arti-
ficiality of the dramatic convention by which the heroine's birth is
revealed, solving the problems of fathers and sons, is itself a warning
that this, after all, is the theatre. In real life things may not turn out
like this. Moreover, as is common, there is just and saddening reproach:
'O Chremes', cries Simo, 'behold the loyalty of my son. Do you not
grieve for me? To have taken so much trouble for such a child! Are you
not ashamed, Pamphilus?' (868–71). But, characteristically, neither
father nor son is right, for Simo does not know the whole truth.
Terentian comedy is truly dramatic in that each man sees the situation
as is appropriate to his years, his character, his knowledge of events, and
hence only partially. This dramatic quality Boileau especially praised.
Because Terence is empirical, he is relativistic and ironic. Absolute truth
is difficult to obtain, perhaps impossible, and hence the tentativeness
which leads to the famous advice that there should be nothing in
excess: *adprime in vita esse utile, ut ne quid nimis.*

Yet if one quality shines through the plays as of unquestioned
value, it is that compassionate feeling for human weakness, leading to
charity, expressing itself in love. Menedemus reproaches himself,
*Coepi non humanitus/neque ut animum decuit aegrotum adulescentuli
Tractare* 'I began unkindly, and not as I ought to have treated an
adolescent failing' – thus he is, justly so, a self-tormentor (100–01).
The hero of *The Mother-in-Law* was at first unhappy in his marriage,
but he came to learn love *uxoris misericordia/devinctus*, constrained by
compassion for his wife. The lesson that Demea learns in old age (in
The Brothers) is that nothing is better in a man than to be easily
tolerant. Thus it is that he will win the love of his sons. In the same way
Pamphilus in *Andria* is moved to love not merely by the beauty of
Glycerium, her modesty, her purity and virtue – words used without
affectation of his mistress – but because she has been entrusted in her
helplessness to him (by a courtesan), because he will not leave her (to
sink to prostitution), because, in his love, he pities her. Thus he shows
his *humanitas*.

Compare with Terence two *loci* from *The Conscious Lovers* on the
nature of man: Isabella to Indiana on the character (as she supposes it)
of Bevil, and Phillis to Tom on the nature of his love.

> There are, among the destroyers of women, the gentle, the generous, the
> mild, the affable, the humble.... They have usurped an exemption from
> shame for any baseness, any cruelty towards us. They embrace without love;

they make vows without conscience of obligation; they are partners, nay, seducers to the crime, wherein they pretend to be less guilty. (303) [10]

Such a lover Isabella fears Bevil to be: 'He is a man, and therefore a hypocrite.' *Homo sum*, said Chremes: because I am a man I would learn human sympathy and morality from experience. What Isabella has learnt from experience, however, is not to trust appearances. Behind a mask of propriety she sees the evil of sexuality divorced from love and responsibility. What she describes in general terms to Indiana is more directly described in the subplot by Phillis, for what high society disguises is laid bare in common life. 'Oh, Tom, you grow wanton, and sensual', Phillis exclaims. 'Oh! foh! you are a man — an odious, filthy, male creature' (316).

Tom, as described by the woman he desires, is not fully a man at all, but an animal, a 'male creature', what Pamphilus would describe as *ferus*; a beast because merely a sensualist, and as merely a sensual animal (to employ the language of a contemporary philosopher on human nature) a Yahoo, 'odious' and 'filthy'. What is particularly shocking is that Phillis is not condemning, but coquetting. Her virtue, as Isabella fears Bevil's to be, is mere hypocrisy, an exterior parade. What she wants is that Tom should be filthy and sensual, and it is, in the end, what Isabella expects of Bevil. She links the words because sex, for her, has become a dirty idea. It is dirty because it has become an end in itself, and thus separated from the proper condition of humanity. One may compare the direct attack of Steele's *The Theatre* no. 21 on the lascivious representation of love (and acts of sex) on the contemporary stage. It is something which he describes as 'monstrous', as filthier than prostitution. 'If we are any longer to march on two Legs, and not to be quite prone, or on all four, like the other Animals,' he writes, 'let us assume Manhood and humane Indignation against so barbarous an Affront.'

More specifically, both Phillis and Isabella are seeing the *mores* of man through the medium of Restoration comedy. Tom and Phillis are explicitly represented as mimics of that degeneracy. Steele's touch is light. After the manner of Mr Spectator he reforms by ridicule, and he has benevolence enough to be kind. He wishes to put immorality out of fashion, not to thunder like a Prynne. There is no doubt, however, that the lovers below stairs have caught a disease which damages, if it has not entirely corrupted, the human heart. Isabella sees that disease palliated by the superficial humanity of Bevil's gentleness, generosity and meekness, but man, for her, remains essentially a rake. Bevil is another Horner or Dorimant disguised, a cold-blooded sexual chauvinist.

In Terentian comedy there are keepers of women in plenty — Pamphilus himself in *Andria* — but a sense of shame, deeply grounded in what is best in human nature, is a powerful source of moral good. *Erubuit: salva res est* cries Micio in *The Brothers*: 'he blushed, we're saved' (643). Does that Prince Charming of Restoration heroes, Mirabel, ever blush for having married his discarded mistress to a man she does not love? In Terentian comedy there are seducers in plenty, but they make love from love, even if hurried away by appetite. Like Chaerea's in *The Eunuch*, the generosity of their nature is touched, and a spirit of loyalty is kindled. It is not only sex, but *amor* and *pudor* which leads Pamphilus to keep faith, to behave, therefore, *humane*, and not like the witty gallant of the Restoration as Steele sees him, a Yahoo with a tincture of reason.

In the fine dialogue between Mr Sealand and Sir John Bevil, the merchant lays his finger on the same corrupt spot. He speaks of deliberate womanisers who pursue sex not because 'their appetites hurry 'em away, but, I warrant you, because 'tis their opinion they may do it' (337). Sir John tries to mitigate the charge in Terentian vein: to err is human, therefore one should not be severe on promiscuity — *at humanum tamen/fecere alii saepe item boni*, 'it is human nature, others have done it, even good men' (*The Brothers* 687–8) — but it is the cold-blooded selfishness of the accomplished whoremaster that Mr Sealand has not the compassion to forgive. When a man calculates in these matters, when he sees no obstacle to the selfish exercise of physical gratification, then neither shame, nor love, nor compassion will ever put an end to his promiscuity. Sealand will not marry his daughter to such a man. 'Commerce with a Woman, without Affection to her, or Concern for her,' wrote Steele in *The Theatre* no. 6, 'is the most inhumane and bestial Action a Man can be guilty of. The Woman's Vice in that Case is humane Frailty, but the Man's is the same, improv'd with Diabolical Malice.'

Steele wrote in what he called a 'degenerate' age. Men had fallen away from proper standards of human conduct. The *humanitas* of Terence, which has to encompass so many weaknesses, can usually expect nonetheless to touch a sympathetic chord in the heart of both the *dramatis personae* and the audience. There is nothing more

beautiful in the comedies than the praise of the discarded mistress in
The Mother-in-Law for the wife who has supplanted her: *recte amasti,
Pamphile, uxorem tuam . . . perliberalis visa est,* 'you are right to love
your wife, Pamphilus, she is truly a gentlewoman' (862—4). Here even
in a whore human nature rises above the norm. Out of human frailties
one sees permanent good coming nonetheless, and a brave new world
may be hoped for which has such people in it, and who are seen not
with the eye of virgin innocence, but with the wisdom of experience.

Steele, however, has to establish humane values in the face of a
dramatic convention which had dressed libertinism with all the graces
of rank and brilliance of wit. Bookwit, in *The Lying Lover*, comes to
town determined to cultivate the image which the mass media, one
might say, had made popular. Dressed in the 'gay habit' of vice 'he
makes false love, gets drunk, and kills [a] man'. Young men of shallow
understanding and lively conceit are addicted to fashion. There is no
genuine life-style in Bookwit (indeed, this is what saves him, for his
true feelings are touched later by the compassion of his father and
friend). Lady Brumpton, likewise, in her villainy is an incomplete being,
but she has degenerated too far to be saved. When she arranges a rape it
is not, in Terentian fashion, a sudden explosion of heedless love, but a
political calculation. Her husband exclaims, 'She never had virginity, to
have no compassion through memory of her own former innocence.
This is to forget her very humanity' (76). When we penetrate behind
the mask of Lady Brumpton's propriety, what we see are merely the
jaded desires for sexual titillation of the rake who recognises the
impulse of sex but is ignorant of love, and the brilliant cerebration of a
wit which can thrash any other character in the play, but seeks no end
except domination. So dreadful does Steele view this degeneration to
be, that we are permitted at moments to gaze into a heart of darkness
too terrible for comedy. When Pamphilus in *Andria* marries his mistress,
his happiness comes close to that of the Gods. Compare what happens
in the world of Lady Brumpton:

> He that is so mean as to marry a woman after an affair with her, will be so
> base as to upbraid that very weakness. He that marries his wench will use her
> like his wench. — Such a pair must sure live in secret mutual scorn of each
> other; and wedlock is hell if at least one side does not love, as it would be
> Heaven if both did; and I believe it so much Heaven, as to think it was never
> enjoyed in this world. (21)

In Sealand's view the same misery results when the woman seduces, then marries the man: 'such a husband soils with his wife for a month perhaps — then good be w'ye, madam, the show's over' (338). To this end sex without love comes.

This is the outcome of those Restoration *mores* against which Steele was seeking to re-establish humane values. The *mores* were Epicurean in reducing sexual relations to the rutting of animals, Hobbist in seeing at the root of things a battle for power between the sexes. Lurking in all the plays, like some ominous spectre waiting for the right moment to appear, is the figure of a hellish man of mode damned beyond forgiveness because there is no humane chord in his nature which can be touched. Lady Brumpton has had commerce with this incubus. Bookwit aspires to his condition, the Clerimonts, Tom and Phillis have heard him whispering in their ear, Isabella and Sealand know of the creature and fear young Bevil accordingly.

It is because of this degeneracy in human nature that the *humanitas* of Steele's comedies, the compassionate sympathy and charitable forgiveness which characterize his model heroes, is driven from the more natural channels in which it flows in Terence. Hardy and Bevil are not formed by Steele to correspond to the essential nature of young men, but are wise with philosophy it seems from the cradle; they are manifestations of an ideal of conduct which is to exorcise the spirit of Horner and Dorimant from society. One must turn, therefore, to the lighter comedies, *The Lying Lover*, and *The Tender Husband*, and the reformation of Bookwit and Mr and Mrs Clerimont, to find sympathetic forgiveness which grows from personal experience. Old Bookwit, especially, is a *senex* of liberal clemency to his son of a kind Terence might have portrayed:

> I do not grudge you your expenses. . . . For I decay, and so do my desires, while yours grow still upon you. Therefore, what may be spared from mine, I heartily give you to supply yours, 'tis but the just order of things. . . . All your just pleasures are mine also; in you my youth and gayer years methinks I feel repeated. (137) [11]

This is to be *pater humanissimus*. But due emphasis must be given to the phrase 'just pleasures'. When Bookwit, in sprightly vein and looking askance at his father, enquires, 'I wonder whence I had this amorous inclination?', the reply is Terentian: 'Whoever you had it from, sirrah, 'tis your business to correct it, by fixing it upon a proper object.'

Terentian also is Old Bookwit's address to his son in prison:

> Thy mother's happy that lived not to see this day. Is all the nurture that she gave thy infancy, the erudition she bequeathed thy youth, thus answered? Oh my son! my son! rise and support thy father! I sink with tenderness, my child. (179)

Here is both *humanitas* and justice, and from experience we learn charity.

Yet it is not *The Lying Lover* which is the heartland of Steele's reformative comedy. The character of Trusty, Hardy's forgiveness of his father, Bevil's succour of Indiana, the refusal of Myrtle's challenge, here in scenes intended to move tears of charitable joy he seeks to refine human nature and destroy the fashionable prestige of the selfish and promiscuous man. If the tone of this study is solemn in dealing with comedies, it is because the central moral issues with which Terence and Steele are concerned are only comic in the sense that the action shows a change from worse to better, and human nature is reformed. The 'joy too exquisite for laughter' of which Steele wrote was moved by scenes such as Bevil's refusal of the duel, or the story of Indiana, and defending his lack of the *vis comica*, Steele writes with reference to the discovery scene in *The Conscious Lovers*:

> I must, therefore, contend that the tears which were shed on that occasion flowed from reason and good sense, and that men ought not to be laughed at for weeping till we are come to a more clear notion of what is to be imputed to the hardness of the head and the softness of the heart. . . . To be apt to give way to the impressions of humanity, is the excellence of a right disposition and the natural working of a well-turned spirit. (270)

He does not conceive of himself as a sentimentalist, but as a humane dramatist. The scene in which Lady Brumpton's squirrel is lamented shows what he thinks of sentimentalism. He insists, rather, upon the rationality of good sense (does not reason distinguish men from brutes?). If men are moral because they are rational beings, it is true reason to recognise the power of natural affection and the workings of the heart. The fact that Steele felt the need to make a programmatic and defensive claim for this play may indicate why his dramatic argument is developed in *The Conscious Lovers* to extremes. Like Bookwit he himself is 'image building', and for this reason he is in danger of losing contact with those essential affections which are a necessary part of the whole human heart.

Consider further the relation of Indiana and Bevil. In Terence their

originals are lovers. What is more, the woman is with child. They have
not married, and Pamphilus has kept the relationship secret because
Glycerium is a penniless girl of uncertain birth picked up at the house
of a courtesan. In Steele, Indiana is still a virgin. Considering the
unhappiness of the position Glycerium and Pamphilus have got
themselves into, the reason and good sense of Steele's lovers would seem
to be preferable. But this is not enough. Bevil has never spoken a word
of love to Indiana, or she to him, although both are deeply enamoured,
and show it. Moreover, although Bevil's relationship with his father is
good, and Indiana is of respectable birth, although now without a
family, he has kept all knowledge of his liaison from his father. Is this
natural or human, or does it betray a punctiliousness, a regard for
appearances and proprieties inflexible, absurd — what is worse, as John
Dennis suggested — even hypocritical? [12]

It troubles Indiana. The continued generosity of Bevil's seemingly
disinterested charity she finds 'prodigious, almost incredible'. Bevil
replies by readjusting the hedonistic calculus of Restoration comedy.

> If pleasure be worth purchasing, how great a pleasure is it to him, who has a
> true taste of life, to ease an aching heart; to see the human countenance
> lighted up into smiles of joy. . . . This is the effect of a human disposition,
> where there is only a general tie of nature and common necessity. What then
> must it be when we serve an object of merit, of admiration! (310–11)

Basically he grounds his argument on the *humanitatis societas*. Human
beings are linked together in one society, and it is right that we should
serve that society. This is the rational benevolence of a citizen of the
world, and, being good sense, natural and pleasurable, why should it be
considered 'a mighty heroic business'? Admirable sentiments, worthy of
a parson in a tie-wig! But the trouble with this refined humanity is that
it neither coincides with general human experience, as Isabella cynically
but truly observes, nor is it true of Bevil. He is head over heels in love
with Indiana. The morality is separated from the dramatic situation,
and Bevil, although he is truly kind, is getting credit where it is not due.

This is not irony on Steele's part. Earlier, in *The Funeral*, he could
laugh a little at Hardy. The scene in which he fails to declare his love to
Sharlot charmingly blends comedy with sentiment. But Bevil is
intended as a compendium of virtues, and he is to be free from any
criticism. How severe Steele's conception is, further comparison with
Pamphilus reveals. The first words of the Terentian hero have already
been quoted: *Hocinest humanum factu aut inceptu? hocinest officium*

patris? He is overwrought. He reproaches, not without reason, the inhumanity of Simo. Bevil, on the other hand, about to receive his father who is urging on a marriage which the son does not desire, appears reading Addison:

> These moral writers practise virtue after death. This charming vision of Mirza! Such an author consulted in a morning sets the spirit for the vicissitudes of the day better than the glass does a man's person. (287–8)

Having steadied his nerve with a draught of literature and moral philosophy, he receives his father with natural politeness and good breeding. This is *humanitas* in its extended sense of the mental cultivation befitting a man of liberal education, expressing itself in good manners and refined language – a sense of the word perfectly suited to Steele's comedies, but so general in its extension that it is difficult to give it local context. Yet, with all this propriety, the exigencies of the plot promptly lead Bevil to lie to his father as to Indiana, when it would be far more natural and sensible to come to an explanation. The excellent Mr Sealand has far more sense and at once cuts the knot. Even in the duel scene where Bevil, because manly, is allowed to lose his temper – 'the infirmity of human nature . . . can bear no more' – it is an odd punctiliousness about revealing the contents of Lucinda's note which lets the crisis develop, and there is something over-refined in the nature of a man who is prepared to risk killing his best friend rather than reveal the contents of a harmless letter.

In Bevil, and in Hardy, Steele is prepared to portray far less, if any, of the weaknesses of human nature than Terence will admit in his heroes, and one feels at times that Steele is not only being implausible, but also unjust. Hardy's father, for instance, even more than Bevil's, has treated him abominably. Hurried away by his lust, Lord Brumpton has acted stupidly and with gross inhumanity. Yet, as the perfect model of filial tenderness, Hardy never complains. As Trusty describes him to his father, 'Though you made him not your heir, he is still your son, and has all the duty and tenderness in the world for your memory' (76). It is right to show *omnia humani ingeni mansuetique animi officia*, but is it not also human to complain under ill-treatment, and just to oppose stupidity and illiberality? This is not permitted in Hardy, lest it should be seen as a fault.

Steele is aware that the effects are extraordinary. He has rejected the counsel *ne quid nimis*. 'Oh, unparalleled goodness!' exclaims Lord

Brumpton of his son at the climax of *The Funeral*. 'If they are both what they would seem,' says Isabella of Indiana and Bevil, 'they are made for one another, as much as Adam and Eve were, for there is no other of their kind but themselves' (350), and the play ends with what is described as a 'scene of wonder'. Even *The Lying Lover* concludes with Lovemore exclaiming at the 'noble friendship' of Bookwit and Latine: 'Let me grasp you both, who, in an age degenerate as this, have such transcendent virtue' (183). In each case we are shown an extreme example of humane charity. Possibly Steele chose to work with such bold strokes because it was necessary to obliterate one image of which he disapproved and forcibly intrude upon the public conscience another type of dramatic hero. One should not discount also the idealism of the Christian religion which, by setting its disciples the task of imitating virtue incarnate, made far greater demands than the easy-going pagan morality of 'nothing in excess'. 'You confound me with all this tenderness and generosity', says Hardy of Trusty (67). The humanity of such a character as Trusty is intended to ravish the spirit, and one has passed beyond Terence to something resembling more the moral heroism of *The Pilgrim's Progress*.

Yet this virtue, soaring towards the height of Christian charity, is not only so perplexed with a delicate sense of impropriety as to become unnatural, but smacks also at times of mere prudery. In *Spectator* 51 Steele reproached himself for writing of the 'struggling — and at last yielding' Harriot. While his general thesis may strike a sympathetic chord in some — that when a piece is very dull the actors either talk bawdy or strip (one wonders what he might think of Mr Warhol) — yet Campley's remark is natural and human, and his love for Harriot is grounded in such good sense that he can readily be forgiven a little lust. There is some need of it compared with the asexuality of Hardy with his love of friendship, constancy, piety, household care and maternal tenderness. Hardy plays Palamon to Campley's Arcite, which is the nobler role, but a more balanced man can love both the 'goddess' and the 'creature' in woman. The extraordinary reticence of Hardy and Bevil on sexual matters, their spotless rectitude, does not spring from a fully rounded sexual consciousness, but from some copybook of propriety which later was to be inherited by the family of Podsnap. It is easy to see how humanity passes into hypocrisy when sexual morality becomes blinkered to human nature. A 'Phantom' made up of 'Religion and Dissimulation, Morality and Fraud', is Dennis's harsh judgement of

Bevil. If one turns to Fielding, and that grossly immoral novel *Tom Jones*, one sees a more truly Terentian young man in the hero, and Fielding, with the warm-hearted indulgence of a just but tolerant father, leads Tom both out of the hands of whores to a romantic marriage, and out of the antiseptic clinic of that castrator and voyeur, Samuel Richardson. If Steele has more of Terence's sentimentalism, Fielding, in *Tom Jones*, has more of a pagan catholicism.

It is the ideal of *humanitas* we perceive in Steele's plays, however, which for something like two centuries, it is fair to suggest, was to be a major element in the English moral conscience, benevolent and charitable to mankind in general, and deeply chaste in its attitude to sexual relations. Some ancient virtues still shine with undiminished lustre in the modern world. In both Terence and Steele fathers and children forgive and are reconciled, men perform their duty through love, and compassion powerfully cements the union of the sexes. Tenderness and tears witness to virtue, not to weakness. But it is for virtue in distress that Steele particularly excites our sympathy, and not for the waywardness of sexual passion. In his plays young men no longer have mistresses (which seems to be the prerogative of the older generation) and big-bellied women no longer bring forth bastards. Terence's humanity, because it is less idealistic, is more liberal, for his comic world shows a greater capacity to tolerate, to absorb, and to turn human nature with all its faults into something good. 'Are you pleased with what has happened?' Demea asks Micio in *The Brothers*. He replies

> non, si queam
> mutare. nunc quom non queo, animo aequo fero.
> ita vitast hominum quasi quom ludas tesseris:
> si illud quod maxume opus ist iactu non cadit,
> illud quod cecidit forte, id arte ut corrigas. (737–41)

No, not if I could change it. But since I cannot, I take it calmly. The life of man is like a game of dice: if the throw you want does not turn up, you must correct by art what comes by chance.

So speaks a humane father seeking to find the right path by which to bring up the young. If one were to choose a motto for the plays of Steele, however, one would not consider a passage like that. Perhaps the first epistle to Timothy (iv.12) offers a more appropriate quotation:

> Let no man despise thy youth: but be thou an example of the believers, in word, in conversation, in charity, in spirit, in faith, in purity.

Haec nosse salus est adolescentulis

Notes

[1] *Terence's Comedies: Made English* (1694).

[2] The text is that of the Loeb edn, the reference to the line number.

[3] cf. *Les Comédies de Térence* (Hamburg, 1732), iii and vii.

[4] *Lectures on Poetry* (1742, originally *Praelectiones Poeticae* (1711), 288.

[5] Cicero in Donatus, cf. the prolegomena to the Delphin Terence (London, 1792), xxvii.

[6] idem, cxx. He is describing 'new comedy' in general as a Graeco-Roman genre. This was common.

[7] idem, cxxxiii.

[8] For Euanthius cf. idem, xxvi; for J. G. Vossius cf. *Institutionum Poeticarum*, 107b in *Opera* III (Amsterdam, 1697).

[9] Echard, op. cit., iv.

[10] The text is that of the Mermaid edn, the reference to the page.

[11] Much of *The Lying Lover* is imitated from Corneille's *Le Menteur*. It is fair to claim with D'Aubignac, however, that the spirit of seventeenth-century French comedy is Terentian. Cf. *La Pratique du Théâtre* (Amsterdam, 1715), 11–12. The last two volumes of this edition are devoted to Terence.

[12] 'Remarks on a Play, Call'd, The Conscious Lovers, A Comedy' (1723), in Edward Niles Hooker, *The Critical Works of John Dennis* (Baltimore, John Hopkins, 1939–43), ii, 251f. For further comparison of Bevil and Pamphilus see *The Censor Censured; Or, the Conscious Lovers Examin'd* (1723). Hooker reviews the long continued discussion as to whether comedy should reform by ridiculing folly or vice, or, as Steele endeavours, by portraying moral virtue. The local critical discussion of *The Conscious Lovers* is presented by George A. Aitken, *The Life of Richard Steele* (1889), ii, 279f.

2 EDGAR V. ROBERTS

The Songs and Tunes in Henry Fielding's Ballad Operas

During his career as a dramatist Henry Fielding wrote eleven ballad operas [1]. For the New Theatre in the Haymarket, his ballad operas were burlesques and satires, while for the Theatre Royal in Drury Lane, they were farces and intrigues. It is not difficult to explain these correspondences. The New Haymarket operated without a patent or licence, and in order to draw audiences it capitalized upon criticism of the establishment, in this respect following the precedent of Gay's *Beggar's Opera* (1728), which had attacked the expensive and 'un-English' Italian opera, exposed the fashionable but hypocritical social and economic world of the day, and affronted the prime minister, Sir Robert Walpole. Thus, for the New Haymarket, Fielding wrote *The Author's Farce; and the Pleasures of the Town* (30 March 1730), a criticism of Colley Cibber and the London entertainment establishment; *The Welsh Opera* (22 April 1731), revised as *The Grub-Street Opera* (not performed), a criticism of Walpole and the family of King George II; *Don Quixote in England* (5 April 1734), a criticism of the parliamentary elections of 1734 but also a general satiric view of the English character; and *Tumble-Down Dick; or, Phaeton in the Suds* (29 April 1736), a burlesque of the fashionable pantomime dramatic form.

When Fielding was forced off the New Haymarket stage in 1731 as a result of Governmental suppression of *The Grub-Street Opera*, he went to the Theatre Royal in Drury Lane, where in addition to other plays he wrote six new ballad operas, wrote a revision of *The Author's Farce*, and had a share in an additional ballad opera. Three of these were the most successful of all his plays on the eighteenth-century stage. Because Drury Lane was favoured with a Governmental licence, Fielding's ballad operas for this theatre avoided the subject of politics, except by remote reference, and concentrated on farcical action and the exploitation of the talents of the very fine actors from whom Fielding was able to choose. For Drury Lane he wrote *The Lottery* (1 January 1732), the third most successful of all his plays; *The Mock Doctor* (23 June 1732), the most successful; *Deborah* (6 April 1733), not published [2]; *The Intriguing Chambermaid* (15 January 1734); *An Old Man Taught Wisdom; or the Virgin Unmask'd* (6 January 1735), the second most successful of all his plays; and *Eurydice, or the Devil Hen-Peck'd* (19 February 1737), a burlesque which ridiculed the 'obvious foibles of fashionable society' [3] . In 1742 he had 'a very small share' in another ballad opera, *Miss Lucy in Town* (6 May 1742). His collaborator in this sequel to *An Old Man Taught Wisdom* was apparently David Garrick [4] .

Fielding's Singing Actors

Even though the texts of Fielding's ballad operas stand up well under repeated readings over a great many years — and this is my personal testimony — one must acknowledge that his ballad operas, like most after Gay's success of 1728, attained greater popularity in the theatre than in the armchair. The actors must have brought Fielding's texts to life brilliantly. There was obviously a close relationship between Fielding and his actors, and, though they apparently parted company politically in 1731, and though in the theatrical war of 1733 and 1734 Fielding stuck with a minority group of actors opposed to the rebelling group led by Theophilus Cibber, he was clearly influenced by the abilities and limitations of the various actors who played the roles he was creating. One may readily grant that the ballad operas, like today's musical comedies, did not require singers of the best capability, but the really successful singing actors owed their success to their voices. These actors sang most of the ballad-opera songs. Although other actors with less musical but more dramatic talent carried the brunt of the character roles, some of these singing actors were also versatile enough to handle fairly complex acting roles.

Among the successful singing performers, by far the best-known was Catherine Clive, née Raftor, who began her career at Drury Lane in 1729, and who was a stage favourite for decades afterwards. She originated leading female roles in eight Fielding ballad operas, if one includes the revised *Author's Farce*. According to Dr Burney, 'her singing, which was intolerable when she meant it to be fine, in ballad farces and songs of humour was, like her comic acting, every thing it should be' [5]. The revisions which Fielding made in 1734 for *The Author's Farce* show how his dramatic creativity was drawn out by Mrs Clive's abilities. Mrs Clive performed the role of Harriot in the first two acts and in the revelation scene, and the role of Madam Novel in the puppet show. In the first version, Harriot had been a colourless, sentimentally-conceived romantic heroine who appeared only in scenes ii and iii of Act I, and in the revelation scene. In the revision, by contrast, she had the same scenes as before, but also had prominent parts in Act II, scenes ix, x, and xi. In the puppet show, Fielding added an air for Madam Novel, and gave her a part in an additional duet. As a result, Mrs Clive sang six solos in the 1734 production, and participated in five duets, a greater task than in the 1730 production Fielding had assigned to two actresses. A measure of Fielding's re-characterization of Harriot especially for Mrs Clive's talents may be seen in the first-act dialogue leading up to the duet. In the first edition Luckless and Harriot indulge in a romantic interchange in couplets, followed by an unmotivated sigh by Harriot, who wishes that she 'were assured of the Sincerity' of Luckless' love for her. Then the two lovers sing their song. In the revision, Luckless teases Harriot about the possibility of his marrying Mrs Moneywood for her money. Harriot responds petulantly, and the following lovers' quarrel is climaxed by this display of Harriot's emotion:

> Stay, Sir, let me acquaint you with one thing; you are a Villain! and don't think I'm vexed at any thing, but that I shou'd have been such a Fool, as ever to have had a good Opinion of you.   [*Crying.*

After this outburst, Harriot's worries about Luckless' love are reasonable, and the song is logical, as it had not been in the first version. Examples could be multiplied, but they would only show what this one does, namely that Mrs Clive was in a class by herself as a singing actress and as an influence on Fielding's ballad-opera songs.

Less heralded, but an extremely important ballad-opera actor, was the tenor Michael Stoppelaer, or Stopler, one of the many Macheaths of the day (and also, for many years, a successful Mat of the Mint, though he also played Polly on one occasion at least) [6]. Probably a native of Ireland, Stoppelaer apparently began his career at Goodman's Fields and at the New Haymarket in the season of 1729–30. In 1730, he appeared as Sparkish and as Signor Opera in *The Author's Farce*, and in 1731 Fielding selected him for the revised part of Owen in *The Grub-Street Opera*. Stoppelaer was not only talented, but independent, for when the New Haymarket Company of Comedians was forced off the stage in the summer of 1731, he was the first from the company to secure new employment at Drury Lane [7]. During the following years he sang in five Fielding ballad operas, and he originated the roles of Lovemore (*The Lottery*), Leander (*The Mock Doctor*), Valentine (*The Intriguing Chambermaid*), and Orpheus (*Eurydice*). In 1735 he switched his major theatrical affiliation to Covent Garden, where in addition to performing in regular productions he became one of Handel's tenors. He was durable, continuing with the company at Covent Garden for the next forty years. The many operatic airs that appear in Fielding's ballad operas are there chiefly because Stoppelaer could sing them, though despite his talent as a singer, his acting ability does not seem to have suggested any unique characterizations to Fielding.

Other leading playhouse tenors of the day who acted in Fielding's ballad operas were Thomas Salway, who acted Coupee in *An Old Man Taught Wisdom*, and John Beard, who was Signor Cantileno in *Miss Lucy in Town*. That all three of these tenors at various times achieved success with Handel indicates not only that they had voices of some excellence — indeed, Beard has been called the 'leading English singer of his day' [8] — but also that good voices were necessary for leading singers in the ballad operas.

Less well-known actors with either good or competent voices had a determining influence in Fielding's selection of music. William Mullart, the original King Arthur in *Tom Thumb*, could take either leading or character singing roles. His voice was at least competent, if not good, and his range was greater than two octaves. He sang as Luckless, Robin, and Sancho for Fielding at the New Haymarket, but was relegated to minor singing roles in Fielding's ballad operas at Drury Lane, being obscured by Harper, Theophilus Cibber, Stoppelaer, and Macklin. After 1734, Mullart left Drury Lane for more prominent parts at Covent Garden. The best-known actress besides Mrs Clive to take a leading singing role in Fielding's ballad operas was Mrs Charke, Colley Cibber's daughter, who was Clymene in *Tumble-Down Dick* at the New Haymarket in 1736. Her talents as a singer, however, probably lay not so much in her voice as in her ability to style her songs satirically. An actress who sang as a romantic heroine was the Mrs Atherton who created the role of Charlotte in *The Intriguing Chambermaid* and Dorothea in *Don Quixote in England*. Since Dorothea is given extensive singing in *Don Quixote in England*, I conclude that Mrs Atherton had a fair or good voice. Mrs Nokes, who sang as Sweetissa in *The Grub-Street Opera*, must also have been a good singer, although she did not act in any other Fielding ballad opera. Because the Miss Jones who sang as Jezebel in *Don Quixote in England* sang only in her disguise as Dulcinea, I am unable to pass judgment on her voice, except to suggest that her abilities lay in using it to comic effect.

While the leading singing actors and actresses were notable primarily because of their voices, some players who had roles in Fielding's ballad operas were unable to sing well. To them Fielding only rarely gave songs, which could probably have been sung at least partly in *parlando*. Mrs Elizabeth Mullart, for example, apparently excellent in boisterously shrewish roles (she was the original Dollalolla and Mrs Moneywood), was to have introduced 'When Mighty Roast Beef Was the Englishman's Food' in *The Grub-Street Opera*, to the tune of 'The King's [Queen's] Old Courtier'. Since this music holds the same note all the way to the refrain, I conclude that Mrs Mullart did not have a promising voice, musically speaking. It is possible that she might have chanted the music, perhaps in imitation of chanting in an Anglican service. A better-known character actor with apparently similar vocal abilities was John Harper, the original Stocks in *The Lottery* and Blister in *An Old Man Taught Wisdom*. Harper performed a large number of songs in these roles, however, and may have been more musical than I have supposed. The famous Macklin, whose interpretation of Squire Badger delighted the audiences at *Don Quixote in England*, sang only one part of one song, and did so while impersonating a drunken sot. His other roles in Fielding's ballad operas are without any music at all. Because Macklin was a well-known Peachum, however, one must give at least some recognition to his power to deliver a song effectively, even though he was apparently a bellower [9]. Hallam, whom one associates with the fatal argument with Macklin, was given the satirical part of Joan in the revised *Author's Farce*. Clearly his voice was used for comic effect. The Mr Jones who acted in seven Fielding ballad operas, and in a total of twelve Fielding plays, was usually only a speaking actor, although as William in *The Grub-Street Opera* he was to have sung extensively in solos and duets. Since William is usually angry in that play, however, the *parlando* voice would probably have been required of Jones rather than the singing voice. The one actor who probably had no singing voice at all was Theophilus Cibber who, acting the parts of both Jack Stocks and Gregory, did no singing. That Fielding gave no music to the title role in *Don Quixote in England* is probably attributable to the fact that Roberts, who performed the role, did not have a singing voice.

When Fielding set out to write his ballad operas, then, he assigned the bulk of his songs to just a handful of singing actors: Mrs Clive, Stoppelaer, Salway, Beard, Mullart, Mrs Atherton, and Mrs Nokes. For especially comic and satiric effects he relied upon the abilities of Harper, Macklin, Hallam, Jones, or Mrs Mullart. For the rest of the players he wrote only supporting speaking parts, although perhaps some of these players sang in the occasional choruses or danced in the inevitable production numbers.

The Orchestra

The most obvious difference between the production of a typical ballad opera and that of a regular play was the integration of the theatre orchestra into the ballad opera. That the Lincoln's Inn Fields Theatre had employed a large orchestra for accompanying Rich's antics as Harlequin made it especially suitable for the first productions of *The Beggar's Opera*. Drury Lane also had a large orchestra; in 1707 there were twenty-one musicians at the theatre [10], and in the 1730s there were probably as many, or more. The anonymous overture to *Penelope* (1728) by Cooke and Mottley may be seen as an example of the orchestra at the New Haymarket, where Fielding's first two ballad operas were performed. This overture, like Pepusch's overture to *The Beggar's Opera*, called specifically for first and second violins and first and second oboes. Instruments for the lower parts must be inferred, but it is safe to say that orchestral balance would have required the violoncello, the bassoon, and the double-bass. The harpsichord was standard in all orchestras, and was played by the musical director. There is no certainty that a flute or recorder was used at the New Haymarket, but the writer of *The Touchstone: or, Historical, Critical, Political, Philosophical, and Theological Essays on the Reigning Diversions of the Town* (1728) mentioned that 'screaming little' flutes (or recorders) were to be heard in the playhouses. If a recorder was in use, however, it may have been alternated with the oboe [11]. Since Air XX of *The Beggar's Opera*, the march from Handel's *Rinaldo*, calls for 'Drums and Trumpets', and since *The Beggar's Opera* was performed at the New Haymarket many times, I conclude that brass and percussion sections were also part of the orchestra. The brass section probably consisted of trumpets, French horns, and a post-horn (or 'Wind-horn'). The percussion section had the snare drums required by Air XX of *The Beggar's Opera*, and also had kettle drums: Luckless, in *The Author's Farce* (Act III), for example, asks that 'Kettle Drums and Trumpets' be sounded in honour of his newly found fortunes. It is clear, then, that the number of musicians and the variety of instruments at the performance of a Fielding ballad opera, even at a minor theatre like the New Haymarket, was great enough to produce an agreeable symphonic effect.

Not all the orchestra members stayed exclusively in the pit. Frequently several of them, usually from the violin section, appeared on stage and performed music to accompany songs and dances. Fielding's *Tumble-Down Dick* has a cast which includes 'Fidlers', and at the end of *The Grub-Street Opera* Owen announces that he has 'prepar'd the fiddles', the players of which presumably were to come on stage to play for the concluding dance and song. One may see evidence in ballad operas other than Fielding's for the regularity with which musicians appeared on stage. In William Rufus Chetwood's *The Generous Free-Mason* (1730), a violinist entered to play what presumably was a solo accompaniment to 'The Black Joke'. Carey's *Chrononhotonthologos* (1734) included a stage direction saying 'Enter King of the Fidlers at the Head of his Band'. This band of musicians stayed in order to play 'The Black Joke' while the Queen and her ladies danced. Carey's stage musicians must have been especially versatile, for the stage direction ending the scene stated 'Musick plays, Queen and Ladies Dance off, Fidlers and all'. On many other occasions musicians must have appeared on stage, as in the village dance scenes in Johnson's *Village Opera* (1729) or in similar scenes in Coffey's *Beggar's Wedding* (1729). Presumably, however, this stage music was augmented by music from the full orchestra in the pit.

Most of the accompaniments to the songs were probably straightforward and serious orchestral compositions. For example, a 'Symph.' is mentioned as an accompaniment to Air IV of the revised *Devil to Pay* (1732). There were orchestral introductions before many of the songs, as is shown by Fielding's direction to Air X of *The Welsh Opera*, indicating that Robin blows his nose 'While the Symphony is Playing' the introduction. Almost all the ballad operas had overtures. Though preliminary speeches between the 'Author' and the 'Manager' specifically call for overtures in only four Fielding ballad operas, there is no reason to assume that his other ballad operas did not also have overtures. In addition, the frequent dances would have needed orchestral music. The ballad operas provided much work for the musical arrangers at the theatres.

It must not be presumed that all the accompaniments were strictly symphonic, for to achieve variation and musically satiric and comic effects, other instruments, producing what the French called 'charivari' and the English called 'Rough musick', were in use. Carey's Chrononhotonthologos was wakened from a deep sleep by 'A Concert of Rough Musick, viz. Salt-Boxes and Rolling-Pins, Gridirons and Tongs; Sow-Gelders Horns, Marrowbones and Cleavers &c &c', and his response to the music was 'What heav'nly Sounds are these that charm my Ears! / Sure 'tis the Musick of the tuneful Spheres' (3rd ed, 1744, p. 21). Hogarth's satirical engraving entitled The Beggar's Opera Burlesqued (1728) shows, in the pit in front of the cast with asses' heads, an ensemble composed of a bladder and string, a salt-box, a jew's harp, a bagpipe, and a dulcimer [12]. Another instrument belonging to this group was apparently the hurdy-gurdy. Many of the sounds which these instruments produced were well known on London streets. For example, the sow-gelder's horn was mentioned by Addison as a street sound [13], and sounds similar to those of the gridirons and tongs could be heard at any blacksmith's shop. Certainly part of the humour caused by these and similar instruments resulted from their identification with common London sounds.

This 'Rough Musick' was most probably the accompaniment for satirical pageantry and for songs sung by burlesque or farcical characters. Odingsels' Bayes's Opera (1730) had an inaugural parade of satirical figures led by a bagpipe player. Although there is no musical notation in the printed editions to support my contention, I believe that many of Fielding's ballad operas also used these instruments. They would naturally have added much to his satirical thrusts. It is not difficult to imagine the theatrical effect of an Italian operatic air being sung to irregular accompaniment. There were many other chances for such burlesque effects. In The Author's Farce, when Signor Opera and Madam Novel sang their travesty of 'Were I laid on Greenland's Coast' from The Beggar's Opera, I suggest that salt-boxes, marrowbones and cleavers, and other instruments like them, might have augmented the musical joke. Part of the musical humour of *Tumble-Down Dick* could have resulted from a 'Rough' accompaniment to Harlequin as he picked pockets on the stage. It is certain that the appropriate instruments and musicians were available for Fielding's use, for *Chrononhotonthologos* was performed on 3 May 1736; that is, during the first run of *Tumble-Down Dick* [14].

On any particular evening, then, the audience at one of Fielding's ballad operas could have expected to be treated to a wide variety of entertainment. They would have heard excellent singing if Mrs Clive, Stoppelaer, Salway, or Beard was in the cast, and they would have heard comic, *parlando*, patter-song-like singing if Harper, Macklin, Hallam, or Mrs Mullart was on stage. The accompaniments to the serious songs they would have heard with interest, and, one hopes, with appreciation. The satirical 'Rough Musick' they would have responded to with laughter. It is impossible, of course, to reconstruct the precise quality of each ballad-opera performance, but since these plays were in vogue for such a long time, the productions must have been colourful, tuneful, and well acted.

Fielding's Musical Preferences

It is difficult to say with certainty that Fielding necessarily liked the music that he used for his ballad-opera songs. He was writing popular plays, using popular music, for a popular audience. As a result his selection of tunes may have been calculated more to satisfy his audience than himself. For his ballad operas he wrote a total of 206 songs, if one includes as separate versions some songs which he used once and then used again later with only slight variation. For these songs there were 151 separate tunes, or apparently there were that many, for some of the tunes are not identified and therefore one cannot know if any of the unidentified ones were ever repeated by Fielding. Among the tunes that can be identified, 108 were popular ballads or theatrical music in the public domain, while sixteen were ascribed specifically to the Seedo who was musical director at the New Haymarket and at Drury Lane when Fielding was writing most of his ballad operas [15]. The origins of twenty-seven of the tunes remain obscure, but probably a few of these were popular ballads, while most were specially composed. The discrepancy between the 151 tunes and

206 songs is explained by the fact that Fielding wrote fifty-five of his songs to tunes that he had already used at least once. The total number of tunes that he repeated was thirty-eight. He used three tunes for four songs, eleven tunes for three, and twenty-four for two [16]. Since he could have selected many other tunes, but chose rather to re-use thirty-eight, he probably had strong preferences for his choices. I consider it unlikely that he was ever too pressed for time to select a new tune, or that he was too lazy to do so. Either he liked these tunes, or else he felt that his audiences liked them. Since he chose to re-use them, they may conveniently be regarded as his favourites.

Judging from these favourite melodies, I conclude that at this ballad-opera stage of his career, Fielding's taste in music, like that of his audience, ran toward brisk tunes in a major key. He apparently liked dance tempos best, for in a rapid, 6/8 time are 'The Black Joke' (the tune which, along with 'Dame of Honour' and 'Buff Coat', he used more than any other) and 'Bessy Bell and Mary Gray'. The marking 6/4 on a dance tune apparently indicated a fast to moderate, but also heavily accented, beat. Among this class of Fielding's repeated tunes are 'Buff Coat', Dame of Honour', 'Free-Mason's Tune', Jeremiah Clarke's 'Hark, hark, the Cock crow'd', and Henry Purcell's 'We have cheated the Parson'. Another favourite melody, in a rapid, cut time, is 'Pierrot's Tune', which was unquestionably a dance in origin. Among the moderate tunes which Fielding liked are 'Sir Thomas I Cannot', in a smooth, 6/4 time, and 'Pinks and Lilies', in cut time. 'Under the Greenwood Tree', which he used twice, is in a stately 6/4 time. The slower melodies that Fielding seems to have liked are 'Now Ponder Well', 'Ye Nymphs and Sylvan Gods', 'Why Will Florella', and the beautiful 'Tweed Side', all in 3/4 time. None of these 3/4 tunes is a minuet; the only minuet among Fielding's favourite tunes was 'Geminiani's Minuet'.

Although he used popular arias and marches from Handel's *opera seria*, like 'Caro Vien', 'Si Caro', 'Son' Confusa', and the march in *Scipio*, it does not appear that Fielding developed a genuine fondness for this sophisticated music until after the time of his ballad operas. The operatic tunes that he knew and used seem to have been confined to those which became most popular with the public. Paradoxically, his use of these melodies was most probably determined by his desire to ridicule the *opera seria*, or by his having the tenors Stoppelaer, Salway, or Beard as leading singers at various times. But he must have had a good musical ear – he could not have been as good a lyricist as he was without one – and his practical experience in the theatre with musicians, singers, and musical directors probably educated him musically. As a result of this experience he came to like Handel, a mark of musical sophistication. In *The Wedding Day* (1743) he made the character Brazen recall the excellence of Handel's operas and then sing 'Si Caro' as an example of this excellence. In *Tom Jones*, six years later, Fielding praised Handel through Sophia, who was 'a perfect mistress of music', who 'would never willingly have played any but Handel's [music]' (III.v). By contrast, he disparaged the taste of Squire Western, who 'never relished any music but what was light and airy; and indeed his most favourite tunes were Old Sir Simon the King, St. George he was for England, Bobbing Joan, and some others' (II.v). Since 'Bobbing Joan' appeared as the music of Air III in *The Pleasures of the Town*, it is certain that Fielding in 1749 had moved far beyond the musical taste evidenced in his ballad operas. Did he direct his criticism of Squire Western's taste also against his own earlier taste? Whether he did or did not, it appears certain that in 1749 he was criticising the popular taste which had earlier made the ballad operas, including his own, so successful.

Regardless of his later attitudes, during the time of his ballad operas he threw his energies wholeheartedly into the creation of catchy, witty songs set to various popular melodies. In doing so he was running a risk as a dramatist, for the need to write ballad songs militated against the dramatic exploration of human personality and social issues, an avenue of creativity down which he wanted to travel. His audiences expected the songs of each ballad opera to be like those in *The Beggar's Opera*: epigrammatic, satiric, and sometimes sentimental. Many of Fielding's fellow ballad-opera writers had used the dramatic form as not much more than a vehicle by which to present such songs. Fielding's good friend James Ralph deplored this situation in his ballad opera *The Fashionable Lady* (1730), saying, in Air I, ''Tis our tunes that we trust, and our Tunes are all made'. Ralph and Fielding had probably discussed this problem, and Fielding's *Author's Farce*, written at the same time as *The Fashionable Lady*, was partly a burlesque of the ballad-opera form itself. Their position was that the writer of ballad operas was at best limited in his treatment of character and plot because of the need for songs, and at worst he merely wrote his dramatic dialogue as a bridge from one song to another. Had the requirement for songs not existed, they argued, the ballad-opera writer would have been forced to write better dramas by emphasizing character and plot.

Fielding's use of the Ballad Tradition

Despite the problems inherent in the ballad opera as a dramatic form, one does not need to resort to special pleading to praise Fielding as a dramatist or lyricist. His songs exhibit to a high degree, and sometimes to a superlative degree, all the skills that are to be found in ballad-opera songs. Everywhere one can see the stamp of his creative and original mind. But the subject of Fielding's lyrics deserves a monograph-length study, far beyond my scope here. I shall therefore confine my remarks about his songs to that aspect which would have been most apparent to his audiences, namely to the relationship between (1) what the audiences probably knew – the original words and music of the tunes – and (2) what Fielding presented to them in song, his lyrics. It was this relationship, so difficult for us to recover today, that was the virtual lifeblood of the ballad operas [17].

All the ballad-opera tunes available to Fielding, some of which I have already mentioned, came to him with an independent and sometimes long history. *The Beggar's Opera*, for example, contained the music of 'Valentine's Day', or Ophelia's mad song from *Hamlet*; Gay also used the music of 'Now Ponder Well', 'Greensleeves', and 'London is a Fine Town', all of which were known in Shakespeare's day. Fielding himself used three of these tunes, and also employed the music of 'Under the Greenwood Tree', which may at some time have been associated with Shakespeare's *As You Like It*. Many other tunes in the ballad operas were of similar vintage. Although there was a paucity of material from the Puritan period, a high proportion of the tunes – about twenty to thirty per cent – dated from the Restoration. By far the greatest proportion of melodies, however, had been composed in the eighteenth century, and the greatest number of these came from the decade of the 1720s. The music of contemporary composers, such as those represented in Watts' *Musical Miscellany* of 1729–31, was seized by the writers of the ballad operas, and served to keep their plays up to date.

The content of these original ballads may be classified under the following headings: (1) love songs, (2) songs concerning familiar aspects of life such as conviviality and drinking, farming, sheepherding, sailing, or begging, and (3) public-life songs, including political and social songs in a satirical vein. These types were important, for subsequent uses of the tunes often corresponded to the particular type. The tune of 'The Abbot of Canterbury', for example, was used for innumerable lyrics on political subjects, as were 'Ye Commons and Peers' and 'To All You Ladies Now at Land'. These tunes would have been considered at the time as political, and so also, to their own categories, for many other popular tunes and songs.

When Fielding wrote his songs, then, he was aware of a tradition, and worked within his knowledge. One way was to make the subject matter of his songs similar to the subject matter both of the original song and of its subsequent versions. In this way, his songs became a part of the tradition of the original. 'Lillibullero', one of the eighteenth-century tunes best known today, had a definite political and social connotation in Fielding's time that could be traced to its popularity in the 1688 Irish rebellion and also to its fame in *The Beggar's Opera*. Keeping within this tradition, Fielding used the tune in *The Pleasures of the Town* as the setting for his attack on 'great men', and in *Don Quixote in England* he used it for a musical discussion between Fairlove and Badger about proper marital adjustments. 'Young Damon Once the Happiest Swain' was originally a song about love, the music of which Fielding used in Sweetissa's reflections about love in Air XI of *The Grub-Street Opera*. In *The Pleasures of the Town*, Air III, the dance music of 'Bobbing Joan', accompanied Punch's declaration, 'Joan, you are the Plague of my Life'. As a mark of Fielding's creativity, he established his own characteristic use for songs that had no such particular traditions. He used 'Pierrot's Tune', 'The Black Joke', and 'Mother Quoth Hodge', for example, exclusively as music for songs on social and political subjects.

Quite common in the relationship of Fielding's subject matter to that of the original ballad is a disparity that he deliberately created. By this means he achieved both ironic and burlesque effects. In *The Lottery*, Lovemore sang about his faithfulness to Chloe to the music of 'Virgins Beware', an irony of which Fielding could not have been unaware [18]. One of the excellences of *An Old Man Taught Wisdom* is the extent to which Fielding employed this device for ironic effect, since in that play the meanings of virtually all the songs were made ironically complex by their contrast with the original ballads. The extremity of contrast is the burlesque, and Fielding wrote two full-scale burlesques; the first, which I have already mentioned, was Air XII of

The Pleasures of the Town, a travesty of *The Beggar's Opera*, Air XVI; the second was Air IV of *Tumble-Down Dick*, a parody of a song in Pritchard's *Fall of Phaeton* (1736) [19].

As in these burlesque songs, Fielding frequently echoed passages of the originals, thereby reminding the listener of the original context for purposes either of evaluative comparison or of highlighting his ironic intention. The full title of 'Buff Coat', for example, is 'Buff Coat has no Fellow', which is a line sung at the end of the first musical phrase. Fielding echoed this line in Air XVII of *The Lottery* in order to denigrate alley brokers like Stocks. Whereas the original words praised buff coats, Fielding's words ironically dispraised stockjobbers:

> In all Trades we've had,
> Some good, and some bad,
> But a Stock-Jobber has no Fellow;
> . . . . .
> Nay, the Devil's to blame,
> Or he'll own to his Shame,
> That a Stock-Jobber has no Fellow.

In the opening ballad of *The Pleasures of the Town*, Punch sang 'Whilst the Town's brimful of Farces' to the music of Monro's 'Whilst the Town's brimful of Folly'. Similarly, Eurydice sang 'Turn oh turn, Dear, do not fly me' to 'Turn, oh turn thee, dearest Creature', itself an adaptation of '*Vieni Torna*' from Handel's opera *Theseus*. A particularly effective type of echo was that of the refrain. Many tunes, like 'Yorkshire Ballad', 'The Jovial Beggar', and 'Tenant of My Own', had refrains, and Fielding used them for comic and satiric effects. A refrain, one might note, is that part of a lyric that most people are likely to remember best, so when they hear a variation on one, they are likely to respond quickly. A refrain that would have been well known by Fielding's audience was that of 'Ye Madcaps of England', which was 'Sing Tantararara, Boys Drink, Boys Drink'. Fielding's echo of this line may be seen in the second stanza of Air LX of *The Grub-Street Opera* [20].

The relationship of Fielding's subjects to those of the original ballads extended also to the mood of the music, though the subject-music relationship was not as common or as pronounced as the subject-subject relationship. The firmness and resoluteness of Weldon's 'Let Ambition Fire Thy Mind' made it a fitting accompaniment to Molly's resolution to love Owen in Air XXII of *The Grub-Street Opera* [21]. A similar wedding of subject and musical mood occurred in *The Grub-Street*

Opera, Air LVII: Susan the cook, agitated about having to cut up the sirloin of beef, sang of her disturbance to the rapid, agitated music of 'The South Sea Ballad'. In Air XVI of *The Lottery*, this same music accompanied Stocks' appeal to pursue Dame Fortune 'with vigour' and haste, the music thus supporting the urgency of the appeal.

Another technique of relating subject to music sometimes employed by Fielding was to set satirical words to a melody more appropriate to love or nostalgic sorrow. He used 'Tweed Side' in this way, once to express Sweetissa's disgust with being virtuous (*The Grub-Street Opera*, Air XX), and another time to express Lucy's bashful promise to have an affair with Coupee after she has married Blister (*An Old Man Taught Wisdom*, Air VII) [22]. Another favourite tune that he used in this way was 'Now Ponder Well', which accompanied both the calling of lottery numbers in *The Lottery*, Air XVIII, and Lucy's promise to marry Blister in *An Old Man Taught Wisdom*, Air IV [23]. A stirring tune, from which Fielding extracted ironic humour in *The Grub-Street Opera* (Air XXIX) by having Robin and Will spar halfheartedly to its music, was Purcell's 'Britons Strike Home'. This ironic technique, it may be noted, was later used successfully by Kurt Weill in *The Threepenny Opera*, most obviously in 'Mack the Knife' and 'The Tango Dance', though the difference is that while Weill wrote his own music, Fielding selected his.

In each of the instances just discussed, whether by similarity or by deliberate contrast, Fielding's ballad-opera songs depended for their entire meaning not only upon the context of his play, but also upon the contexts, both topical and musical, of the original street or drawing-room ballads. The topical relationships would have been immediately and obviously apparent to his audience, whose knowledge of popular culture would have been at least modestly extensive. We may imagine that his audience, recollecting Polly's song to her parents in Air XII of *The Beggar's Opera*, would have been doubly amused at hearing Mrs Clive sing Air IV of *An Old Man Taught Wisdom*, particularly because they also knew that Mrs Clive had frequently played Polly. Because it was conventional in all ballad operas to utilize this technique of comparison and contrast, it should not be inferred that Fielding's use of original contexts was unique. But the extent to which he employed the technique, and the degrees of irony he achieved by it, are noteworthy, and were certainly among the reasons for the popularity of many of his ballad operas throughout the eighteenth century.

Notes

[1] See Edmund McAdoo Gagey, *Ballad Opera* (New York, Columbia U.P., 1937), for a complete discussion of ballad operas. I have been over some of the ground covered in this paper, but briefly, in 'Eighteenth-Century Ballad Opera: The contribution of Henry Fielding', *Drama Survey*, I (1961), 77–85.

[2] See My 'Henry Fielding's Lost Play *Deborah, or a Wife for You All* (1733): Consisting Partly of Facts and Partly of Observations Upon Them', *Bulletin of the New York Public Library*, LXVI (1962), 576–88.

[3] Wilbur L. Cross, *The History of Henry Fielding* (New Haven, Conn., Yale U.P., 1918, reprinted by Russell & Russell, Inc., 1963), I, 206.

[4] See Charles B. Woods, 'The "Miss Lucy" Plays of Fielding and Garrick', *Philological Quarterly*, XLI (1962), 294–310.

[5] Charles Burney, *A General History of.Music* (New York, Dover, 1957), II, 1000.

[6] Herbert Stoppelaer's painting of Stoppelaer as Tubal, with Macklin as Shylock (apparently an exact copy of John Zoffany's portrait of Macklin and Stoppelaer in these roles), is now hanging in the American Shakespeare Festival Theatre in Stratford, Connecticut. Raymond Mander and Joe Mitchenson, in *The Artist and the Theatre* (London, Heinemann, 1955), discuss Zoffany's original (pp. 58–60) and reproduce it (p. 62).

[7] Arthur H. Scouten ed., *The London Stage, 1660–1800*, Part 3: *1729–1747* (Carbondale, Southern Ill. U.P., 1961), indicates that on 6 July 1731, Stoppelaer first performed at Drury Lane in the role of Hunter in *The Beggar's Wedding* (I, 147). This role was a familiar one to Stoppelaer, who could have played it with little rehearsal.

[8] Winton Dean, *Handel's Dramatic Oratorios and Masques* (London, Oxford U.P., 1959), 652.

[9] William Appleton, *Charles Macklin, An Actor's Life* (Cambridge, Mass., Harvard U.P., 1961), 14.

[10] Allardyce Nicoll, *A History of English Drama, 1660–1900*, Vol. II, *Early Eighteenth-Century Drama*, 3rd edn (Cambridge, Cambridge U.P., 1952), 77.

[11] Adam Carse, *The Orchestra in the XVIIIth Century* (Cambridge, W. Heffer & Sons, 1940, reprinted 1950), 34.

[12] A print of this engraving can be found in Dane F. Smith, *Plays About the Theatre in England, 1671–1737* (New York, Oxford U.P., 1936), facing p. 138, and also in Frederick Antal, *Hogarth and His Place in European Art* (New York, Basic Books, 1962), plate 22a.

[13] *Spectator*, No. 251.

[14] Scouten, op. cit., I, 571.

[15] See my 'Mr Seedo's London Career and His Work with Henry Fielding', *Philological Quarterly*, XLV (1966), 179–90.

[16] The tunes he used four times were 'The Black Joke', 'Buff Coat', and 'Dame of Honour'. Those he used three times were 'As Down in a Meadow', 'Bessy Bell', 'Hunt the Squirrel', 'Lass of Peatie's Mill', 'Now Ponder Well', 'Pinks and Lilies', 'Pierrot's Tune', 'Sir Thomas I Cannot', 'Tweed Side', 'We

Have Cheated the Parson', and 'Ye Nymphs and Sylvan Gods'. The reader
who verifies this list may question 'As Down in a Meadow' as one that
Fielding used three times, but since the publication of my edition of *The
Grub-Street Opera* (Lincoln, Nebr., U. of Nebraska Press, 1968), I have
discovered that 'As Down in a Meadow' was Air XLVII of *The Grub-Street
Opera*. The tunes Fielding used twice were 'Bush of Boon', 'Celia My
Dearest', 'Chloe is False', 'Country Bumpkin', 'Dimi Caro', 'Dutch Skipper,
Part II', 'Free-Mason's Tune', 'From Aberdeen to Edinburgh', 'Geminiani's
Minuet', 'Have You Heard of a Frolicksome Ditty', 'Hark, Hark, the Cock
Crows', 'In Porus [Son' Confusa]', 'King's Old Courtier', 'London is a Fine
Town', 'Lillibullero', 'Mother Quoth Hodge', 'O Hasten My Lover' (this is
Fielding's title, and the tune was probably composed by one of the musical
directors with whom he worked), 'Polwarth on the Green', 'Si Caro', 'South
Sea Ballad', 'There Was a Jovial Beggar', 'Under the Greenwood Tree', 'Why
Will Florella', and 'Ye Madcaps of England'.

[17] Because of the popularity of *The Beggar's Opera*, much scholarly attention
has been given to the histories of the tunes used in it. I have included a
bibliography of this scholarship in 'A Note on the Origins of the Tunes' in
my edition of *The Beggar's Opera* (Lincoln, Nebr., U. of Nebraska Press,
1969), xxvii *f*. Similar attention to Fielding's tunes has not been published,
but the interested reader might consult my unpublished dissertation, 'The
Ballad Operas of Henry Fielding, 1730–1732: A Critical Edition' (*The
Author's Farce, The Grub-Street Opera, The Lottery, The Mock Doctor*), U.
of Minnesota, 1960, II, 409–584, for historical notes to the tunes in the
first four ballad operas.

[18] This tune was also called 'Claspt in My Dear Melinda's Arms', but it does not
appear that Fielding knew the tune by this name.

[19] Pritchard's song is as follows:

> Thus when the Nightingale has found
> Her young, by some disaster slain,
> O'er the sad Spoil she hovers round,
> And views it o'er and o'er again:
> Then to some Grove retires, alone,
> Filling with plaintive Strains the Skies
> There warbles out her tuneful Moan,
> 'Till o'er th'unfinish'd Note she dies.
>
> (London, 1736), 13.

Fielding's song is an amusing parody:

> Thus when the wretched Owl has found
> Her young Owls dead as Mice,
> O'er the sad Spoil she hovers round,
> And views 'em once or twice:
> Then to some hollow Tree she flies,
> To hollow, hoot, and howl,
> Till ev'ry Boy that passes, cries,
> The Devil's in the Owl!
>
> (Air IV)

[20] One might note that 'Bob' in the refrain of this stanza would have been immediately recognized as a reference to Walpole:

For   if you will be such a   hus-band of pelf,   To

be serv'd by cheats, you must   e'en serve your-self;   The

world   is   so   cramm'd brim - full   of   de -ceit,   That if

Rob - in be___   a   name for   a cheat,   Sing

tan - ta-ra - ra - ra, Bobs   all,   Bobs   all,   Sing

tan - ta - ra - ra - ra, Bobs   all._____

Music adapted from Roberts, ed., *The Grub-Street Opera*, p. 140.

[21] Molly's song is as follows:

Hap - py   with___ the   man___ I___ love,

I'll   ob - se - quious watch his   will;

Hot-test   pleas - ures I___   shall_ prove,

While his   pleas - ures I   ful - fill.

Dames, by   proud - est tit - les   known,

Shall de - sire___ what we___   pos - sess;

And while they'd   less   hap - py   own

Grand-eur is___   not   hap - pi - ness.

Music adapted from ibid., III.

[22] Lucy's song is the following:

Music adapted from ibid., 110.

[23] The two versions are amusing:

Music adapted from Charles B. Woods, ed. (and completed by Curt Zimansky), *The Author's Farce* (Lincoln, Nebr., U. of Nebraska Press, 1966), 136.

3 GEORGE TAYLOR

'The Just Delineation of the Passions': Theories of Acting in the Age of Garrick

My interest in the Acting Revolution associated with the names of Garrick and Macklin was revived when I saw a number of shelves in our University library gradually filling up with the smart green bindings of the Scholar Press reprints of works on Grammar, Philology and Language, particularly as many of them, dated from between 1750 and 1780, dealt with Oratory, Elocution and the Nature of Speech. My concern is not primarily with the details of speech — although these works may hold many of the clues to canting, ranting and the tones — but with the imaginative processes that lay behind acting at that time. Not so much how actors spoke, but why they spoke as they did. My particular paradox of acting is why, in the last couple of centuries, each actor has been greeted as more 'natural' than the one before, and how the naturalism of one generation becomes the 'ham' action of the next. It cannot be entirely due to changing techniques of speech and gesture, but to the underlying creative method. Once such a method has been recognised by an audience, it no longer convinces them. They may still be moved, excited and impressed by a performance, but they call it art rather than nature. My parents remember Gielgud's Hamlet as one who talked and did not declaim, which is something few students would believe today. Another example more readily, and more vividly, appreciated is that of seeing the famous clip from *On the Waterfront*, in which Brando and Steiger grunt at each other in a taxi, and scratch their ears. What was once pure naturalism now seems rather indulgent contrivance.

Garrick himself was hailed as a miracle of naturalness and a master of realistic psychology, yet by the end of his career, although his understanding of his characters seems to have deepened, there were many critics who could analyse his pieces of stage business and indeed attack his notorious 'clap traps'. What is more, Diderot could use him to illustrate his own paradox that even in his most natural and pathetic points, Garrick was in complete control of his sensibilities and contriving the whole effect. Perhaps this phenomenon can be explained in terms of changing techniques and dramatic conventions, in response to an audience's demand for novelty, but I think the key is somewhere in the thought that lies behind performance. To understand how Garrick could be both a miracle of nature and a consummate craftsman, we should not begin by studying the details of vocal technique, gesture or stage business, but the theory of psychology which lay behind the technique, a theory not perhaps consciously incorporated into a specific method, but one vaguely shared by all intelligent men of the age. In other words, we ought to look more closely at the preconceptions of the age with regard to the working of the human mind and emotions. Once we become conscious of this underlying rationale, we become conscious of the actor's art, we begin to admire his imitation of what he believed to be natural, rather than being uncritically astonished that audiences could ever have thought such behaviour was 'natural'.

I am confirmed in this opinion by what I have read in the handbooks of theory published by the Scholar Press. There was a revolution in the understanding of speech and the nature of communication, which parallels the revolution in acting. This is recognized by the editor of these reprints, R. C. Alston, in his brief introduction to John Mason's *Essay on Elocution*, first published in 1748 and which has, Alston says,

> a particular historical significance because it represents a renewed interest in a neglected art. The interest in pronunciation which was so characteristic of writers on English in the second half of the eighteenth century, and finds expression in numerous treatises on pronunciation and elocution as well as in dictionaries of English, can be traced back to sixteenth century manuals of pulpit oratory, but the movement which was to reach fruition in the work of writers such as Sheridan and Walker has its origins in a complex coincidence of interests: among which are the improvement of dramatic speech (to which Garrick contributed so effectively) and parliamentary debate; the public recitation of poetry; and a concern to 'fix' pronunciation and formulate a universal standard. [1]

In fact Mason's *Essay* was preceded by the essential translations of the classical authorities to which nearly all the works of the century refer. Longinus was translated by William Smith in 1739, Cicero's *De Oratore* by William Guthrie in 1742 (with further versions by George Barnes in

1762 and Edward Jones in 1776), while Guthrie's translation of Quintillian appeared in 1756.

Many of the original theoretical works were merely school hand-books, but, as Alston indicates, the most important works were by Thomas Sheridan and John Walker. Both were for a time actors before they turned scholars. Sheridan was manager of Smock Alley and father of the playwright; his *Lectures on Elocution* appeared in 1762, accompanied by the outline of his *General Dictionary of the English Language*, which was eventually published in 1780. It was Sheridan's apparent presumption in planning this dictionary that caused the greatest lexicographer of the century, Dr Johnson, to exclaim, 'Why, Sir, Sherry is dull, naturally dull; but it must have taken him a great deal of pains to become what we now see him. Such an excess of stupidity, Sir, is not in Nature!' This, of course, is unfair. His work may not be very profound but it is thorough, fairly well written and has rather more common sense than Walker's exhaustive works. Walker played for a while at Drury Lane, where 'he usually filled the second parts in tragedy, and those of a grave sententious cast in comedy' [2]. He joined Barry and Woodward in their Dublin adventure of 1758, and left the theatre ten years later. His main works include *Elements of Elocution* (1781), *A Rhetorical Grammar* (1785) and *The Melody of Speaking* (1787). Much of his effort was spent in trying to formulate a method of notation to indicate intonation as well as the pauses of punctuation, and his *magnum opus* was a *Critical Pronouncing Dictionary* published in 1791. Other notable contributions to this field of study include John Rice's *Introduction to the Art of Reading* (1765), William Cockin's *Art of Delivering Language* (1775), Joshua Steele's *Prosodia Rationalis* (1775) [3], and that universal genius, Joseph Priestley's *Lectures on Oratory and Criticism* (1777). To these works we should add those of Aaron Hill and the self-styled 'Sir' John Hill, which are the most essential treatises on the art of acting during the middle years of the century, although of course many other critics and writers have made significant comments which have contributed to this study.

Obviously Sheridan and Walker, as one-time actors, must have made use of their experiences of the theatrical art, but how far, one might ask, did these theories affect other full-time actors? Significantly, Macklin took up lecturing himself in 1754, although the combination of his own lack of pedagogic talent and the vicious ridicule he suffered because of this from Samuel Foote, brought his ambitions to a swift conclusion. Nevertheless, he was no mean scholar and indeed Tom Davies described him as 'the only player I ever heard of that made acting a science', [4]. After the failure of his lecturing he of course returned to the theatre and continued to influence many young actors. Garrick, too, prided himself on his intellectual accomplishments. After all, he was allowed to join Dr Johnson's famous Club. Moreover, he figures in some of these theoretical treatises. William Cockin, although a school teacher in Lancaster and Nottingham, must have got to know Garrick at some time and discussed his theories with him. for his *Art of Delivering Language* is dedicated to the actor; he claimed that 'the doctrine laid down in the following essay agrees exactly with your own sentiments' [5]. John Walker also acknowledges Garrick's interest in his work and indicates that during his retirement the great actor might even have assisted him. In the Introduction to his *Elements of Elocution* he describes how he was trying to apply his form of notation,

> to convey such turns and inflexions of voice as accompanied the pauses and emphasis of a good speaker, and this, had that great actor and excellent citizen Mr Garrick lived, I should have exemplified in some of his favourite speeches; but death which deprived the stage of its greatest ornament, bereft me of a most valued friend and patron; a loss I have the greater reason to lament, as his advice and assistance was always open to the feeblest attempt of genius, and had been often afforded to the beginnings of the present work. [6]

We must assume from these dedications that Garrick was at least aware of the theories of Cockin and Walker, and also those of his one-time rival, Thomas Sheridan, for he is on the list of subscribers to the *Lectures on Elocution*. We may also assume from the authors' acknowledgements that he was rather more in sympathy with the approach of Cockin and Walker than with that of Sheridan; which may seem rather surprising when we examine and compare their arguments.

Throughout his *Lectures on Elocution*, Sheridan argues for naturalistic delivery. He attacks the usual method of school teaching, which encourages children to read in a sing-song tone, giving an impression of mechanical learning and boredom; he attacks also the use of theatrical tones, which give an impression of bombast. After examining the correct use of Articulation, Pronunciation, Accent, Emphasis, Tones, Pauses and Stops, Key or Pitch and the Management of the Voice, by which he means voice production, he concludes:

The chief end of all public speakers is to persuade; and in order to persuade, it is above all things necessary, that the speaker should at least appear himself to believe, what he utters; but this can never be the case, where there are any evident marks of affectation, or art. On the contrary, when a man delivers himself in his usual manner, and with the same tones and gestures that he is accustomed to use, when he speaks from his heart, however ill-regulated his tones, he will still have the advantage, of being thought sincere, which of all others, is the most necessary article, towards securing attention and belief, as affectation of any kind, is the surest way to destroy both [7].

And what is true for the orator, he implies, is the same for the actor. Some of his analysis may seem pedantic to the modern actor, but in comparison to the work of Cockin and Walker it is common sense itself. Cockin specifically claims that he wrote in order to refute Sheridan, and maintains in opposition to him that;

in *theatrical declamation* in order to give it more pomp and solemnity, it is usual to dwell longer than common upon the unaccented syllables, and the author before quoted [i.e., Sheridan] has endeavoured to prove the practice faulty. . . . But that this deviation from ordinary speech is not a fault, as our author asserts, nay, that on the contrary it is a real beauty, when kept under proper regulation, the following observations I hope will sufficiently prove. . . . To keep pace and be consistent with the *dignity* of the tragic muse, the delivery of her language should necessarily be dignified. [8]

Cockin, as we have seen, claimed that the doctrines laid down in the essay 'agreed exactly with Garrick's own sentiments'. If this is so, I find it surprising, since the theory of Sheridan seems to explain the practice of Garrick, while the theory of Cockin might explain the practice of Sheridan, whose own acting was often considered stiff and pedantic. However, the real point that seems to emerge from this apparent contradiction is that Garrick was rather more aware than Sheridan of the importance of the use of artifice in creating the impression of naturalism.

A specific example of both Garrick's precision of performance and his acquaintance with at least the terminology of rhetorical theory, can be seen in his answer to criticism of his delivery of certain lines in Hamlet. He wrote to the critic who accused him of stopping injudiciously in the middle of the sentence, 'I think it was to see — my mother's wedding', that he did not make a 'real *stop* (that is close the sense) but I certainly *suspended* my voice, by which your ear must know the sense is suspended too; for Hamlet's grief causes the break, and with a sigh, he finishes the sentence — 'my mother's wedding' [9].

However, it is obvious from all the sources that Garrick's main contribution to the development of acting was to dispense with the tones of Booth, Wilkes and Quin, and, despite Cockin's desire for 'dignified' language, I could quote many passages from these books condemning the old fashioned theatrical whine, and the canting tones of heroic tragedy. But this development is well known and indeed fully expounded in Bertram Joseph's *The Tragic Actor* (London, 1959) and Alan S. Downer's paper 'Nature to Advantage Dressed' [10]. The only really notable comment I came across on this point was in John Rice's *Art of Reading*, where he gives an amusing example, not of tones being ridiculous, but of the perils of being too natural in delivery.

> Nothing can be more ridiculous than the affected Airs of Dignity and Importance with which most Readers recite oratorical and poetic Compositions. ... On the other hand, I have seen some Actors, aware of the Impropriety, run into the other extreme, and affecting Ease and Simplicity, converse in the characters of Heroes, of the Fate of Kingdoms, with as much Familiarity as if they were chatting of theatrical Affairs in the Green-Room. I remember, in particular, to have heard the whole Audience burst into an immoderate Peal of Laughter, on *Romeo's* saying to his Man — *You know my Lodgings*, so excessively Ludicrous did a familiar Tone of Voice make this short Sentence. I well remember also, that, to avoid the like Error the next Time the Character was played by the same Actor, he pronounced these Words in a plaintive and sad Tone as if the Circumstance itself was to be remembered among his greatest Misfortunes. [11]

What has attracted my notice time and again in these handbooks of oratory, and which is to be found also in the treatise on acting and in many of the theatrical criticisms of the time, is the analysis of the Passions. It is the phrase, 'the just delineation of the passions', which appears so often and which I have made the title of this paper, that I wish to explore in more detail, for it is almost entirely in terms of 'the passions' that they discuss the creative and psychological techniques of acting. What we must first do is to find out what the eighteenth-century writers meant and understood by the term Passion, and then consider how they thought an actor should go about imitating or recreating these passions. That this concept is the key to the art of acting can be seen, not only from the oratory and elocution books, but also from the writings of the actors themselves. In 1744 in his *Essay upon Acting*, Garrick himself defined the art as 'an entertainment of the stage, which by calling in the aid and assistance of articulation, corporeal motions and ocular expression, imitates, assumes, or puts on the various mental and bodily emotions arising from the various humours, virtues and vices, incident to human nature', and he ends the essay with a promise of 'a more complete and expanded treatise upon acting, with an accurate description of each humour and passion, their sources and effects' [12] . Macklin, too, at the end of the century wrote on *The Art and Duty of an Actor*, where he not only defines acting in terms of passions, but makes a plea for the actor to understand intellectually the theory behind them: 'If the actor has not a philosophical knowledge of the passions, it is impossible for him to imitate them with fidelity . . . unless he knows the *genus, species* and characteristics that he is about to imitate, he will fall short in his execution' [13] .

It is necessary therefore to say something about the general theories of psychology that were commonly accepted in the eighteenth century. This will take us back to the philosophers of the seventeenth century who formulated these concepts, and in particular to John Locke's *Essay concerning Human Understanding*, which was the most influential work of philosophy throughout the century. To understand Locke we need also to say something of Descartes and Hobbes, within the context of whose ideas he was himself writing. The Cartesian dualism made a clear distinction between the Mind and the Body. The Mind, or Soul, could think rationally, remember and make choices by the exercise of the will, the Body, or the Animal Spirits, was responsible for fantasy, the instincts and what he called common sense. Physical sensations were transmitted by these animal spirits along the nerves and caused automatic responses or 'reflex actions'. Thus certain appetites and instincts were automatic and physiological. However, some emotions were internal sensations, not resulting from the external stimulus of the five senses, but from the activity of the mind alone. These Descartes called the Passions. This meant that he used the term passion to cover all internal sensations and activities, such as perception, emotion and the processes of thought. These activities were not the reflex actions of the body, but activities of the soul. It is a cardinal point of Descartes, and one shared by Locke, that the mind could control the passions. In other words, good judgement and the exercise of reason can control a man's conduct. The soul is the operator of the physical machine; it is only animals, which lack Man's soul, which automatically behave in response to the activity of their animal spirits.

Hobbes was less confident in the overruling power of the mind, and he tended to explain man's behaviour, not in terms of a Rational Morality, but as a response to one chief irrational passion, the passion for power, the power to achieve pleasure and avoid pain. His philosophy claimed that this was the sole motivation for action, but the powerful religious preconceptions of the age were hostile to his idea of an active psychology, fundamentally based on the gratification of selfish passions and appetites for power, pleasure, and the avoidance of pain. Spinoza too saw the passions as being a reflex response by the body to circumstances which are either pleasant or unpleasant, but, unlike Hobbes, he did not feel that Man should motivate all his actions in response to these passions. In fact, he stressed the conflict between the emotions, which were concerned with physical gratification, and the mind, which was capable of moral choices and decisions.

Spinoza's important contribution to this study was the way in which he precisely classified the different passions – the prime passions being Wonder and Desire. Wonder is a physiological reaction to a shock to the system and causes agitation, whilst Desire is the motivating cause of action, which leads to the secondary passions, the states of emotion such as joy, pleasure, love, grief, anger or hate. Even the activities of the intellect, to which he gave a higher moral value, Spinoza analysed in terms of passions. These were the rational emotions of virtue, nobility, fortitude, sobriety, etc., which were controlled by the chief intellectual passion, the Will. It will be seen that Spinoza, like Descartes, seems to include all mental activities and psychological states under the term of Passion, and perhaps this may explain why the 'delineation of the passions' was held to be so important by our theatrical commentators, for, to follow these philosophers, it would seem that the whole personality was the sum of all the passions. But in the formation of eighteenth-century English thinking, the Continental philosophers had nowhere near the same influence as John Locke, and in his *Essay on Human Understanding* the term passion does not even appear in the index.

Locke's *Essay* is primarily concerned with perception, understanding, and learning, rather than with the psychology of behaviour, but he does make some important points about the passions. Firstly, of course, his famous concept of the *tabula rasa*, 'that the mind is a blank sheet at birth', denies all possibility of there being such a thing as an innate emotion — even apparent instincts have to be learnt from experience, even if only in the first few hours of life. This meant that he believed a passion was created by the experience of pain or pleasure, but he tended to underrate the Hobbesian active desire for pleasure, and stress the impelling need to avoid or escape from a state of pain or unease. The most important thing about his attitude towards the passions is not that it underrates their power or denies that they exist, but that he thought of a passion more as a psychological state than an internal motivating force. Locke continually stresses the static nature of perception and experience; for example, he points out that when we say 'I see the moon' or 'I feel the heat of the sun', although we are using an active verb, 'It does not signify any action in me whereby I operate on those substances, but the reception of the idea of light, roundness and heat'. He goes on to say that this sort of reception 'will be found rather a passion than an action'. The passion is a passive state.

A further interesting concept, one that was popularized in the 1760s particularly in the novels of Laurence Sterne, is Locke's theory of the Association of Ideas. We see one thing and it reminds us of another by association; we experience some situation which once caused us pain, and when a similar situation arises we experience an irrational emotion of fear or anger. If this association is not recognized as being irrational and combated by the proper use of reason, then, Locke argues, it can become so habitual as to be a Ruling Passion. Such is the miser's irrational glee at the sight of gold. However, among the most significant features of Locke's teaching are, firstly, how little he says about the nature of emotion, and secondly, how far he subordinates its power to the power of reason:

> Nor let anyone say, he cannot govern his passions, nor hinder them from breaking out, and carrying him into action; for what he can do before a prince or a great man, he can do alone, or in the presence of God, if he will. [14]

During the eighteenth century the philosophers Berkeley, Hartley and Hume continued to be fascinated by Locke's theories of perception, and all contributed to the increasing study of psychology. The period began to see the specialization of the scientist, who studied the Laws of Nature in the physical world, leaving to the philosophers that proper study of Mankind, Man. Dr Johnson, in the preface to his *Shakespeare*, comparing the Elizabethan times with his own, could write that

> speculation had not yet attempted to analyse the mind, to trace the passions to their sources, to unfold the seminal principles of vice and virtue, or sound

the depths of the heart for the motives of human action. All these inquiries, which from that time that human nature became the fashionable study, have been made sometimes with nice discernment, but often with idle subtilty, were yet unattempted. . . . Mankind was not then to be studied in the closet.

Hartley had modified the concept of the animal spirits into a theory of the nervous system based on Vibrations, by which certain passions became contagious, thus helping to explain the so-called Natural Sympathy, which was the growing concern of the Sentimental Movement. Hume had categorised Locke's theory of the Association of Ideas into associations of resemblance, contiguity, cause, and effect. He had also sophisticated Spinoza's classification of the passions by showing how many of them were in fact mixed passions; for example, the idea of impending evil leads to fear, but also arouses the idea of escape, which leads to hope, in many ways the opposite of the original fear. An emotional response is therefore very complex. Nevertheless, even though he had recognized their complexity, Hume was still thinking of the passions as individual states of mind or of spiritual agitation, each in some subtle way different from the other.

We can now see something of the meaning of the term Passion for our philosophers of acting. It is a mental state, not necessarily an emotional motive; it is a state recognized and controlled by the mind, not, as a modern psychologist would maintain, a subconscious response controlled by unconscious memories and physiological reactions. Thus it is that we find our actors approaching the recreation of these passions rationally, through the exercise of the intellect, and by the scientific observation of those outward symptoms of a passion, the gestures and the tones of voice. It was in this scientific spirit that the scholars of elocution tried to find methods of notation to record inflection, and made their exhaustive lists of natural, reflex actions of the face and body.

What I think this interpretation of behaviour in terms of passion also explains, is the practice of eighteenth-century actors of making isolated and individual points, rather than seeking the overall development of the character. The actor who could convey one specific passion in a single line or gesture caused the whole audience to applaud that one 'stroke of nature', unlike a modern audience which watches the gradual unfolding of a personality through the development of the action of a play, withholding their applause until the whole process, or life of the performance, has been completed. A fine example of this is Garrick's famous start at seeing the ghost in *Hamlet*. He was not concerned primarily with the significance of the ghost as his murdered father, but with the expression of the passions of fear and amazement. It was these that convinced the audience that he saw a ghost, not his overall interpretation of the Prince of Denmark. That he also saw the difference between characters in terms of passions, can be seen from his comparison of the parts of Macbeth and Able Drugger. Although both are frightened — one reflects on the consequences of murder, the other on the breaking of a chamber pot — the passion is similar, but the expression must be different [15]. It would seem that Garrick looked first for the passion, and only then considered a method of expression suitable to the character and to the genre of the play. That he was a complete master of these means of expression can be seen from Davies' description of his performance of Lear:

> We should reflect that Lear is not agitated by one passion only, that he is not moved by rage, by grief and indignation singly, but by a tumultuous combination of them all together, where all claim to be heard at once, and where one naturally interrupts the progress of the others. . . . Garrick had displayed all the force of quick transitions from one passion to another: he had, from the most violent rage, descended to sedate calmness; had seized, with unutterable sensibility, the various impressions of terror, and faithfully represented all the turbid passions of the soul; he had pursued the progress of agonizing feelings to madness in its several stages. [16]

This brings us to another point frequently mentioned in the criticism of performances, the transitions between passions. If, as I have suggested, the passions were thought of as individual states of mind, the process of altering from one passion to another was conceived of as a decisive change, rather than a gradual progression. Clearly this was the case in Garrick's Lear; it was also true of Macklin's Shylock, where, in the scene with Tubal, the transitions between delight and despair, revengeful glee at Antonio's losses and piteous regret for his daughter and ducats, were so extremely striking and sudden. Yet the audience's delight in these transitions of passion was no more connected with a recognition of really naturalistic behaviour than a modern audience's amusement at the exaggerated 'double-take' of the Whitehall farceur. John Hill in his treatise *The Actor*, first published in 1750, showed that he at least was aware that the theatrical transition was part of the actor's technique, used to link the various passions together into a consistent characterization, and yet keep them distinct, so that they might be recognized by the audience:

> As in the landscape, so in the representation on the stage, things in their own place very remote, are obliged to be represented in a small compass; the field is large that affords the view for the one, and the human mind, which is represented in the other is yet more extensive. Where so many things, so distant in themselves, are to be thrown together, there requires great art to shew that they are not joined to each other: in the scene, as well as in the picture, there is required what is called *keeping*; but as the painter's principle skill is to mark the distances, the player's is to shew the removes thro' which the transitions are made from one to the other: and great care is to be taken not to confound one with another, because they happen to succeed. [17]

I have not studied the techniques of John Philip Kemble or Sarah Siddons to the same extent as Garrick's but I would like to suggest that their greatest advance on his technique was that they did not always think of a performance in this way – as being made up of distinct passions separated by spectacular transitions – but considered instead the Ruling Passions of a part, the way in which the emotions naturally led from one to another, following what Stanislavski would later call a 'through line' of feeling. Sarah Siddons evidently continued her emotional involvement in a part throughout a performance, even when off stage, and from her analysis of Lady Macbeth, it would seem that the part was interpreted so as to reach a climax or turning point after the banquet scene [18] . Similarly, Kemble's performance of Macbeth seemed reserved, or at least held back, until the dreadful news of his wife's death; the whole performance was preparing for the famous 'Tomorrow and tomorrow' speech. Maybe he was saving his voice, as Bertram Joseph suggests, but perhaps the reason was that his sense of consistency of character was preventing him from trying to make a 'point' out of every passion as it came along, in the way that both Garrick and Edmund Kean tended to do. Henry Siddons, in his *Practical Illustrations of Rhetorical Gestures*, first published in 1807, quotes Hume's comments on the complexity of passions and the phenomenon of transitions, equating the passion with the vibrations of a string which continue after the stroke of the bow, unlike the pipe, whose note dies with the breath;

> and though the fancy may change its views with great celerity, each stroke will not produce a clear and distinct note of passion, but the one passion will always be mixed and confounded with the other. . . . It is necessary to introduce a pause, and even a very long one, to connect and bind together sentiments so extremely opposite to their intermediate conditions. [19]

Siddons concluded his essay by trying to apply this theory of complex passions to Shylock's scene with Tubal:

> Two opposite sentiments alternately succeed in the soul of the Jew: grief seems to take the place of joy, and joy to assume that of grief, without any intermediate sentiment. I use the word *seems*, since grief, in succeeding to joy, no longer manifests itself with the same violence as in its original; and so joy, likewise, in its sudden triumph over grief, cannot, in its first instants, efface the wrinkles from the forehead. . . . With a feeble light, it smiles, as we may say, through a cloud, still leaving something of pain and chagrin in the first mien, and probably in the first tone of Shylock's voice; but the essential circumstance to be observed here is, that in joy there is found an accessary sentiment, which serves for its point of union with grief: I mean that joy arising from the misery of another person; consequently the joy of *hatred* closely approaches grief. The two alternate sentiments are not then simple, though they appear to be so. – But we are beginning to lose ourselves in subtilties, which appear to remove farther and farther from us in practice. It is time then to terminate our researches. [20]

Thus it would seem that by 1807 the eighteenth-century theory of the passions was no longer of practical use to the actor, although probably most of them continued to act according to it, or at least according to the clichés into which the method declined once the theory behind it was exhausted or discredited.

Having discussed the way in which the actors and theorists of acting conceived of naturalistic behaviour and expression, I want now to look at what they suggest about the actual creative processes of acting. They saw emotional reality in terms of passions, but how should the actor recreate or imitate these passions so as to convince his audience of their reality? As has already been suggested, there was a great reliance on the intellectual approach of observation and analysis. Any modern teacher of acting would be horrified by the number of times these authorities advise practising before a mirror, or studying the graceful gestures of painting and sculpture. We are disturbed when we recognize self-consciousness on stage, and it seems that this is precisely what the eighteenth century often valued; but I think this arises not from a desire to encourage affectation, but from their preconceptions of psychology. Descartes said that the Soul, by definition, is always thinking, and no other philosopher really opposed this idea with a consistent theory of subconscious motivation. Nevertheless, they were aware, to some extent, of the automatic, reflex, irrational processes of creative imagination and imitation.

Aaron Hill tries to give a fully scientific explanation of this irrational creativity in his *Essay on the Art of Acting*, published in 1746, the earliest of a number of theoretical works inspiring and inspired by the new 'naturalistic' acting. Hill was himself a dramatist, and for a while administrator of Drury Lane, but it was really in his detailed criticism of performances, which appeared in *The Prompter* between 1734 and 1736, that he had made his chief contribution to the theatre. In these criticisms he had consistently attacked,

> the puffed, round mouth, an empty, vagrant eye, a solemn silliness of strut, a swing-swang slowness in the motion of the arm, and a dry, dull, drawling voice that carries opium in its detestable monotony – these are the graces of the modern stage! These are the fruits of the two royal patents! [21]

However, in his *Essay* of 1746 he regularized his ideas into a systematic exploration of the art of acting. The concept of the passions is quite clearly central to it. His first principle for the actor is,

> To act a passion well, the actor must never attempt its imitation, 'till his fancy has conceived so strong an image, or idea of it, as to move the same impressive springs within his mind, which form that passion, when 'tis undesigned and natural. . . .
> 1st. The imagination must conceive a strong idea of the passion.
> 2nd. But that idea cannot be strongly conceived, without impressing its own form upon the muscles of the face.
> 3rd. Nor can the look be muscularly stamped, without communicating, instantly, the same impression to the muscles of the body.
> 4th. The muscles of the body (braced or slack, as the idea was an active or a passive one), must, in their natural, and not to be avoided consequence, by impelling or retarding the flow of the animal spirits, transmit their own conceived sensation, to the sound of the voice, and to the disposition of the gesture.

It would seem that, beneath all the scientific jargon, he was in fact relying upon the unconscious functioning of the mind and body to help recreate the passion. But unfortunately he goes on to leave unconscious creativity behind:

> It should be noted, that there are only ten dramatic passions:– that is, passions, which can be distinguished by their outward marks in acting.

He then describes in detail the gestures and tones which are the signs of Joy, Grief, Fear, Anger, Pity, Scorn, Hatred, Jealousy, Wonder and Love. Finally, he advises the actor that the whole creative process can in fact be bypassed by the use of rational technique:

But there is a shorter road, to the same end, and it shall in due place be shown him. When he believes himself possessed of the idea of joy, that would not fail to warm a strong conception, let him not imagine the impression rightly hit, until he has examined both his face and air, in a long, upright, looking glass; for there, only, will he meet with a sincere and undeceivable test of his having strongly enough, or too slackly, adapted his fancy to the purpose before him. . . for these are nature's own marks, and impressions, on the body, in cases where passion is produced by involuntary emotions. And when natural impressions are imitated, exactly, by art, the effect of such art must seem natural. [22]

So much for moving the 'same impressive springs within his own mind, which form the passions, when it is undesigned and natural'!

John Hill's translation and adaptation of Saint-Albine's *Le Comédien*, published in 1750 as *The Actor: a Treatise on the Art of Playing*, is probably the more profound and sensible work of acting theory. Unfortunately, however, and despite his friendship with Macklin, his failure as an actor, his reputation as a quack herbalist and as a Grub Street parasite, had made him unpopular in the best theatrical circles, as can be seen in the fact that he is probably the hero not only of a number of Sam Foote's satires, but even Garrick went out of his way to attack him in the press and in his poem 'The Sick Monkey'.

But *The Actor* is not merely a hack translation; it has so many perceptive examples drawn from the English stage, that I think we must credit John Hill with a good understanding of the histrionic art. To begin with, he discusses the actor's need for both Understanding and Sensibility. Understanding is necessary for the actor to appreciate what he ought to be doing, sensibility is necessary for him to do it well. His first point is to combat the vague idea that the new acting was based entirely on nature:

Playing is a science, and is to be studied as a science; and he who, with all that nature ever did, or can do for a man, expects to succeed wholly without the effects of that study, deceives himself extremely. (p. 12)

He then attacks the completely unnatural approach of the actor, who merely copies what his predecessors in the role have done:

It will be said, that imitation will supply the place of understanding, and that having observed in what manner another pronounces any sentence, the performer may give it utterance in the same cadence: an ear answering the purpose of understanding. Too ma..y players are of this opinion; but it is setting their profession very low, it is reducing that to a mechanical art which was intended to exert all the force of genius; but as it is contemptible, it is also imperfect. (p. 21)

What John Hill feels is necessary is a balance of understanding with what he calls sensibility, 'a disposition to be affected by the passions which plays are intended to excite'.

Unfortunately Hill does not really distinguish the creative sensibility of the actor, who has to recreate the emotion working only from the script, from the sensibility of the members of the audience, who are moved by his performance. Perhaps rightly, he assumes we know what he means by sensibility and merely stresses that it is a gift of nature, which must be exercised by the actor in passages of sentiment, yet be controlled by a critical understanding of the play as a whole. He points out that it would be quite wrong to expect to find both great understanding and a deep sensibility in the same person, since that is a rare gift shared only by the greatest actors.

> We find people of both sexes who have excellent understandings, and who have very little of this sensibility. Nay, perhaps the greatest understandings of all are most exempt from it. It is in reality, no other than giving way to passions, and philosophy would teach us to get the better of it. (p. 51)

He recognizes too that an actor must not be overcome by the passions he is portraying, so that he is himself reduced to tears or paroxysms of rage, and so unable to communicate clearly what he feels. All in all, Hill's work is a good guide to the criticism of acting; but it does not set out a method for actors. He points out how Garrick had too much natural fire to make an ideal Romeo, and Barry too little to capture the violence of a Richard III. Mrs Pritchard alone receives his complete approval, as an actress who could portray all the passions of her role; she had

> the ductility of mind... that is the only true, as it is the only general sensibility. It were best that the heart of the player had no reigning passion of its own with this ready sensibility of all. Then he would receive them all as the writer offered them, in an easy and unconstrained succession. He would be the body, the author, for the time, the soul: And thus he would represent all well, because he would first feel all properly. Few enjoy this sensibility perfect; all are excellent, very nearly in proportion to the degree in which they enjoy it: and it is like the understanding, one of these qualifications the player must have from nature; for art will never give it. (p. 61)

As for how the actor can improve his natural sensibility, Hill makes two suggestions which, if followed by the modern actor, would once again seem to increase his self indulgence. His first suggestion is very interesting for various reasons; he proposes that, to increase his sensibility to tragedy, the actor ought to read *Paradise Lost*, for in it 'there are passages that will affect the heart that has true sensibility, more strongly than any that occur in our best tragedies.' This says little for the purely dramatic qualities of eighteenth-century tragedy; yet when he describes the effect it should have on the sensitive actor, I feel I ought to read Milton again myself:

> for, if he will in a perfect retirement, and with a mind divested of all other thoughts, read daily, parts of this great poem, stop at the passages which affect him, most of which fill his heart with greatness, and his eyes with tears of admiration, which raise him from his seat, and carry him out of himself: he will soon find those seeds (of sensibility) dilate and grow to maturity. . . . Let him give nature her full scope, when they affect him. I have said, let him stop at them; but let him never read them over again. The first effect is the greatest, and all he has to do is to give way to it. Let him give himself up without restraint to the emotions he feels on this occasion, and without addition, or abridgement, throw everything into action. (pp. 96—7)

This, I think, confirms the impression that one gets from reading many sentimental tragedies and comedies, that their inspiration is more often literature than life itself. But then Hill does make some observations rather more sensible than many of the other theorists. He says, for example, that to try and observe and recreate every minute article of one's reaction to the poem,

> were as contemptible as to practice attitudes in a glass; But let him repeat and encourage the whole, and by a practice like this, he will fall into a way of giving a loose to himself upon the stage, on the like occasions. The action and the expression will arise from the occasion, unstudied, unpremeditated, and as it were natural to him; and being natural as well as great it will affect everybody: And this is the character of sensibility. (p. 97)

When Hill talks of what the actor can learn from life itself rather than from literature, his approach once again indicates the selective, idealizing nature of eighteenth-century sentimentality:

> the next thing to inciting into the mind thoughts which are great and proper is, the banishing from us such as are unworthy. Among these come almost all that concern the actor in private life. He should, as much as possible, alienate himself from these, and obtain an entire command over them, otherwise they will blend themselves with those of his character, and debase and spoil all his expression. (pp. 102—3)

I cannot help comparing this with Stanislavski's advice that the actor ought to store up *every* feeling and reaction, however base or trivial, in his 'emotional memory', but perhaps the difference is more to do with the nature of drama in their different periods, than with the nature of acting.

The rest of John Hill's observations on acting need not delay us long, except to point out, firstly, that he, unlike his namesake Aaron Hill, and the other writers on elocution and reading, recognized that extraordinary, compelling personality which we would call 'star quality' and which he defines as Fire — 'that glorious heat' which makes him 'glow with transports not his own'. He of course pointed out that 'Mr Garrick has more fire than any actor in the world probably ever possessed'. Secondly, he is also fully aware of the technical tricks and the terminology of the performer. He tells us how an actor must be 'rotten perfect' in his lines — a lovely phrase — and how he must be a master of stage business and be capable of 'finesse'. By finesse he means the ability to improve on a play for the sake of good theatre, to know when a speech is tedious and must therefore be hurried, or when a seemingly insignificant line must be given extra emphasis in performance, either vocally or by a significant piece of by-play.

Hill's essay does not seem to have received much notice in England after its second edition of 1755, although in my opinion it is the best book on the subject, and even theatrical historians have tended to go to *The Actor* for factual information on Macklin, rather than for Hill's own criticism and theory. However, in 1769 it was translated back into French by one Antonio Fabio Sticotti, under the title *Garrick, ou les acteurs Anglais*, and it was this edition that provoked Diderot's famous *Le Paradoxe sur le Comédien* of 1773. Diderot takes up the apparent contradiction between understanding and sensibility, and comes down heavily against the actor's sensibility. My own feeling is that he was overly impressed by Garrick's party-pieces, and the ease with which an actor is able to guide and control his sensibility. Hill had pointed out that 'with the power of feeling, he must have the power of quitting them instantaneously, or of changing one for another, or all his sensibility is nothing' (p. 68). Diderot, seeing this as a mechanical skill controlled at will and by the use of reason, argued that the actor was not really exercising his sensibility at all. But although this attitude, which stresses rationality, may be more typical of the eighteenth century, the modern actor would tend to see that John Hill was groping towards the use of, and control over, emotions, which finds its classic expression in Stanislavski's search for 'an inner spiritual technique, without which one cannot find true psychological and physiological approaches to the soul of man, for the natural and conscious birth of a superconscious creative impulse in it' [23]. Even Garrick himself recognized that 'the greatest strokes of genius have been unknown to himself, till circumstances, and the warmth of the scene has sprung the mine as it were, as much to his own surprise as that of the audience' [24].

The last theorist whom I wish to look at seems to come somewhat nearer to a systematic examination of the subconscious creativity of the actor, which Hill seems to recognize but cannot explain. John Walker, already cited (p. 53) as an extremely pedantic actor/scholar whose main desire was to formulate a method of notating inflections by the use of accents, acute, grave, and circumflex, does have a significant chapter on how the actor can begin to awaken and control the unconscious passions of his sensibility. In the second volume of *Elements of Elocution*, published in 1781, after having stressed the importance of passions in speaking he continues:

> But it will be demanded, how are we to acquire a feeling of this passion? The answer to this question is rather discouraging, as it will advise those who have not the power of impassioning themselves upon reading or expressing some very pathetic passage, to turn their studies to some other department of learning, where nature may have been more favourable to their wishes. But is there no method of assisting us in acquiring the tone of the passion we want to express; no method of exciting the passion in ourselves when we wish to express it to others? (pp. 273–4)

Walker's first answer is that of Quintillian, who suggested conjuring up all the details involved in what he had to speak about, until the sheer elaboration of detail began to fire the imagination — for example, if he wished to complain of an assassination, he would first imagine all the gory mess and the dying agony of the victim, so as to become passionate in his denunciation of the murderers. Walker's second example from the classics is that of Polus, the actor who took his son's ashes onto the stage in order to enact Electra's mourning. So the actor should use his own experience to awaken his sensibility:

> Calling to mind such passages of our own life as are similar to those we read or speak of, will, if I am not mistaken, considerably assist us in gaining that fervour and warmth of expression, which, by a certain sympathy, is sure to affect those who hear us. (p. 276)

Finally, Walker refers to Burke's *Origin of our Ideas of the Sublime and Beautiful*, in which,

> he observes, that there is such a connection between the internal feeling of a passion, and the external expression of it, that we cannot put ourselves in the posture, or attitude, of any passion, without communicating a certain degree of that passion itself to the mind . . . hence it is, that though we frequently begin to read or speak, without feeling any of the passion we wish to express, we often end in full possession of it. (pp. 278–9)

This idea is, in fact, an elaboration of Locke's Association of Ideas, which was indeed the only way of explaining the subconscious springs of creative imagination at this time, linking it with the reflex actions of the nervous system or animal spirits. Stanislavski himself moved towards a position that, similarly, was more physiological than psychological, when in *Creating a Role* he wrote a chapter entitled 'From Physical Action to Living Image'; but whereas he is thinking of the naturalistic action of the plot and of stage business, Walker is thinking of those gestures and tones of voice which he, like all the eighteenth-century theorists, believed were the universal expressions of the internal passion. And so, although one feels he might have got somewhere had he followed up Burke's theory of inspiration through action rather than through thought, he in fact became one of the most precise and pedantic observers of those external expressions of a passion;

> Fear violent and sudden, opens wide the eyes and mouth, shortens the nose, gives the countenance an air of wildness, covers it with a dreadful paleness, draws back the elbows parallel with the sides, lifts up the open hands with the fingers spread, to the height of the breast, at some distance before it, so as to shield it from the dreadful object. One foot is drawn back behind the other, so that the body seems to be shrinking from the danger, and putting itself in a posture for flight. The heart beats violently, the breath is fetched quick and short, and the whole body is thrown into a general tremor. The voice is weak and trembling, the sentences are short and the meaning confused and incoherent. (pp. 328–9)

This is detailed observation, but I fear it sounds more like a description of Garrick and the ghost than a genuine experience of life itself.

It has been said that actors have always acted the same way, and that Stanislavski's only contribution was to give the art a vocabulary and a method. But I hope that this survey of some of the eighteenth-century ideas about acting shows that this is a short-sighted analysis. I do believe that man's emotions cannot have changed much, but as his understanding of them changes, so must his acting, which is of course the recreation and portrayal of those emotions. If actors thought in terms of passions as separate states of mind, and if their whole approach tended towards external imitation, rather than internal recreation, then it is not surprising that we find descriptions of what actors of the past actually did on stage unconvincing and smacking of technique, even though their audiences acclaimed them as being natural. We must remember that these audiences too shared the common preconceptions of a more primitive psychology; it was a terminology and an expression which rang true for them, as for the actor and the critic. It was not until the popularizing of new concepts by Freud and the Viennese psychologists in the late nineteenth century, that a further revolution in naturalistic acting became possible. In the meantime there was a tendency for Garrick's passions and strokes of nature to become refined into the clichés that Stanislavski attacked with scorn:

> Can one sit in a chair, and for no reason at all be jealous? Or agitated? Or sad? Of course it is impossible. Fix this for all time in your memories; on stage there cannot be, under any circumstances, action which is directed immediately at the arousing of a feeling for its own sake. To ignore this rule results only in the most disgusting artificiality. When you are choosing some bit of action leave feeling and spiritual content alone. Never seek to be jealous, or to make love, or to suffer, for its own sake. All such feelings are the result of something that has gone before. Of the thing that goes before you should think as hard as you can. As for the result, it will produce itself. [25]

Notes

[1] *English Linguistics: Collection of Facsimile Reprints* (Menston, Scholar Press, 1968–71), No. 102.

[2] *Dictionary of National Biography* (*DNB*) (London, 1885), LIX, 74.

[3] Published by Scholar Press as *Melody and Measure of Speech* (*Eng. Ling. Reprints*, No. 172).

[4] *Dramatic Miscellanies* (London, 1785), quoted in Toby Cole and Helen C. Chinoy, *Actors on Acting* (New York, Crown, 1954), 121.

[5] *Eng. Ling. Reprints*, No. 132, iv.

[6] *Eng. Ling. Reprints*, No. 148, introduction to Vol. I.

[7] *Eng. Ling. Reprints*, No. 129, 121.

[8] William Cockin, *Art of Delivering Language* (London, 1775), 25–9.

[9] D. M. Little and G. M. Kahrl, eds, *Letters of David Garrick* (London, Oxford U. P., 1963), I, 350.

[10] Downer's paper was first published in *Publications of the Modern Language Association* (*PMLA*), LVIII (1943), 1002–37, and republished in *Restoration Drama*, a collection of essays edited by John Loftis (New York, Oxford U.P., 1966).

[11] *Eng. Ling. Reprints*, No. 161, 364.

[12] Quoted in Cole and Chinoy, op. cit., 133.

[13] See J. T. Kirkman, *Memoirs of the Life of Charles Macklin* (London, 1799), where the essay is quoted.

[14] John Locke, *Essay on Human Understanding*, Book 2, XXI, para 53, in *Works*, Vol. I (London, 1728), 152.

[15] See Cole and Chinoy, op. cit.

[16] Davies' is among the best of the many informative contemporary comments on Garrick's Lear. See Cole and Chinoy, op. cit.

[17] John Hill, *The Actor: a Treatise on the Art of Playing*, 2nd edn (London, 1755), 36–7. All later references are to this edition.

[18] Mrs Siddons, 'Remarks on the Character of Lady Macbeth', are quoted in Thomas Campbell, *Life of Mrs. Siddons* (London, 1834), II, 10–34.

[19] Henry Siddons, *Practical Illustrations of Rhetorical Gesture in Acting* (London, 1822 [1st edn 1807]), 345 and 348.

[20] ibid., 355–6.

[21] W. A. Appleton and K. A. Burnim, eds, *The Prompter* (New York, 1966), 85. This excerpt is from No. 66, June 1735.

[22] *The Works of the Late Aaron Hill* (London, 1754), IV, 339–46.

[23] C. Stanislavski, *My Life in Art*, trans. J. J. Robbins (London, Bles, 1924), 475.

[24] Little and Kahrl, op. cit., II, 635.

[25] C. Stanislavski, *An Actor Prepares*, trans. E. R. Hapgood (London, Bles, 1937), 40–1.

4 KATHLEEN BARKER

William Powell — a Forgotten Star

O yes! O yes! O yes!

THIS is to give Notice, that Mrs PROSE is lately elop'd from her Husband (well known by the Christian Name COMMON SENSE) and suppos'd to be secreted somewhere between Bedminster and the lower part of Small-street — she went off in a Phrenzy Fever, and has been thought delirious ever since Mr POWELL first perform'd the part of LEAR. [1]

That little piece of satire from a Bristol newspaper is a not unfair comment on the kind of adulatory notice which William Powell's acting drew; while I am convinced that no actor ever inspired a greater quantity or a more dismal quality of tributes in verse than did Powell in the bare six years of his theatrical career, from 1763 to 1769. This kind of writing makes it in some ways more than usually difficult to assess him as an actor; but at the same time it is in itself something of an assessment, because the most obvious and dominant feature of his acting was the effect, emotional almost to the point of irrationality, which he had on his audiences.

William Powell was born in 1735 at Hereford, and after attending the Grammar School there was nominated to Christ's Hospital (the Blue-Coat School), where he completed his education. Sir Robert Ladbroke employed him in his City office, and Horace Walpole heard that he was 'so clever in business that his master would have taken him in partner' [2]. Certainly one can assume that he was reasonably able, since he must have spent at least ten years with Ladbroke; and this educational and business background needs to be borne in mind and weighed against the rather derisive remarks made by Garrick and some of his biographers about Powell's lack of culture and qualifications for theatre management.

All accounts of Powell agree, however, that his attention was very much divided between his office duties and the 'Spouting Clubs' he frequented in his spare time; and ultimately, as usual, it was the theatre which won. Charles Holland, who had been playing some of the leading roles in Garrick's Drury Lane Company, was sufficiently impressed by Powell to introduce him to Garrick, and Garrick in his turn sufficiently impressed to groom the twenty-eight-year-old amateur to make his debut as leading man at Drury Lane in October 1763 while Garrick himself went on his Continental trip.

Wisely, the part chosen for Powell was virtually a new one — that of Philaster in a revision by Colman of Beaumont and Fletcher's play — and his success was sensational. Hopkins the Drury Lane prompter wrote:

> A greater reception was never shown to anybody, — he was so very much frightened, he could not speak for some time, and, when he did, the tears ran fast down his cheeks, — but he soon recovered himself, and went through the part with a great deal of nature and feeling, — continued claps and huzzas of bravo! &c. &c.

Walpole reported to Sir Horace Mann that 'the audience, not content with clapping, stood up and shouted'. The one dissentient, apparently, was Samuel Foote, who Davies says 'endeavoured to laugh those who sat near him out of their feelings, but the power of nature was too strong for the effects of spleen'. [3]

Nor was this a nine-days' wonder; throughout Garrick's two years' absence Powell was the acknowledged mainstay of Drury Lane and continued to draw packed houses; while in the summers he went down to the Jacob's Wells Theatre at the Bristol Hotwells and repeated his success there. Richard Jenkins recalled:

> Powell was the chief subject of conversation at our coffee-houses, taverns, and tea-tables, and anyone who had not seen and applauded his performances, must (like Lady Teazle) never have pretended to any taste again [4].

When the King Street Theatre superseded Jacob's Wells in 1766, Powell became its leading man and principal manager.

On Garrick's return to the stage Powell continued at Drury Lane, but was misguidedly persuaded in 1767 to break his articles and make one of the ill-fated 'Four Kings of Brentford' whose rule at Covent Garden proved such a sorry farce. At this theatre, however, he had no Garrick to show up his lack of technique, no Holland entrenched in the romantic leads; as at Bristol, the whole range of principal parts lay open to his choice. But he had only two seasons at Covent Garden before his death in the summer of 1769, an event which produced at least as much theatrical sensation as his life.

Well into the next century, Richard Smith, surgeon, antiquary and dedicated theatre-goer, could write in his notes for a history of the Bristol stage:

> No man was more beloved in private life or admired in public – He was a good natured man, an exceedingly affable & entertaining companion, his merit as an Actor was superlative & his name will last to the exeunt Omnes of the British stage.

It has not done so, of course.

> Who then to frail mortality shall trust
> But limns on water, or but writes in dust

Yet certainly for decades Powell was something of a legend – a sort of eighteenth-century James Dean – and his importance at the time was sufficient, I think, to make it worth examining the characteristics of his acting and the nature of its appeal.

The descriptions of Powell give one a very fair idea of his physical resources as an actor. His deep voice, though he often forced it beyond its natural range, is repeatedly described as 'sonorous' and 'melodious'; his face was exceptionally mobile and many tributes are paid to the extent to which his expression reflected the passions of the part. In Posthumus, for example,

> the Versatility of Jealousy, Love, Tenderness, and Resentment, so variously interspersed throughout this Tragedy, were very strongly marked in the Features of his Face and Tones of Voice; which, like Strings upon Musical Instruments, justly answered to the Impression made on them by the mind [5].

Powell was not, judging from the pictures remaining of him, particularly handsome, and all accounts agree that he was, or by bad posture appeared to be, round-shouldered – a defect which in the engraving of him as Posthumus makes him look deplorably like Uriah Heep. His movement too was awkward; as his admirer Mellifont put it

> His Figure's bold, his Eye is keen,
> But he wants Dignity of Mien,
> And that free, untheatric Air,
> Which, off the Stage, is very rare. [6]

Arthur Murphy says, more pedestrianly, 'He ought to have frequented a school for grown gentlemen to dance; for, though he walked the stage with ease, he wanted grace in all his motions'. [7] 'Spouting Clubs' were not exactly a breeding ground of restraint in acting, and it is abundantly clear that in basic techniques — in voice production, movement and gesture — Powell was sadly wanting at times. Hopkins comments repeatedly on his being 'wild', on his voice going unmanageably high, on his stamping too much; and even favourable newspaper reviews repeat these criticisms, although most admit a great improvement after the nervous tensions of a first night.

It was not, then, by the physical gifts of a Barry or the finished technique of a Garrick that Powell won his audiences over, but by a direct assault upon their feelings, much more in the style of the best melodramatic acting of a later century. Perhaps the clue to his enormous success lies in the half-submerged struggle in mid eighteenth-century culture between the classic formalism which is today popularly associated with the term 'Georgian' and the stirrings of Gothic romanticism. This is particularly noticeable in the ambivalence of critical attitudes to Shakespeare and his contemporaries, but it is equally apparent in the response to acting styles. Powell represented 'Nature' — untutored, instinctive, passionate, untamed. Every major actor seems to begin by arousing this reaction, however formal and inhibited he comes to appear by the end of his career, but given such an attitude even Powell's lapses could be interpreted as 'Nature', if perhaps Nature in the raw.

> For young *Philaster feels* his Part,
> And follows Nature more than art

claimed one poetaster, typically [8]. Colman, with that unhappy ambiguity which characterized his friendship with Powell, put it thus:

> When, like the Paphean Maid of old
> Thy Gesture, Voice, and Eye,
> Lost in wild Transport, we behold,
> "*Orestes* raves", we cry.
> Such *strong Emotions* from the *Heart*,
> All Mockery exceed;
> You do not *act* the Madman's Part,
> But *you* are *mad indeed.* [9]

More happily, another critic summed up:

> No Actor ever entered deeper into the Spirit of his Part than he, nor had a more sympathetic Feeling for those Characters which required it [10].

So often do his admirers stress the apparent identification of Powell with his best roles that it is clear this was a major factor in creating the sympathy of the audience. It is of course a claim which could be made for any fine actor, but in Powell's case it could be taken one stage further – for his histrionic reputation it might rather be said, one stage too far. For him the line between himself and the character he played was perilously thin and sometimes seemed to vanish altogether. Cape Everard describes how, only rehearsing the part of George Barnwell, Powell's feelings 'so overcame and distressed him, that he declared he never would play the part again', and he comments shrewdly on the adverse effect of so much sensibility:

> I remember a great tragedian, Powell, . . . performing the part of Jaffier, and when he said,
>> "I have not wrong'd thee – by these tears I have not."
> His feelings were so great that they choaked his utterance, his articulation was lost, his face was drowned in tears. – The audience from these causes, not understanding what he said, the effect was of course lost. When Garrick in the same part, spoke the same line, every eye in the house dropt a tear! If he did not feel himself, he made everybody else feel. [11]

However, it takes quite a sophisticated audience to resist such an obvious display of feeling, and most of the auditors succumbed readily enough. As I have written elsewhere, it became an apparently boundless love affair between actor and spectator, to which each gave himself too easily. The tears of the one were matched, if not overmatched, by those called forth from the other. A correspondent of the *Gazetteer* claimed that 'during the last two acts [of *Venice Preserv'd*], the tears of the whole audience spoke their sympathy with the sorrows of Jaffier and Belvidera' [12], and hardly a versified tribute is printed without some similar reference.

Not surprisingly, it was in tragic and pathetic parts that Powell was most popular. He did play quite a number of 'juvenile leads', creating the characters of Lovewell in *The Clandestine Marriage* and Honeywood in *The Good-Natur'd Man*; Lord Townly in *The Provok'd Husband* was a favourite part with him. Where he could seize on some vein of feeling, he was effective, but aristocratic polish was beyond him. Hugh Kelly put it:

> But, when in gay Lothario he wou'd shew
> The sprightly airs of libertine and beau;
> Or gay in Townly, to a modish wife,
> The nicer touches of superior life,
> Not all the scrapes or cringes which he tries
> Those paltry arts of little men to rise,
> The scorn of sense and judgment can remove,
> Or touch one honest blockhead to approve. [13]

Even his Romeo and Hamlet aroused little or no comment — Holland held these parts at Drury Lane, so it was only when Powell was his own manager, at Bristol and later at Covent Garden, that he could appear in either.

Undoubtedly his finest part was Lear, which he first played at Jacob's Wells for his benefit in August 1764, and there were not wanting flatterers to tell him he outdid even Garrick in the part. Repeatedly his admirers singled out for especial praise the curse at the end of Act I, which revealed 'the most convuls'd and really agonizing Heart-felt Distress, and the utmost Sensibility that shook every Nerve of the most susceptible Powell' [14]. The mad scenes and the reconciliation with Cordelia in the last act, where he fell on his knees to beg forgiveness, were other great 'points'. One critic objected to his business when, overcome with exhaustion after killing two of the would-be murderers of Cordelia and himself,

> instead of supporting himself against any part of the stage, where there is a possibility for the audience to see his face, [he] falls plump against the flat scene, and, with a politeness equal to his accuracy, shews nothing but his back view to the company. — By this means he throws away an admirable opportunity of adding both to the general satisfaction, and of acquiring a reputation for himself — flags in one of the most capital incidents in the whole play, where he ought to exert his utmost abilities; and instead of endeavouring to heighten the pathos of the Poet by the energy of action, he thinks it totally unnecessary to shew any action at all.

The critic was not impressed by the modern-sounding argument of Powell's friends, that this new business was in the cause of realism [15]. But there were more to agree with the admirer who thus described the storm scene:

> Powell fill'd up his Circle midst the Roar,
> Great Shakespear's Mantle in his Right he wore,
> An equal Portion of his Spirit felt,
> And all the Climax of his Terrors dealt.
> With such Variety! such Strength! such Taste!
> That in quick Whirlwinds more and more increas'd;
> Till Reason like a shatter'd Vessel tost,
> Amid the Mind's mad Hurricanes was lost. [16]

Othello was the one major Shakespearean tragic character which Powell created in London; he chose it for his first Benefit at Drury Lane, an occasion which caused such a chaotic crush that having started the play, the company had to ring down again and recommence a quarter of an hour later when the ladies had been able to get to their seats. Hopkins called it 'one of the greatest overflows that ever was known', and not surprisingly the delay and confusion affected Powell's performance adversely, so that he had to be warned against 'overstraining his Voice and throwing his Body into ungraceful Contortions' [17]. In later performances his tenderness to Desdemona and the contrasting scene with Iago were especially praised.

> Mr. Powell's artful Disposition of the rich Colouring in this Piece; his just Proportion of Light and Shade, his very minute Attention to the smallest Tinct that gives it Life and Beauty, is truly deserving a Testimony of public Approbation. [18]

His Macbeth seems to have been uneven, mainly because of lack of imaginative perception. When he first played it, at Jacob's Wells, he was praised for the realism with which he spoke the dagger soliloquy, and another Bristol admirer exclaimed

> In guilty Macbeth, when amaz'd he stands,
> With the drawn Daggers in his trembling Hands,
> How just his Features! how well-timed each Start!
> Betray the Fear of that great Tyrant's Heart. [19]

Unfortunately, when at last he was able to play the part in London at Covent Garden in 1768, he was not in good health, and the *Theatrical Monitor* accused him of ignorance of the sense and spirit of the words he spoke, 'and the violence of his passion, with the *air-drawn dagger*, was so great, that it deprived him of his powers, where there was a real occasion to shew them' [20]. Even in Bristol objection was taken to his greeting the news of his wife's death in an 'elevated tone of voice' — and if this means that he took 'She should have died hereafter' at the full stretch of his voice, then he deserved everything the *Monitor* said of him.

Outside his Shakespearean roles, Lusignan in *Zara*, Castalio in *The Orphan*, and particularly Jaffier in *Venice Preserv'd* appear to have been the most artistically successful, calling forth abundant tears from the audience. In *Venice Preserv'd* it was, predictably, the most emotional moments which seized the spectators' imagination: the 'Strokes of Phrenzy' in Act IV, the later scenes with Belvidera. 'The fourth and fifth Act I shall never forget" wrote a correspondent to the *Public Advertiser*,

> his Distraction on hearing his Friend was to die — his Prayer for Belvidera — his Execution at the tolling of the Bell — his last parting from his Wife, I think

were the most masterly strokes of Acting I ever beheld; and indeed the Audience seemed full as sensible of it; for profound Silence and Attention filled the House, while the big Drops rolled down from almost every Eye. [21]

Less appreciated by those who saw in Powell Garrick's successor in carrying on the torch of the classics was his success as Alexander in *The Rival Queens*. Here his tendency to fall into rant made him almost too much at home in meeting the requirements of the part. Powell brought the play back into temporary popularity; but it perturbed Garrick that Powell should lend himself to 'such fustian-like Stuff': 'If a Man can act it well, I mean to please ye People, he has something in him a good actor shd not have' [22].

Garrick was freely accused of being jealous of Powell, and so perhaps he was; but his criticism was shrewd; Powell's enthusiasm for acting — one feels he remained stage-struck all his life — and almost Bottom-like willingness to attempt any taking part, carried with it a lack of discrimination. During the benefits at the end of his first season he sometimes played every night of the week, and each night a different, major, character, giving himself no time to assimilate the parts. No wonder Garrick was worried that he was 'playing himself to rags'.

In addition to this, there are continual hints that Powell, his head turned by success, was dissipating far too much of his strength in his social life. Garrick had warned him:

You must therefore give to Study, and an Accurate consideration of Your Characters, those Hours which Young Men too generally give to their Friends & fflatterers. The Common excuse is, that they frequent Clubs for the Sake of their Benefit; but nothing can be more absurd or contemptible. . . . Study hard, my friend for Seven Years, & you may play the rest of your life. [23]

The advice, as Garrick feared, seems to have been thrown away; George Anne Bellamy, admittedly a biassed witness, says Powell 'would have proved an ornament to the stage, had he had time to acquire that knowledge which is requisite to make the profession a science. But very few give themselves leisure, or take the trouble, to arrive at the goal' [24].

The same temptations surrounded Powell in Bristol; Cape Everard remarks how much Powell was courted by the leading civic figures and merchants of the city, and in less favourable vein there are satiric references in the press to 'the Entertainment he afforded us openly at the W[hit]e-H[art], in B[roa]d-st[ree]t, Saturday was se'nnight in the

Evening: Which was a Proof superior with him to the Possession of the most finish'd Phaeton, or superb *Coat of Arms*, that he was born and bred *a Gentleman.*' It appears that Powell in his cups could not forbear indulging himself in witty comment on his colleagues behind their backs [25].

The accumulation of exhausting professional demands, a hectic social life, and the managerial quarrels at Covent Garden eventually took their toll. During his last two seasons Powell was several times out of the bills with a 'severe cold' or other illness; even in Bristol he missed a fortnight of the 1768 season. In the summer of 1769 he had performed only twice when, overheated by a game of cricket, he stripped off his clothes to cool himself in the grass, caught a chill which turned to pneumonia, and after an illness lasting a month, died at his lodgings next to the theatre, aged only 34. The shooting star had burned itself out.

I said earlier that Powell's death produced as much theatrical sensation as his life. It is difficult sometimes to sort out legend from fact; the one is not less likely than the other. It is said that straw was thrown over the cobbles of King Street to reduce the noise of traffic outside Powell's lodgings, it is certain that the performance scheduled for Friday 30 June was cancelled for the same reason.

Powell rallied that weekend, and *King Richard III* was played as billed on the Monday, but he died just as the play began. Various accounts have been handed down, some, like Bernard's, obviously embellished in the passage of time, but all agree that the news of Powell's death had a shattering effect on the company, their manifest grief making it difficult for them to finish the performance. In the end Holland made a public explanation and apology, and by common consent the idea of an afterpiece was abandoned [26].

On the following Thursday the funeral procession set out for the cathedral, where no less a person than the Dean of Bristol was to take the service. The hearse was carried from College Green, preceded by the choir singing an anthem, but the cathedral was so packed that it was only with difficulty that the coffin-bearers could make their way through, and the doors had to be closed to prevent the pressure of the crowds.

The burial service was performed by the Dean with the most animated devotion, but the spectators were too numerous to observe silence and decorum. After the body was deposited, another anthem was to have been sung over it, but this intention was frustrated by the impatience of the throng multitudes, who press'd forward to take a final look at him, to whom they had been indebted for so many hours of elegant entertainment. [27]

To crown all, Ned Shuter, late and very probably rather drunk, came rushing up, clad in a scarlet waistcoat trimmed with broad gold lace, and a gold-laced hat, and finding the doors closed, beat upon them with the butt of his cane, bellowing, to the horror of the more decorous,

> Thou detestable maw, thou womb of death,
> Gorg'd with the dearest morsel of the earth,
> Thus I enforce thy rotten jaws to open,
> And, in despite, I'll cram thee with more food! [28]

Nearly twenty years later, John Bernard found that a group of Bristol amateurs still met annually at the Bush Inn to commemorate Powell's death [29]. It must always be an open question whether, had he lived longer, Powell would have fulfilled his initial promise, or whether he had not sufficient self-discipline to mature as Garrick matured, and as Henderson, with whose career Powell's was often compared, showed signs of doing. I am afraid I suspect the latter.

Nevertheless, no personality is negligible which can attract such warmth of feeling from both fellow-professional and lay public as, it is clear, Powell inspired; no actor is negligible who can repeatedly move his audiences, London as well as provincial, so deeply as did Powell. If sometimes there was something meretricious in the generation of this too easy emotionalism, more often it was an instinctive recognition of genuine feeling going beyond the craft of acting.

Obituaries are always suspect, but there is a ring of sincerity, as well as of almost Johnsonian phrase-making, about this:

> His superlative eminence in his profession will ever be remembered by those who had refinement of taste, and sensibility of mind, to relish those admirable strokes – those inimitable touches – that transfusion of the soul into the expression – that intimate congeniality of sentiment with which he breathed every line of his own Shakespeare – those elegant graces – that undefinable pathos – that energetic emphasis – that nicely happy conception – that effusion of feeling in the expression which captivated the affections of his hearers. These and other distinguishing and characteristical excellences will live in the remembrance of every lover of that profession of which he was so brilliant an ornament. [30]

Tom Davies said of Powell, 'Had he restrained his impetuosity, he certainly might have been twice the actor he was.' Maybe; but in his impetuosity lay much of his charm for audiences; without it, it is equally probable that he would have been only half the actor he was.

Notes

[1] *Sarah Farley's Bristol Journal*, 8 December 1764.
[2] H. Walpole, *Letters*, ed. P. Toynbee (Oxford, Oxford U. P., 1905), V, 379.
[3] T. Davies, *Memoirs of the Life of David Garrick, Esq.* (London, 1780), II, 69.
[4] R. Jenkins, *Memoirs of the Bristol Stage* (Bristol, 1826), 49.
[5] *Public Advertiser*, 3 December 1763.
[6] ibid., 18 October 1763.
[7] A. Murphy, *Life of David Garrick* (London, 1802), 7–8.
[8] *Public Advertiser*, 18 October 1763.
[9] *Sarah Farley's Bristol Journal*, 29 December 1764.
[10] *Public Advertiser*, 11 March, 1766.
[11] E. C. Everard, *Memoirs of an Unfortunate Son of Thespis* (Edinburgh, 1818), 5–6, 9.
[12] *Gazetteer*, 10 October 1766.
[13] H. Kelly, *Thespis, or, a Critical Examination into the Merits of all the Principal Performers belonging to Drury-Lane Theatre* (London, 1767).
[14] *Public Advertiser*, 28 November 1765.
[15] *Lloyd's Evening Post*, 16–18 January 1765.
[16] *Felix Farley's Bristol Journal*, 15 August 1767.
[17] *St. James's Chronicle*, 31 March to 3 April 1764.
[18] *Felix Farley's Bristol Journal*, 18 July 1767.
[19] *Sarah Farley's Bristol Journal*, 16 November 1765.
[20] *Theatrical Monitor*, 6 February 1768.
[21] *Public Advertiser*, 31 January 1764.
[22] D. M. Little and G. M. Kahrl, eds, *Letters of David Garrick* (London, 1965), Letter 329 of 11 April 1764.
[23] ibid., Letter 345 of 12 December 1764.
[24] *Apology for the Life of George Anne Bellamy, written by Herself* (London, 1785), IV, 105.
[25] *Sarah Farley's Bristol Journal*, 4 and 18 July 1767.
[26] The most credible account is that which appeared in the *St. James's Chronicle*, 11–13 July 1769, and was adopted almost verbatim by Richard Jenkins (op. cit., 93–4).
[27] *Sarah Farley's Bristol Journal*, 8 July 1769.
[28] Jenkins, op. cit., 94–5.
[29] J. Bernard, *Retrospections of the Stage* (London, 1830), II, Ch. 1.
[30] *Sarah Farley's Bristol Journal*, 8 July 1769.

5 PAUL SAWYER

John Rich's Contribution to the Eighteenth-Century London Stage

It is a commonly accepted scholarly practice to make judgements based on facts and not facts based on judgements. But with John Rich the facts in some areas of his life are non-existent, well hidden, and often where available difficult to interpret. Where his contemporaries and historians of the theatre provide their personal opinions of him, they are frequently contradictory; we find conflicting evaluations by people associated with him, responding to a personal experience with Rich, satisfying at one moment, disappointing at another. I therefore submit my assessment of Rich's contribution to the eighteenth-century London stage with an appropriate degree of humility and tentativeness. It is subject to review and reassessment by myself, as the research on my biography of John Rich progresses, and of course it is subject to constant review and reassessment by other scholars.

Let me briefly detail some of the problems I have alluded to. The fund of misinformation about Rich is only slowly diminishing. It is still repeated that John Rich was born circa 1682 [1], a non-fact given almost sacerdotal authority by the *Dictionary of National Biography*, despite newspaper and magazine reports of his death, and his tombstone in the churchyard of St John's Church, Hillingdon, which state he was 69 or 70 when he died in 1761 and hence born circa 1692, not 1682 [2]. This decade difference assumes some importance when one realizes that Rich was 22, not 32, when he took over Lincoln's Inn Fields theatre upon his father's death in 1714. The ten-year error is important also when one remembers that Rich, under the name of Lun, was still performing as Harlequin in the early 1750s, although infrequently. It is doubtful, especially since he tended to corpulence, that he could have retained sufficient agility past the age of three score to display a pair of heels as eloquent as most actors' tongues. I say this fully aware of such death-defying performers as Charles Macklin, whose immortality was perhaps more literal than figurative [3]. Indicative of the penumbra in which Rich has dwelt is the fact that he is called Henry Rich and Thomas Rich in some works [4]. He is termed illiterate by several of his contemporaries, yet that he could write more than his name is proven by two holographic, or seemingly holographic, documents, one relating to the building of Covent Garden theatre and one a two-page letter to his daughter [5]. He could read, and well enough to lead John Hill to complain about his effectiveness during the well-known quarrel between them in 1740 over the paternity of *Orpheus*, the libretto for one of the successful pantomimes staged by Rich. His literacy granted, there can be no denying his education was neglected, although some critics state he had a good understanding [6]. Since his father was an attorney, who had been admitted to Gray's Inn in 1676 but never admitted to the bar [7], one wonders why John the son did not receive a good schooling. Because the first twenty-two years of his life are shrouded in mystery, no one has been able to explain the anomaly, but it is manifest that Rich was a notoriously poor speller, pronouncer, and mistaker of one word for another [8]. One wonders, too, why someone who ordinarily would have grown up in and around the theatres with which father Christopher was so much involved, could not act well enough to equal the many mediocre talents which were employed at his playhouses, but we know he turned to pantomime only after two failures in the role of Essex in John Banks' *The Unhappy Favourite* [9].

There are conflicting views on his honesty, and generosity. As a result of his role in support of Fleetwood against the actors in the 1743 revolt, Rich is described as a liar of considerable ability [10], yet Charles Dibdin, usually one of Rich's harshest critics, wrote that Rich 'took care to satisfy, to the letter, his performers, and all those with whom he made engagements' [11], and the author of a life of James Spiller concurred that Rich was 'a most religious observer of his own words' [12]. On the one hand we learn that Rich was 'not by any means liberal to his actors' [13], on the other, that Rich seems to have been more liberal in allowing benefits than was Drury Lane, gave free benefits to the impoverished widows and children of deceased actors, on occasion took to himself certain benefit nights which had brought very little money to poets and players and allotted them another, and paid to bury actor James Spiller 'in a very decent manner' [14].

I shall give two further illustrations of the problems surrounding any study of Rich. The charters in the British Museum are almost all of legal as well as historical value. However, there is one long document (Add. Ch. 9320), dated 1759, in which Rich attempted to buy the one-quarter interest of his younger brother, Christopher Mosyer, in the patent, Covent Garden Theatre, and its scenes and clothes, for an annuity of £200 or, at John's option, £5000 upon the sale of the theatre. Christopher Mosyer, who wanted the lump sum and free admission to the theatre for himself and his family, refused to sign and the indenture was never executed. It is revealing, certainly, of the relationship between the brothers, but it is dangerously easy to mistake this document for a valid agreement. Even more confusing is a twice-executed painting by William Hogarth, a friend of Rich. One version, alternatively entitled 'A Garden Scene at Cowley' (Rich's villa was in Cowley) or 'A Scene in Mr Rich's Garden', shows Rich in a prominent, reclining position. The other version, 'The Fountaine Family', is almost identical, save that Rich is absent [15]. Figures in both paintings are usually identified as Mrs Rich, Christopher Cock, the auctioneer, Mrs Cock and Sir Andrew Fountaine. One may ask whether the background is indeed Cowleyan and why the Fountaine family portrait is so named when it contains only one member of the family. Did Hogarth paint Rich into the first version, or excise him from the second?

Let us now turn to the chief burden of this paper, John Rich's contribution to the eighteenth-century London stage. What we should consider first, I suggest, is London without the Riches' theatrical ventures. Would there have been a second legitimate theatre? Well, not necessarily, if he had sold his theatre and the letters patent to Drury Lane. But there was hardly much chance of that. Howls of monopoly would have caused, I think, either granting of another patent or, more likely, a licence similar to the one under which Drury Lane operated. But the possibility exists. What prevented Rich from so doing, other than his desire to try his hand at managing and, I think, acting, was the knowledge that his father expected his sons to carry on his struggle against the theatre he had once controlled and from which he had been ejected. Although the will [16] does not prohibit such a sale, it would have violated the spirit of Rich's last testament and also involved some financial juggling to satisfy not only Rupert Clarke, who with Rich père owned 17 of the 36 shares in the playhouse, but also the owners of the

other shares, purchased probably at or about £120 per share, except for
the two shares in the possession of the Rich brothers [17]. We know
that Rich not only kept one theatre open, but he built another and for
a while, a brief while, operated both. This in itself represents a
contribution, independent of any judgement about the quality of his
management. For viewed in perspective the presence of a second
legitimate theatre, providing opportunities for playwrights, actors,
dancers, musicians, scene painters, carpenters and sundry other person-
nel to work, is a good thing. Although it may be argued that
competition can vitiate the nature of the programme a theatre without
competition is able to offer, it may also engender a healthy rivalry
among the companies and encourage more careful dramaturgy and
more skilful acting. The finest flowerings of the drama the western
world has known – in Greece, England, France – support my
contention. Even a poor second theatre is generally better than no
second theatre at all, and I say this not only with regard to the human
factors – the number of jobs it creates, the additional entertainment
possibilities it offers – but also because it tends to elevate the total
theatrical product.

We shall never know what would have happened had Rich sold out,
but we are fortunate, at least for my purposes, that he farmed out
Lincoln's Inn Fields to Christopher Bullock and Theophilus Keene for
the 1717–18 season, and to Bullock for the following two seasons.
Thus we are able to see how another management performed. The
result was disastrous in many ways; Keene did not survive the season,
and Bullock died only four years after surrendering control. Financially
they did so poorly that Rich was forced to retake possession by
obtaining a judgement for non-payment of rent and, incidentally, 'to
submit to the loss of £2000 Value in his Wardrobe, etc' [18]. Let us
consider what Keene and Bullock produced and how they produced it.

In general, the season 1717–18 is distinguished by an effort to bring
out a variety of Shakespearean plays, but they were less numerous than
Drury Lane's (7 to 11; in performances, 15 to 21). There was much
opera, old and new, with one one-act opera – *Pan and Syrinx* by
Theobald – surviving for several seasons. Its most noteworthy play, one
of three new comedies, was *A Bold Stroke for a Wife* by Mrs Centlivre,
popular for many years. There were two tragedies. One was *Mangora,
Kingdom of the Timbusians* by Thomas Moore, and it is both amusing
and revealing to read what Benjamin Victor says of it. Moore, he writes,

gave the performers 'many good Dinners and Suppers during the Rehearsals of the Play, which they all laugh'd at as ridiculous'. Since the company was composed of young actors and was but little encouraged by the public, 'it may be justly said, their Necessities compelled them to perform this strange Tragedy, which stood some chance to divert from its Absurdities' [19]. The other tragedy, *Scipio Africanus* by Charles Beckingham, had to be deferred twice because of a principal actor's illness. Despite the postponement, the leading character's lines had to be read the first night and the next principal character's lines the second night [20]. Violence was not confined to the stage, however. In a duel Quin, who had joined the company that season, killed another actor, Bowen, over who was the honestest man [21], and Lacy Ryan, another member of the company, ran his sword through the left side of a drunken gentleman named Kelley in a tavern dispute some months later [22]. And there was some sword play among the audience, too [23]. The two following seasons were less tempestuous, although not entirely free from disturbances of course, but the most remarkable (and I use the word in its original meaning) event was the introduction of a company of French comedians in the 1718–19 season, who played very successfully, and provided many lucrative benefits for the Rich brothers and for Christopher Bullock. I come to the conclusion that by whatever reasonable criteria one adopts – the number of good new plays presented, the quality of the acting and staging, the number of Shakespearean offerings and how well they were performed – there was not any significant improvement in the theatre for these seasons. This does not necessarily mean that inevitably the manager or managers of any second theatre must repeat Bullock's experience, or Rich's, but in the early years it is difficult to envisage a second theatre concentrating on drama and performing it without Wilks and Booth and Cibber and other members of their fine company, and managing to survive for more than a few seasons. The implication is that to compete with Drury Lane, especially but not only in the beginning years, there had to be some resort to extra-dramatic entertainment. Enter pantomime.

Rich, of course, did not initiate pantomime on the English stage, and although he talked of borrowing the hints from the ancients (whom he does not seem to have identified!), critics have said that he knew nothing of them [24]. The early harlequin dances, the Italian night scenes, the more or less complete, coherent entertainments like John

Weaver's *The Tavern Bilkers* or *The Cheats* (1702), all these preceded Rich. It is difficult indeed to state positively just what Rich contributed, but probably he deserves credit for combining the early *commedia dell'arte* type of Harlequin intrigue, the so-called comic or grotesque part, with the serious part as found in Weaver's 1718 pantomime, *Orpheus and Eurydice*, which had numerous and impressive backgrounds to support its 'serious' mood. He seems to have added recitative and song to the serious part, with dialogue sometimes included, and based the story on some mythological account. The grotesque part, dealing with the love adventures and misadventures of Harlequin and Columbine, was very largely in dumb show, but there was an occasional song with one of the traditional dances of the time [25]. *Amadis*, composed by Rich in 1718, may be the first of the 'mixt' kind of pantomime which was to become the distinctive and infinitely popular type of pantomime for so many years. *Amadis* was not immediately popular, however, and not until 1723 with John Thurmond's *Harlequin Doctor Faustus*, did pantomime receive its great impetus. It seems to have been the prototype and cause of Rich's first famous pantomime, *The Necromancer*, or *Harlequin Dr Faustus*, which made its debut less than a month after Thurmond's pantomime at Drury Lane. But whatever Rich's place in the birth of that peculiar combination of mythology and harlequinade, of operetta and dance, surely his is the prominent name in its development.

It had been his father's opinion, and it became his, 'that Singing and Dancing or any sort of. Exotick Entertainments, would make an ordinary Company of Actors too hard for the best Set who had only play Plays to subsist on' [26]. He quickly came to appreciate that '. . . in spite of all the rhetoric . . . the pantomime is a kind of stage entertainment which will always give more delight to a mixed company than the best farce that can be written' [27]. Rich was shrewd enough to recognise that pantomime was one of those areas in which he was equipped to compete successfully with Drury Lane. He had a newer theatre than Drury Lane, one capable of handling, with some adaptation, the scenic effects upon which a good share of pantomime's appeal depended. He had an interest in, and some talent for, envisioning and building these effects. Although never affluent, Rich was willing to invest large sums of money in the necessary scenery, machines and clothing. He believed — and this is a point too often ignored — that pantomime needed no apology, no condescension, that it was a kind of entertainment as demanding as tragedy. Rich made no compromise with his principles. Like Anatole France's *Jongleur de Notre Dame*, in pantomime he was giving his best. Cibber called pantomime a 'monstrous medley', but he put them on. Garrick scorned them, but he put them on. We may question Rich's judgement, but his morality, if we may call it that, in staging them is superior to theirs.

Rich's trump card was himself. The tributes to his acting of Harlequin are so numerous that I shall have to content myself with only two. Thomas Davies said that in fifty years no one had approached him:

> ... his gesticulation was so perfectly expressive of his meaning, that every motion of his hand or head, or of any part of his body, was a kind of dumb eloquence that was readily understood by the audience. Mr Garrick's action was not more perfectly adapted to his characters than Mr Rich's attitudes and movements to the varied employment of the wooden sword magician. [28]

Arthur Murphy, surely no friend to Rich, described how he made three thousand steps in running in a circle around the stage,

> the Movement of each Leg was so small and quick, that in going the length of one Foot, he minced it so as to make three hundred steps .... they may say what they will of the Hero of Drury Lane [Garrick]; he only imitates Men, whereas the Covent-garden chief converts himself into a wild Beast, a Bird. or a Serpent with a long Tail, and what not . . . [29]

Such panegyrics are echoed by men as diverse as David Garrick, John Hill, John Jackson, Benjamin Victor, Tate Wilkinson and others. indeed practically everyone who had the good fortune to see him on the stage. They often expressed contempt for Rich's management, intelligence, idiosyncracies, but never for his performance as Lun. Of his rivals as Harlequin, Henry Woodward alone seems to have come near him, and Woodward was himself one of Rich's pupils. Rich, who had a compulsion to 'larn' others how to act, seems to have made little impression with his tuition of actors in the traditional lines, but many of the better Harlequins of the period — Arthur, Nivelon, Hippisley, Laguerre, as well as Woodward — profited from his training.

Rich did not allow a pantomime, once staged, to become static. He introduced new features into some, he pruned others of parts that were not liked, he withdrew them after a time and then, with great hullabaloo and new scenes, machines, and costumes, he brought them triumphantly back, able to attract an audience which had enjoyed the same and yet not quite the same thing a few years earlier. He was resourceful, prodigal, painstaking. It was his concern, his 'baby', and he exercised tight control over all parts of it, a control which he often relaxed in other aspects of his theatres.

The name of Rich has been so intimately linked with pantomime that one emerges from a superficial reading of theatre history of the time with the idea that he monopolized pantomime and that Drury Lane ignored it. Nothing could be further from the truth. In the seasons spanned by Rich's management, Drury Lane produced thirteen more new pantomimes than he did [30]. Under Cibber, Wilks and Booth, under Fleetwood, under Garrick, Drury Lane was constantly trying to cope with Rich at what had become recognized as his own game. Thumbing through the bills for the 1750s, one wonders whose forte it was when it is seen that Drury Lane produced six new pantomimes from 1750 to 1756, all by Henry Woodward. For an opinion of one of these, see *Drury Lane Journal* X, 19 March 1752.

> ... it almost moves my contempt; when I reflect that a mob of unmeaning two-legged creatures, the mere apes of humanity, will venture their precious limbs in jostling one another, to have an opportunity of staring at the pretty feats of a dumb Harlequin, while the empty benches reproach their deficiency of understanding, when Shakespeare or Jonson in vain exert the affecting powers of reason and judgment. To the disgrace of common sense be it remembred that OTHELLO has been play'd at *Covent-Garden* to the rejected refuse which has been disappointed of places at the other crowded house, because forsooth 'twas the twentieth night of QUEEN MAB.

Notice that it is Rich who is staging the Shakespeare and Garrick the pantomime. Imitation is the greatest form of flattery, and envy, and the popularity of pantomime at Drury Lane, as well as at the unlicenced theatres and at the summer fair booths, is an accolade which Rich undoubtedly appreciated, and deplored when it cut into his profits.

Rich's role in the production of processions and coronations is essentially similar to what it is in pantomime: primarily developer, to a lesser extent initiator. Since a stage coronation seems to require a real one, which in turn requires a new monarch, Rich's opportunities were limited. Unaware of the attraction of this kind of theatrical embellishment, he let his first opportunity slip by when he prepared nothing to celebrate the coronation of George II in 1727. Instead, he had to content himself with a pantomime farce, called *Harlequin Anna Bullen*, satirizing Drury Lane's expensive (it cost almost a thousand pounds) and very lucrative entertainment [31]. In the 1750s he exploited the procession very successfully in productions of *Romeo and Juliet*,

Coriolanus, and *The Rival Queens*. We know that Rich was proud of his interpolations, and attributed the popularity of *Romeo* to a funeral procession for Juliet to the accompaniment of a solemn dirge with words by Shakespeare and music by Thomas Arne [32]. When Mrs Bellamy switched allegiance and came to Covent Garden to play Juliet, she told Rich that she thought the large crowds came to see her. Rich disabused her. 'It is', he declared, 'owing to the *procession*' [33]. Garrick, incidentally, did not hesitate to introduce a procession of his own, and he anticipated Rich with the spectacle of a coronation in 1761 upon the accession of George III. But about a month and a half later Rich was ready with such a splendid coronation that one enthusiastic magazine reviewer wrote, 'If, in many instances, it must be inferior to the real Coronation, in some it is universally acknowledged to exceed it' [34]. It was so immensely popular that one foreign visitor felt that there could hardly be anyone in London who had not seen it [35]; it put Garrick's to shame. The 'God of Pantomimes, Jubilees and Installations' was what Richard Warner called Rich in 1770, stating flatly that he was as much superior to Garrick in 'fancy and taste for magnificence' as Garrick was to him 'in the talents of a good actor' [36].

In the ballad opera, that engaging and ephemeral species that could never overcome the misfortune of having what is often regarded as its first born vastly superior to later offspring, Rich played the part of a midwife, but probably an unwilling midwife. He staged *The Beggar's Opera* with some reluctance, more impressed by its sponsor, the Duchess of Queensberry, than its unusual content and format. There seems to be some historical basis for assigning to Rich at least some of the credit for suggesting the airs be set to music [37]. Its reception we know — I shall be the first theatre historian in the last 200 years to refrain from quoting the famous pun linking the names of Gay and Rich — and it quickly spawned a flock of lesser ballad operas, more of them introduced by Drury Lane than by Rich. Anyone who helped, even in a minor way, to give us such a sparkling work as *The Beggar's Opera* during a century in which playwrights spent as much time cursing the darkness as lighting a candle, deserves our gratitude.

You will note that Rich seems to have been an afterpiece-man — in pantomime, in coronations, in the ballad opera which in its most common form was performed as an afterpiece. This statement may be more of an epitome of Rich than his biographer should care to make, but honesty compels my hazarding it. When Rich became a theatre manager in 1714, the afterpiece was little known, the programme usually consisting of a mainpiece and sometimes a dance. Rich, who could not equal Drury Lane's standard dramatic offerings during many of the seasons at Lincoln's Inn Fields and Covent Garden, as has been stated before, developed the afterpiece into a much more frequent and important part of the evening's bill, thus lengthening and varying the century's theatre programmes [38].

Considering Rich's affinity with attractions that were not literary, we are not surprised that he produced a number of English operas, usually to audiences more numerous than those which attended tragedies, comedies and farces [39]. *Camilla*, *Thomyris*, and *The Prophetess*, or *The History of Dioclesian*, were three of his favourites. They are, of course, rarely heard today, but except for *The Beggar's Opera*, how often are the plays of Rich's time performed? He brought out a very successful burlesque of the Italian operas, *The Dragon of Wantley* by Henry Carey, in 1736. The finest music of the period flowed from the pen of Handel, and Rich seems to have had a good relationship with him for many years. He rented Lincoln's Inn Fields and Covent Garden to him, he subscribed to his published works, and in 1749 he was about to enter more actively into an association with him which would have been something of a departure for both. He commissioned Handel to write incidental music for a production of Smollett's play, *Alceste*. Servandoni was hired to provide the scenery. But for some reason, either because it was too expensive (which seems a good one) or, the more commonly given explanation, because he found the music 'too good for his performers' [40], *Alceste* was abandoned, and Handel used most of the score in *The Choice of Hercules*. (Handel liked Rich sufficiently to will his organ to him at his death.) Rich experimented in 1753 with burletta but it did not prove attractive enough for him to continue. Purists may resent any intrusion of opera into what was essentially a playhouse, but they may wish to recall one of John Genest's final observations on Rich's management. Disgruntled by the increase of music and song with the advent of John Beard, who came into Rich's family by marrying his second daughter, Charlotte, in 1758 and into his theatre a year later, Genest wrote '. . . let it be ever remembered to his honor that it was not till a little before his death that C. G. was turned into an opera house' [41].

The managers must have been convinced of the appeal of dancing, because it was so frequently part of the programme. Rich, himself a dancer although of a special kind, went to considerable expense (as did Drury Lane) to provide dancers, both foreign and domestic, to regale the spectators. He was a regular employer of the ever young Mlle Sallé, and helped make the reputation of the famous Nancy Dawson. When Garrick enticed her away from Covent Garden for the 1760–1 season, Rich replaced her with Mrs Vernon, whereupon ensued the much publicized hornpipe rivalry when the two theatres offered competing versions of *The Beggar's Opera*. It is difficult to discern any specific contribution that Rich made to dancing, other than to embrace it and incorporate it into his bills, usually as *entr'acte* entertainment. I would not care to state that his theatre's dancing was better than Drury Lane's.

But it would be true to assert that in such attractions as acrobatics, on the rope and off, animal acts of various sorts, and cries of London, Rich was superior to Drury Lane. Maddox, the famous wire dancer, Swarts and his famous dogs in 1717 [42], the bear, the lion, monkey, serpent and ostrich, not to mention the dog and cat, in his much satirized pantomime-raree show, *The Fair* (1752), all attracted large audiences. Although Rich was personally so fond of cats as to house perhaps as many as twenty-seven [43], his interest in animals was largely professional. He knew that people crowded to see Mrs Midnight's display of dogs and monkeys, and the wild beasts on view at the Tower of London and in various private rooms. Rich himself dressed as a dog and barked when he played Harlequin in the comic part of *The Rape of Proserpine* [44]. Drury Lane never did find anyone who could equal the droll Ned Shuter in his amusing impersonations of street vendors crying their wares [45].

This is small beer, of course, although undoubtedly it enhanced the box office receipts. But what about the meat of the theatre, literary drama? I do not believe Rich made a significant contribution, but his reputation in this area is probably worse than he deserves. It is true that he did not always treat playwrights particularly well, but what manager ever did? On occasion they expressed their appreciation to him in dedications – William Shirley in *The Parricide* (1738/9) and George Sewell in *Sir Walter Raleigh* (1718/19) can be cited – but more often he was heavily attacked, especially after the first fifteen years of his management, during which period he was more solicitous of dramatists because more in need of their products. Then, we are told, he had 'cajoled' [46] the playwrights and received with 'Civility and good Nature' [47] pieces scornfully rejected by Drury Lane. With the popularity of pantomime and *The Beggar's Opera*, his character seemed to change, for he developed the 'Pride of a Grand Vizier, and the Breeding of a Bombaily' [48] and presumed to 'mangle' plays presented to him. Mixed in him, said his critics, were the vanity of Wilks, the arrogance of Booth and the pertness of Cibber without any of their good qualities, and he used poets so hard that only obscure ones would show him a play, and then they would be forced to wait for years while he 'reduc'd it to his own taste' [49]. In the later years of his management, handicapped by age, poor vision, increasing weight, he seems to have kept plays even longer than he had formerly, promise-feeding the authors, and ultimately rejecting them with a 'Sir, it will not do' [50]. At times he did not even read the plays [51]. His rivals Cibber and Garrick, were themselves prolific and successful dramatists, which provoked the wrath of the less fortunately placed authors. Rich avoided that kind of envy; the one play in which he may have had some part, *The Spirit of Contradiction* (1760), was played and published anonymously. But he made no friends among the dramatists (so many of whom turned to pamphleteering upon their plays being refused) when he used to say that no living poet had any ability, that all those who could write were dead [52]. Rich, then, was certainly not an object of veneration, or even respect, to the playwrights, but he did not undergo as much abuse from them as did his fellow managers to whom they preferred to submit their plays first, because at Drury Lane, in general, they could be assured of a better production and a better chance of a substantial benefit night. As a result, Rich did not suffer the humiliation that Cibber and Garrick, particularly, underwent upon seeing a manuscript they had rejected become a great success on another stage. Elijah Fenton's *Mariamne* (1723), John Home's *Douglas* (Covent Garden, 1757) and *The Beggar's Opera* had both literary and dramatic appeal; Robert Dodsley's *Cleone* (1758) was perhaps lacking in poetry; but all enjoyed the kind of reception which delighted Rich and tormented his rivals.

However, Rich's record of new productions is not, compared to Drury Lane's, a good one. Using Allardyce Nicholl's handlist of plays, I have determined that in each of the five most frequent types of production, he was second to the Old House. Drury Lane presented 62 tragedies to Lincoln's Inn Fields and Covent Garden's 42; 42 comedies to 38; 48 farces to 28; 37 pantomimes to 24; 32 ballad operas to 13; a total of 221 for Drury Lane, 145 for Lincoln's Inn Fields and Covent Garden [53]. Of course there are reasons for the disparity. As we have shown, Rich's interest often lay in the non-dramatic or the non-literary. He knew that to be successful plays needed powerful patrons more than powerful lines, and the Old House was favoured by these patrons. He was aware that new plays could be costly experiments, whereas Shakespeare and Fletcher, Otway and Congreve, long in repertory, never asked for a third night's benefit; their pieces did not require many rehearsals, new scenes, or new clothes, although they were sometimes refurbished. With less capital than Drury Lane during many seasons, with his growing conviction that success for him lay in areas other than literary drama, with an indolence in part attributable to age and lassitude (in the first fifteen years of his management, he *was* more productive than Drury Lane), his disinclination to try new plays is understandable. And it should be remembered that statistics can be deceiving. Drury Lane's more numerous pantomimes could not be sustained as long as Rich's; he could renovate one and bring it back while the Old House was forced to seek a completely new one.

No one can seriously maintain that John Rich had an abiding love for the plays of William Shakespeare. I think that he regarded them chiefly in terms of their attractiveness at the box office, but then who in his century ignored that aspect of the theatre? Shakespeare's works gave his playhouse some *ton*, drew some of the higher classes such as the Shakespeare Ladies to it, were relatively easy to produce since the actors were familiar with the lines (although they might have to adjust their memories to allow for altered texts), and his wardrobe usually contained adequate costumes for them. They sometimes provided an opportunity for a procession or two, and there was no third night's toll, except for an alteration when the author might receive the sixth night's proceeds. Shakespearean pieces were not particularly successful for Rich; and he often had to supplement them with an afterpiece, the most effective of which was pantomime [54]. What is commonly held, that Shakespeare was the darling of the Old House and the pariah of the New, has little basis in fact. The performances at Drury Lane of Shakespeare's plays were, in the main, superior, but there seems to be no appreciable difference in either house's fidelity to the pristine Shakespearean text. David Garrick was undoubtedly a great Shakespearean actor and was often credited with an alleged renascence of interest in the bard's plays during the years of his management. However, the renascence began before Garrick became partner with Lacy, and as Professor Scouten maintains, 'David Garrick simply rode the wave of the rapidly increasing popularity of William Shakespeare' [55]. Essentially the rival theatres produced the same plays, twenty-seven, with four put on by the Old House not staged by the New, and three presented at Lincoln's Inn Fields and Covent Garden not acted at Drury Lane. The frequency of productions is not significantly different, with Drury Lane staging a total of 1,759 Shakespearean plays to its rival's 1,627 from the 1715–16 season to the 1760–1 season, an average of about 38 to 35 per season [56]. Thus Rich did not neglect Shakespeare, and among his memorable productions *The Merry Wives of Windsor* (with Quin as Falstaff) and *Romeo and Juliet* merit special mention.

It is difficult to evaluate Rich's contribution to the acting of the period, but if his role was significant at all, it must rest upon his willingness to pay competitive salaries (whether he could have avoided not doing so is questionable), his relatively fair treatment of his performers, his occasional acts of generosity towards them, and a laissez-faire policy which meant that frequently the casting and direction and sometimes the choice of the plays were in somebody else's hands. James Quin, Lacy Ryan and Theophilus Cibber were among the better known surrogates for Rich, and Isaac Ridout and William Gibson also served as Rich's 'deputies'. The relationship between Rich and his assistants is perhaps revealed in George Anne Bellamy's account of her debut at Covent Garden, when Quin 'governed the theatre with a rod of iron'. Rich, she says, 'was, through indolence, a mere cypher'. She adds, however, that Rich was, 'when he had resolved on any thing, the most determined of men' [57]. Probably he gave, or was forced to give, Quin a greater measure of control than the others. It is noteworthy that there were no revolts against his management, while Drury Lane, under Highmore in 1733 and Fleetwood in 1743, experienced severe interruptions. He employed some of the greatest acting talents of the century and gave some performers their first chance. We have already mentioned that he dearly loved to teach but fortunately he does not seem to have affected the styles of his company. It is sometimes asserted that he could have kept Garrick on his payroll, but a perusal of Garrick's correspondence demonstrates Garrick's determination to strike out on his own and his disinclination to work for Rich. In common with other managers, Rich did not hesitate to make cartels limiting an actor's freedom to choose his theatre. The superiority of Drury Lane acting has already been pointed out. Only in two seasons was Rich's company the finer one: in 1746—7 when Garrick, Quin, Mrs Pritchard, Mrs Cibber and Woodward adorned it, and 1750—1 when Barry, Mrs Cibber, Quin, Woffington and Macklin were the stars.

Rich built, or as the legal documents have it, caused to be built, the Theatre Royal in Covent Garden. This was no mean achievement. Larger and better than Lincoln's Inn Fields, although patterned after it, it has become possibly the most famous name in the entertainment world of the United Kingdom and beyond, even though it is used to house opera and ballet, not drama. One may remark that it is not an inappropriate evolution for a theatre founded by Rich. That he seems to have made some shrewd and profitable arrangements in the financing of its construction may indicate that had he not found people willing to assume the risks of playhouse ownership he might have abandoned the project, and that Rich had motives other than theatrical glory and adulation [58]. For him the theatre was very importantly a business. In his justification can we not state that the theatre was a business, primarily, for most of the other managers? Is not one of the best known and oft repeated quotations of the period the concluding couplet from Garrick's prologue spoken at the opening of Drury Lane in 1750:

If want comes on, importance must retreat;
Our first, great, ruling passion, is . . . . to eat. [59]

If any reader wishes to suggest that this is an architectural rather than a dramatic achievement, if he wishes to suggest that a number of Rich's contributions are minor, or even negative, I would not disagree. I am not sure that his efforts to clear the stage of spectators, motivated in part by their interference with his pantomime machinery, is of major consequence either. His more substantial contributions I have enumerated. If they seem small, I am prepared to be Rich's apologist. I think he suffers by comparison with the Cibber, Booth, and Wilks management of Garrick's, but I think there are not many managements, and I include other centuries, which could equal theirs. Place Rich against Highmore and Ellys and Mrs Wilks. Place him against Christopher Bullock, and Charles Fleetwood and James Lacy; against the managements that succeeded him at Covent Garden and the managements that succeeded Garrick at Drury Lane. With the average he can hold his own.

To a large extent, final opinions on Rich derive from the viewpoint of the observer. For those concerned with the stage as a source of literature, he draws distinctly negative judgments. Robert Lowe's terse summation is typical. After paying a brief homage to his ability as a Harlequin, Lowe states, 'As a manager, he did great harm to the drama' [60]. By those concerned with the stage as entertainment and business, Rich is regarded more appreciatively, sometimes even enthusiastically. The annalist of Covent Garden theatre uttered this paean:

> There is little doubt that he deserves to rank among the great theatre managers of all time. He doubtless had the faults common to his day ... But he did what few of his successors have done since, he bore the responsibility of successfully managing the great theatre on his own shoulders for nearly thirty years. [61]

This is a 1906 judgment. Let me quote a 1970 evaluation, twice rendered, in a work of sound and detailed scholarship. Rich 'proved to be one of the most successful and long-lived London theatre managers in the whole of the eighteenth century' [62]. In the other rendering he is called 'the most successful theatre manager of the century' [63].

I feel the balanced judgment lies between the two extremes. I believe that whatever harm he did to the drama – and for me this is too pejorative a phrasing – was largely the result of circumstances beyond his control: the nature of the audience, of the written drama, of the competition, of the accident of birth which placed him in a position for which he was not adequately prepared. I am not yet ready to accept the statement that he was the most successful manager of the century. He was the defendant in too many law suits for debt in King's Bench and Common Pleas, involved too frequently in mortgaging his patent and leasing his 'messuages' – the final one as late as 1760 – to have been so very successful. He refused, or was unable, to pay too many widows – even recognizing his seeming love for litigation – to have been so very successful. Yet – and here again is one of the anomalies surrounding John Rich – he lived the good life, raced horses for a decade, associated with nobility, pursued women before his third and final splice of life, savoured good wine and good food: witness his founding of the Sublime Society of Beefsteaks. He left a theatre and patents, or a good part of them, which brought £60,000 six years after death, a tribute to the inflationary increase in the value of the patent as well as Rich's management.

There is one question, fascinating to speculate on, impossible to answer, which keeps running through my mind. If, in the fall of 1715, John Rich, aged 23, had stepped onto the stage of his new playhouse in Lincoln's Inn Fields and had been greeted, not with the apathy that history suggests but with acclamation, how would the course of the eighteenth-century London theatre have been altered?

Notes

[1] See *Correspondence of Thomas Gray*, ed. Paget Toynbee and Leonard Whibley (Oxford, Oxford U.P., 1935), I, 69. *Eighteenth-Century English Literature*, ed. Geoffrey Tillotson, Paul Fussell, Jr. and Marshall Waingrow (New York, Harcourt, Brace, 1969), 680, lists Rich's birth date as 'c. 1692'.

[2] *Lloyd's Evening Post*, 25–7 November 1761, says Rich was 'in the 70th year of his age'. *The Gentleman's Magazine*, November 1761, 603, says he was 'aged 70'. 'Rich's Register', the original of which is in the Duke of Devonshire's Library at Chatsworth, microfilm copy in the Folger Shakespeare Library, Washington D.C., records that he died 'in the 70 [sic] Year of his Age' (Vol. III, 1750–73, after 26 November 1761; there is no pagination).

[3] He is supposed to have lived to the age of 107.

[4] See John Timbs, *Club Life in London* (London, 1866), I, 133, where he is called Henry; J. B. Nichols, ed., *Anecdotes of William Hogarth* (London, 1833), 371, calls him Thomas. Also see Samuel Ireland, *Graphic Illustrations of Hogarth* (London, Vol. I, 1794, Vol. II, 1799), *passim*.

[5] The account of the progress of work at Covent Garden theatre is reproduced, from a Harvard Theatre Collection original, by Howard P. Vincent, 'The First Covent Garden Theatre', *English Literary History*, XVII, No. 4 (December 1950), 300–1. The letter is referred to by Henry Saxe Wyndham, *The Annals of Covent Garden Theatre from 1732 to 1897* (London, 1906), II, 304.

[6] See John Hill, *Orpheus, An English Opera* (London, 1740), preface, 5. Hill says Rich read 'with his best Grace of Diction, and not without some Flourishes of Action'. Thomas Davies, *Memoirs of the Life of David Garrick, Esq.*, new edn (London, 1808), I, 370, states that because of a 'grossly neglected' education, his language was vulgar and ungrammatical.

[7] See *Gray's Inn Admission Register*, 1521–1887.

[8] *Grays Inn Journal*, 5 January 1754, records that he confused 'adjutant' for 'adjective', and that he pronounced 'emphasis' 'emphersis'.

[9] He tried twice, once advertised as 'a Gentleman for his Diversion', on 22 October 1715, and under his own name on 9 November 1715. See *The London Stage 1660–1800*, Part 2, 1700–29, ed. Emmett L. Avery (Carbondale, Ill., 1960), 372 and 375.

[10] See *The Case between the Managers of the Two Theatres and Their Principal Actors, Fairly Stated and Submitted to the Town* (London, 1743), 15–16.

[11] Charles Dibdin, *A Complete History of the Stage* (London, 1795), V, 125.

[12] George Akerby, *The Life of Mr. James Spiller, The Late Famous Comedian* (London, 1729), 11.

[13] James Thomas Kirkman, *Memoirs of the Life of Charles Macklin, Esq.* (London, 1799), I, 426.

[14] Akerby, op. cit., 47. Tate Wilkinson, *Memoirs of his own Life* (York, 1790), IV, 183, relates some of Rich's generosities.

[15] R. B. Beckett, *Hogarth* (London, 1949), 43, dates the Fountaine portrait as circa 1730. The earliest connection of Rich with Cowley that I have traced is 1737, when his second wife Amy and two of their children were buried near there in St John's Hillingdon churchyard.

[16] PROB. 11/543/228. Recently it was moved from Somerset House to the Public Record Office.

[17] BM Add. Ch.9303.

[18] *An Impartial State of The Present Dispute Between The Patent and Players, Late Belonging to his Majesty's Company at the Theatre-Royal, in Drury-Lane* (n.p., n.d. [1733]), 5. A copy is in the British Museum.

[19] Benjamin Victor, *The History of the Theatres of London and Dublin* (London, 1761), II, 144.

[20] See *The London Stage*, Part 2, 474.

[21] ibid., 491.

[22] ibid., 498.

[23] ibid., 493.

[24] See *Garrick in the Shades, or A Peep into Elysium* (London, 1779), Act I, 2–3.

[25] For one of the better discussions, see the article by Mitchell Wells, 'Some Notes on the Early Eighteenth-Century Pantomimes', *Studies in Philology*, XXXII, 598 (October 1935).

[26] Colley Cibber, *An Apology for the Life of Mr. Colley Cibber, Written by Himself*, ed. Robert W. Lowe (London, 1889), I, 335.

[27] Thomas Davies, op. cit., I, 131.

[28] ibid., I, 368–9.

[29] *Gray's Inn Journal*, 1 September 1753.

[30] Allardyce Nicoll, *A History of English Drama 1660–1900*: Vol. II, *Early Eighteenth-Century Drama* and Vol. III, *Late Eighteenth-Century Drama*, 3rd edn (Cambridge, Cambridge U.P., 1952). See 'Hand-list of Plays, 1700–50', 293–400, 430–52; 'Hand-list of Plays, 1750–1800', 261–363, 377–408.

[31] Theophilus Cibber cites the cost in *The Lives and Characters of the Most Eminent Actors and Actresses of Great Britain and Ireland, from Shakespear to the Present Time* (London, 1753), 64.

[32] *Gentleman's Magazine*, September 1750, 427.

[33] Bellamy, op. cit., II, 194–5.

[34] *The Court Magazine*, November 1761, 120. *The London Gazette*, 22 September 1761, contains an elaborate description of the real coronation.

[35] Count Frederick Kielmansegge, *Diary of a Journey to England in the Years 1761–1762*, trans. Countess Kielmansegg (London, 1902), 194.

[36] *A Letter to David Garrick, Esq. – on his conduct and talents as Manager and Performer* (London, 1770), 36.

[37] Victor, op. cit., II, 153–4.

[38] *The London Stage*, part 2, cxvii–cxviii.

[39] For a fuller discussion of the appeal of opera, see my article, 'The Popularity of Various Types of Entertainment at Lincoln's Inn Fields and Covent Garden Theatres 1720–1733' *Theatre Notebook*, XXIV, No. 4 (Summer 1970), 154–63.

[40] Winton Dean, *Handel's Dramatic Oratorios and Masques* (London, Oxford U.P., 1959), 579.

[41] *Some Account of the English Stage. From the Restoration in 1660 to 1830* (Bath, 1832), IV, 656.

[42] Robert Wilkinson, *Theatrum Illustrata, Graphic and Historic Memorials of Ancient Playhouses...* (London, 1825), no pagination; see under 'Lincoln's Inn Fields Theatre', talks about Swarts.

[43] *Memoirs of the late Celebrated Mrs. Woffington*, 2nd edn with additions (London, 1760), 19-21 offers a graphic (if exaggerated) picture of Rich at home, eating his breakfast.

[44] See E. Curll, *The Life of that Eminent Comedian Robert Wilks* (London, 1733), 14.

[45] George Winchester Stone, Jr., *The London Stage 1747–1776; A Critical Introduction* (Carbondale, Ill., 1968), cliii–cliv.

[46] See *The Daily Courant*, 26 February 1732.

[47] *Grubstreet Journal*, 16 March 1732, summarized by the *Gentleman's Magazine*, March 1732, 650.

[48] *Daily Courant*, 26 February 1732.

[49] See above, note 47.

[50] James Quin, *The Life of Mr. James Quin* (London, 1766), 33, mentions this judgement by Rich as inevitable. Garrick and Cibber used the same words in rejecting plays.

[51] For vigorous complaints against his failure to read a play, see *The Theatrical Examiner; An Enquiry into the Merits and Demerits of the present English Performers in General* (London, 1757), 18–19; and *The Present State of the Stage in Great-Britain and Ireland* (London, 1753), 17–18.

[52] *Tyranny Triumphant! ...* by Patrick Fitzcrambo, Esq. (London, 1743), 15–16.

[53] See Nicoll, op. cit.

[54] See above, note 39.

[55] Arthur H. Scouten, 'Shakespeare's Plays in the Theatrical Repertory when Garrick Came to London', *Studies in the Department of English, The University of Texas* (Austin, Texas, 1944), 258.

[56] Charles Beecher Hogan, *Shakespeare in the Theatre, 1701–1800* (Oxford, 1952). Even if the number (80) of Shakespearean plays presented by the Bullock-Keene management and by Bullock himself from 1717–18 to 1719–20 were deducted, the amounts would not be much affected. Rich's average would then be about 36 per season.

[57] Bellamy, op. cit., I, 49.

[58] For details of the building, see Basil Francis, 'John Rich's "Proposal" ', *Theatre Notebook*, XII (Autumn 1957), 17–19. Howard P. Vincent, op. cit.; PRO C11 2662/1; BM Add MS, 32, 248; and Arthur Scouten, *The London Stage 1729–1747: A Critical Introduction* (Carbondale, Ill., 1968), xxvii–xxxi.

[59] The entire prologue is quoted in the *Gentleman's Magazine*, September 1750, 422.

[60] *A Bibliographical Account of English Theatrical Literature From the Earliest Times to the Present Day* (London, 1888), 279.

[61] Wyndham, op. cit., I, 140.

[62] F. H. W. Sheppard, *Survey of London, XXXV, The Theatre Royal Drury Lane and The Royal Opera House Covent Garden* (London, Athlone Press, 1970), 4.

[63] ibid., preface, vii.

6 CECIL PRICE

Thomas Harris and
the Covent Garden Theatre

In the eighteenth century, the managers of the Drury Lane and Covent Garden theatres included some of the period's most interesting personalities: the names of Colley Cibber, John Rich, David Garrick, George Colman and Richard Brinsley Sheridan, arouse attention. That of Thomas Harris, a man who controlled a patent theatre for longer than any of them, is barely remembered. The *Oxford Companion to the Theatre* gives him no separate entry, the *D.N.B.* notice is thin and pallid. I shall now try to discover what manner of man he was, and what contribution he made to the theatre of his day.

I think the simplest way of doing this will be to look at his relationship early in his career with the other members of the managerial board, to consider his dealings with some authors and actors later in his reign, and to examine in general his collaboration with his opposite number at Drury Lane, Richard Brinsley Sheridan.

When John Rich died, he bequeathed his interest in Covent Garden Theatre to his wife and his son-in-law, with directions that they were to sell it 'as soon as a sum adequate to the value thereof' could be obtained. In 1767, enquiries were made about purchasing it by Thomas Harris and John Rutherford, who hoped to find sixty thousand pounds but were uncertain about their own ability to run a theatre. Harris's father had been in trade, and it seems likely that the son's approach to the playhouse was that of a business man: I have found no record to suggest that he had any ambitions as an actor or author.

Harris and Rutherford then approached the actor, William Powell, and asked him to become a sharer and leading player, but he hesitated because, he said, his associates would be 'two inexperienced young men, who perhaps might know but little of the world, and certainly could know nothing of the internal management of a theatre' [1]. He suggested therefore that George Colman the elder should also be invited to join them, and Harris and Rutherford rather reluctantly agreed to the proposal. At one of their early meetings, Colman remarked

> managing a Theatre was like stirring a fire, which every man thought he could do better than any body else. 'Now, gentlemen,' said he, 'I think I stir a fire better than any man in England.' To this they replied, 'Do you manage; let Mr Powell act; all we want is to have good interest for our money'. [2]

This report comes from Colman; Harris himself did not want the words taken seriously: 'That indeed we laughed at, as a conceit of intended wit and pleasantry, but could not imagine that you meant it as a serious and conclusive argument to which we had agreed' [3]. Harris was supported in his view by the legal instrument for the purchase, in which all four partners were held jointly and equally responsible for the management; but in actual practice, its day-to-day running was in Colman's hands. The two young men went away on holiday for six weeks, and left Colman to make his own arrangements. When they returned, they complained about hearing nothing from him, but he excused himself on the ground that they were moving about and that he had taken only two material decisions: he had accepted a comedy by Goldsmith, and had engaged Macklin as a performer [4]. Colman afterwards alleged that they were conspiring to check his authority, and they accused him of being dictatorial. He responded by suggesting hat Harris was opinionated: 'Mr Harris must be humoured, and has in his nature, among many worse qualities, the tyranny of a school-boy, who will have every-thing his own way' [5]. Harris's irritation, however, increased when he found that Colman had engaged Mrs Yates and her husband without consulting him, and that the cast of parts for his (Harris's) mistress, Jane Lessingham, was not at all to her liking [6].

The quarrels became bitter. Colman went so far as to say that they had 'no further right to act in the management than occasionally to signify their disapprobation in writing unto the said George Colman' [7]. Harris saw himself 'involved in a vast and insupportable expense, lavished away, in defiance of our most solemn protests, upon superfluous servants, greedy favorites, and a numerous standing army of undisciplined and useless performers' [8].

Colman shut Harris and Rutherford out of the theatre, so they went there with some soldiers and some pugnacious assistants and broke in and carried off in carts its books, music, and costumes. As may be imagined, this stimulated public controversy, and Harris accused Colman of filling the newspapers and particularly 'your *St. James's Chronicle*' with 'libellous and unmanly insinuations' [9]. Colman retorted that Harris was

> continually running to all the news-printers in town with his own scurrilous letters and paragraphs, and his friend Mr Kenrick's dirty epigrams in his pocket; having absolutely opened an account current with the publishers, and undertaken to pay a round price for their suffering their papers to become the registers of his falsehood, and journals of his malignity. [10]

The disagreements went on for some time, but since Colman succeeded in making a profit on his seasons, he could not really be charged with neglecting his business, and a decision in his favour was returned in court in July 1770. He was continued in the management, subject to the advice, though not the control, of the other proprietors. In the meantime, William Powell had died and John Rutherford had sold his share to a solicitor and a bookseller named Dagge and Leak [11].

When Harris quarrelled with Jane Lessingham, he became better friends with Colman, and they worked together more happily between October 1771 and May 1774. Then Colman withdrew from the management of Covent Garden, leaving Harris as the only surviving member of the original quartet of managers and a much more knowledgeable one than the novice of 1768. Colman had been trained in the law, and Harris learned from him to safeguard his legal rights very jealously. In time, too, he learned not to worry too much about people who were quixotic enough to forget their own.

This is obvious from some serious charges made against him by Thomas Holcroft. Apparently Harris accepted Holcroft's comic opera, *The Choleric Fathers*, and a comedy named *Seduction*, and agreed to the author's conditions that they were to be performed in, respectively, November 1785 and February 1786. Harris wanted some parts of *Seduction* altered, so Holcroft made the necessary changes. Then Harris thought that it might be dangerous to represent one of the characters, and called for further amendment. The comedy in its finally corrected state was delivered to Covent Garden in December 1785, but no word was received from Harris for a month. The play was eventually returned rather rudely, and Harris said afterwards that it could not possibly succeed. Holcroft concluded that the failure of *The Choleric Fathers* had made Harris uneasy about the success of *Seduction*, and had led to its being rejected.

Early in their negotiations, the agreement to produce *Seduction* had been put down in writing but Holcroft, with typical open-heartedness, had torn it up, saying that he thought it impossible that men who meant honestly should differ in trifles and that their word should be sufficient. He found that he had no redress now, and wrote angrily of Harris's lack of principle:

> If men in similar situations might act thus *always* with impunity, as they *too often* do, what means could the weak and unprotected find of obtaining redress; what security in their dealings with a man, who, regardless of probity, and yielding to the caprice of opinion, the dictates of pride, or the narrow motives of self-interest, does not scruple to break his word, so pledged, and engagements thus formal.

He went on to contrast Harris's behaviour with that of the proprietors of Drury Lane Theatre, who behaved to him 'like Gentlemen, and men of honour' [12].

Harris's relationships with most of his playwrights were rather better than this, but in general, I suppose, his businesslike methods verged on the grasping. He seems to have made a practice of buying the copyright of successful plays from their authors and of selling the texts to publishers when they were no longer topical or were out of copyright. The late Cyprian Blagden informed me that he had found in Longman's archives a record of the sale by Harris to that publisher, in 1800, for £420, of *The Duenna* and a miscellaneous collection of twenty-five other plays. This does not work out as a large sum per play, but it does show that Harris knew how to capitalize on every resource.

At least one of his authors grumbled about the financial rewards of dramatic authorship. On 20 January 1797, *The Times* reported that Thomas Morton had received £400 for his play, *A Cure for the Heartache*, and £150 from Harris for its copyright. Some seven years later, Morton wrote to Harris about this payment and others he had received for his successful comedies: he thought himself

> under the most indelible obligations for the very kind and gentlemanly attentions, you have ever favoured me with, yet the pecuniary compensations I have received for plays seem *now* to me, below par. – The four Comedies I have had the pleasure of presenting to you, have each on an average run the first Season 37 nights – and the Sum taken from the Theatre for each averaged £450. . . .
> Perhaps you may have heard, that I have often been applied to by the

proprietors, and managers of Drury Lane Theatre for a Comedy. My answers ... have been that your conduct has been so gratifying to my feelings, as to render my writing for any other theatre than yours impossible. . . .

But Sir tho I declined the flattering invitation to visit Drury Lane, I did not forget what they proposed to treat me with — suffice it to say that my remuneration would have exceeded that I have got by my most successful efforts. . . . [13]

He ended by saying that he would consider £450 for his new play 'inadequate compensation'. I have not seen Harris's reply but there is sufficient information in Morton's letter to suggest that while Harris had personally been very agreeable, his payments had been on the stingy side. Harris realized, however, that common sense dictated a better deal for Morton, and by 1807 the dramatist drew as much as one thousand pounds for a new play.

Harris's policies and personality are also revealed in his relations with his actors, and nowhere better than in the squabble over benefit charges that took place in 1800. The actors were informed on 26 July 1799 that charges would now amount to £160 and that only three weeks' notice would be given of the date of the benefit night. Since the charges had been only £64.5.0 within living memory, the performers were irritated by these innovations and claimed:

Want of success had been the plea of former Proprietors for encroachments on Actors' emoluments; that certainly cannot be urged in the present state of Covent-Garden Theatre when the profits of the concern, to justify the rate of a late purchase in it, must be nearly trebled since Mr. Harris commenced Proprietor. [14]

There had been an immediate increase in benefit charges of £20 to meet what Harris said were theatre expenses of over £160 a night. The actors asked to see the figures and when this was refused, worked out for themselves that this would mean expenses of over thirty thousand in the season. Yet the salaries of the leading players, usually considered to be a large part of the total sum, only came to £3,205. Harris responded by saying that the increase of size in the theatre cost much money; but the actors were of the opinion that the proprietor had 'of late years . . . made the most exorbitant, and, as it manifestly appears, the most unfounded pecuniary demands on our benefits' [15].

They also argued that the increase in fines from £5 to £30 for refusing a character, allowed managers to make the leading actors do the work of inferior ones [16]. On the question of orders (or free admissions allowed to actors), they maintained that Harris had called them, in his dispute with Colman, 'an established privilege', but now termed them 'a gratuitous indulgence', and had even deducted the cost of them from the performers' salaries. At this point one must feel some sympathy for Harris, if only because the 'order' system was grossly abused at this period; yet he did not mind taking advantage of Drury Lane in this respect and frequently 'sent in towards 30 of a night'. Of course, on some nights as many as 547 people went in free at that badly-run institution [17].

Harris's actors, however, wished to make the point that they were unfairly treated:

> This latitude in giving written Orders was enjoyed by Performers till about the year 1787, when a habit commenced, contrary to former practice, of charging a portion of them as cash whenever the receipt of the House should accidentally amount to a certain sum — we believe £290. As this capricious deduction from Performers' salaries depended on a casualty, there was no security from it by any human foresight; and, independently of its being a violation of established usage, it was considered as the most obvious injustice, that the attraction of particular Performers, to which alone the high recepits were frequently to be attributed, should be actually converted to the diminution of their incomes. [18]

The emphasis here, as in Holcroft's grievance, is on the capriciousness of the proprietor's behaviour. Harris certainly appears to have been a very changeable character.

The last important complaint by the players was that Harris had 'of late years, (without any apparent shadow of right)' demanded that a play given at a benefit should be the theatre's property, without allowing the usual terms, 'or *any* terms of satisfaction, to the Author' [19]. Sir St Vincent Troubridge defends Harris to a certain extent by noting that this was far from being true of Thomas Dibdin's dealings with him, and goes on to describe the relationship. W. T. Lewis, by this time deputy manager of Covent Garden, asked Dibdin to write a play for his benefit night and Dibdin regarded it as a favour that Lewis 'stipulated that in case of success the theatre should pay for the play, which Mr Harris confirmed'. Harris went even further than this, for after its performance he said, 'Dibdin, you may ask the treasurer for £300, two for the play, and one for the copyright' [20]. There is a certain ambiguity in the use of the word 'favour', but it seems to me to suggest more capriciousness on Harris's part. Perhaps he paid for some benefit plays and not for others, as the fancy took him. His attitude increased the actors' sense of injury, as summarized in their saying, 'the passive admission of unaccounted-for charges and new restrictions only sanctifies oppression, and encourages still greater attempts to diminish our incomes' [21].

Harris took care to see that his point of view on all these subjects was justified to the public for, as Colman had said, he was ready to pay well to put over his case. Other examples of this are to be found in his career. In 1786, he gave 'a great dinner' for 'all the people concerned in the *Morning Post* and . . . made them all drunk' [22]. Ten years later, Joseph Farington confided to his diary that Harris had paid the publisher of *The Times* a hundred pounds a year so that 'his play-house may be well recommended in that paper' [23]. He knew, quite as well as Sheridan, the value of favourable publicity.

At this point, I move to consider Harris's relations with Sheridan for, on the whole, they show him in a more favourable light. Sheridan's early indebtedness to the principal proprietor of Covent Garden Theatre is acknowledged in a letter of 17 November 1774, written to Thomas Linley. A comedy he had written was done at Harris's request and though it was at least double the length of any acting comedy, he had advised Sheridan on the way in which he could improve it for presentation [24]. When this piece, named *The Rivals*, was put on, a critic noted that it was '*a full hour* longer in the representation than any piece on the stage. – This last circumstance is an error of such a nature as shows either great obstinacy in the author, or excessive ignorance in the managers' [25]. Neither was true according to Sheridan, who said of Harris, 'I believe, his feeling for the vanity of a young Author got the better of his desire for correctness, and he left many excrescences remaining, because he had assisted in pruning so many more'. Sheridan was anxious to withdraw the piece after the first performance, but Harris had more confidence in the play and was determined to put it on again as soon as the text had been revised. Its success is well remembered, and obviously owed something to Harris's intervention.

The manager's confidence in Sheridan's ability was even more justified by the success of *The Duenna*. Well before it was produced, Harris was 'extravagantly sanguine of its success as to plot and dialogue' [26], and gave Sheridan eager assistance. It became the rage of London for many months.

Then, by an astonishing transformation, Sheridan became principal proprietor of Drury Lane and was very soon involved with Harris in plans for the creation of a third winter theatre. They were attracted to this idea by the need to interest 'a higher class of people' who dined late and lived at quite a distance from the patent theatres. A small fashionable playhouse in one of the politer streets was required. Rather than wait for someone else to forestall them and find use for the dormant 'Killigrew' patent, they proposed to build a new one themselves. According to the *London Evening Post*, 29 November– 2 December 1777,

> the idea . . . was started by Mr. Sheridan, on the remonstrances of many of the nobility and gentry at the west end of the town. The scite [*sic*] of it is to be somewhere about Portland square, the architect Sir William Chambers. The sum subscribed is to be seventy thousand pounds. . . .

The preference to be given to Covent Garden in the sharing of the profits of the new venture is noted by Sheridan:

> All the Proprietors . . . of Drury Lane and Covent Garden shall share all profits from the Dramatic entertainments as above specified exhibited at the New Theatre – that is each shall be entitled to receive a Dividend in proportion to the shares he or she shall possess in the present Theatres – First only deducting a certain nightly sum to be paid to the Proprietors of Covent Garden Theatre, as a consideration for the licence furnished by the exercise of their present dormant Patent. [27]

Harris, it would appear, had everything to gain by this association.

Years later, Sheridan declared that George III had given his full consent to the exercise of the Killigrew patent in the new theatre which they contemplated building, and went on to add some significant words: 'A subsequent suggestion from His Majesty respecting the Opera House occasioned their purchasing that property also' [28] . I think we may conclude from this that the King's suggestion made them obey his wishes, and that they put off the building of a small, fashionable theatre for the time being. The union of the managers was not confined to the Opera House, but took in the patent theatres and their companies as well. It was greeted with indignation: 'Atticus', writing in the *St. James's Chronicle*, 19–22 September 1778, thought they were given a monopoly that was 'unfavourable to dramatic excellence and the honest effort of genius'. He preferred rivalry between the houses because it made them strain to excel. 'A Poor Player' remarks in *Coalition. A Farce* (1779), p. v.:

> That a conspiracy has been formed against the independence of the stage and performers, cannot be denied. . . . Some have had their salaries reduced, and those who are under articles for a time, have no better treatment to expect,

when the term of their agreement expires. . . . Writers of dramatic pieces and
of music are in the same predicament. . . .

The rationalizing mind of Thomas Harris seems to have been busy
cutting costs, and both managers attempted to strengthen their
positions in other ways. They agreed to take over the quarter-share of
William Powell's widow for twenty-one years at an annuity of
£1,600 [29], and at Drury Lane Sheridan bought out Willoughby Lacy's
moiety in a similar manner. Sheridan would have gone on adding to his
liabilities endlessly in the hope that money would flow in from all
quarters, but Harris wanted greater security, and when the Opera House
season showed a heavy loss, he decided to quit.

They had purchased the Opera House on 24 June 1778 from James
Brooke and Richard and Mary Yates for £22,000, paying ten thousand
on being given possession, and promising repayment of the rest in
regular payments over four years. In a later memorial to the Lord
Chamberlain, Harris noted that this theatre was also subject to a rent of
£1,270, 'which, though a price notoriously beyond the value of the
property, your Memorialist was induc'd to give in the intention of
exercising in that Theatre a dormant Patent now in his possession,
under the authority of which it was proposed to open that Theatre on
more than two nights per week' [30].

In 1779, Brooke and the Yateses were dissatisfied with what they
had received and they obtained judgments against Sheridan and Harris
for the penalty sum of £24,000 and costs. Harris's alarm at their action
was increased when he saw that the accounts of the Opera House at the
end of its first season showed a loss of £7,200. So he sold out to
Sheridan (whose serenity on the subject of high finance was unshake-
able) at the same rate as he had purchased the share. No conveyance
was actually executed but in the following season it was reported that
Harris 'hath not intermeddled in the said theatre but the said R. B.
Sheridan hath been considered as the sole proprietor'.

On 21 August 1781, their positions were reversed. In consideration
of ten shillings paid by Harris to Sheridan, the Opera House reverted to
Harris with the proviso that Sheridan should take it over if he were able
to pay the £12,000 and all the other debts that had been incurred.
What these highly complicated dealings mean, I think, is that once
Harris and Sheridan were convinced that the Opera House would not
pay, they rented out their holdings to others: Sheridan's went
eventually to Taylor, and Harris's to the dancer Gallini [31].

Strangely enough, their experiences at the Opera House did not convince them that a third theatre for fashionable people was too costly a venture for them to undertake. Harris, in fact, pursued the idea almost immediately afterwards, and in a memorandum dated 'Novr. 1782', we find some unpublished information about his intentions. This time he was to work in conjunction with Henry Holland, the architect, and not with Sir William Chambers:

> Messrs Harris and Holland being desirous of building and opening to the public one large elegant and spacious Theatre and Gardens capable of comprising and exhibiting all or any Amusements suitable to the public at large, or to such of the Nobility and Gentry as might choose to enter into subscriptions for more confined Entertainments *they* proposed entering into such engagements with each other as were likely to produce mutual advantages.
>
> Mr. Harris being possessed of a patent the authority of which is absolutely necessary for exhibiting such entertainment – and Mr. *Holland* being possessed of some land at Knightsbridge very properly situated for the purpose and willing to engage for so much more as may become necessary and proposing to subscribe largely to the Scheme and to promote the subscription as his connexions may enable him to do, these were the inducements for sharing any advantage that might arise. [32]

The document also notes that Holland's main concern was to develop the land he owned and to be employed as architect of the new playhouse. Another document, dated London, 10 April 1783, lists his proposals for this 'scheme at the back of Grosvenor Place'. He would let the piece of ground he held from Lord Cadogan and others for five pounds a year clear of taxes, would provide two roads of communication, and would himself subscribe a quarter of any necessary sum of money. In return, he would expect to be the architect, and would also receive an annuity of £200 for thirty years, 'provided the profit of the undertaking amounts to so much after allowing £1,000 per annum for the exercise of the patent' [33]. In other words, Harris's interests were to be carefully safeguarded.

The proposals were consolidated in a document dated 22 March 1784, from which it is clear that Harris had acquired the lease Holland had offered, and now intended to build

> a Spacious, elegant Edifice, to be called (By Authority) The Prince of Wales Theatre with a grand assembly Room, and other Rooms for Suppers, Balls, and Concerts; the whole to communicate with Gardens and Grounds laid out in the most approved modern taste – the theatrical and other Exhibitions will commence at a later Hour, and in all respects be more accommodated to

Persons of Rank and Fashion than can now be effected at any other Place of Public Entertainment. [34]

The desire to satisfy aristocratic patrons who were forsaking the patent theatres is clear and much more ambitious than the scheme for a Pic Nic Theatre [35] put up by Greville in 1802.

Difficulties were encountered later, when William Taylor claimed that he alone had a right to open an opera house, so Sheridan, resourceful in everything but money, tried to remove them all with a new plan. The Grosvenor Place scheme was to be abandoned, and the Opera House, supervised by nominees of Sheridan and five leading noblemen, would be allowed a monopoly of opera. In turn, Harris was to be compensated for the loss of any advantage he might have gained in using the Killigrew patent at Grosvenor Place.

Then Albany Wallis, solicitor to Drury Lane Theatre, raised doubts about the validity of the Drury Lane patent. To make things worse, the Duke of Bedford refused to renew the ground lease unless he could be assured that another patent could be obtained. This all came to a head when Sheridan was trying to raise funds to rebuild the old playhouse, as he had to make some immediate provision before the news of the Duke of Bedford's attitude could reach the prospective shareholders in the new theatre. The simplest answer to this problem was to buy the Killigrew patent from Harris [36]. The Covent Garden proprietor offered it for £15,000, and at a later date, White and Warren (who owned the remaining fourteen-sixtieths) claimed a further five thousand. Sheridan willingly agreed to both demands, and actually paid £11,667 to Harris. The other amount was not paid until 1813 [37]. Once his immediate troubles were over, he went on in his usual desultory way until the bankruptcy of the theatre occurred in 1801. George III thought his purchase of the Killigrew patent 'rather a swindling transaction', but I can find no evidence that this was so [38].

Sheridan was grateful for Harris's help, and remarked that the Covent Garden proprietor appeared always to have paid the fairest attention to the interests of Drury Lane in every plan for reviving the idea of exercising this patent [39]. Harris's aid, however, seems to me to have been dictated as much by self-interest as by friendship. On 28 August 1788, he and Sheridan had pledged to maintain 'their just monopoly' [40], and Harris knew better than to encourage other competitors by dangling the Killigrew patent in front of them.

If Sheridan was satisfied with Harris's fair dealing, his wife certainly was not. In about April 1790, she wrote to Sheridan to say,

> I can't make out what business you are settling with Harris. Is it good or bad plagues? I have no opinion of Mr. H. nor ever had. He is selfish, that is, quite the man of the world. Of course *you* are no match for him; but I trust you do not·deceive me when you say you shall settle things *well*, though (as the poor sailor said) I'll be hanged if I see how, for you seem all poor and pennyless. [41]

Sheridan's incredible optimism and his ability to persuade people to do whatever he wanted, must not blind us to the fact that in the end he gained nothing from these constant manoeuvrings, though Harris was richer by at least £11,667. In financial matters, Sheridan was so concerned about immediate advantage that he could never be a match for an astute business man like Harris; and though he was a very penetrating judge of character, Sheridan mistook this man very badly on at least one occasion.

This occurred right at the beginning of the new century. J. P. Kemble had shown interest in becoming part-proprietor of Drury Lane Theatre. On 1 February 1800, he agreed to buy a quarter-share for £25,000, and Sheridan seems to have been confident that he would go on with the transaction in spite of the fact that Drury Lane was on the verge of bankruptcy.

Sheridan's certainty sprang from a belief that Kemble would never leave Drury Lane for Covent Garden, and would therefore wish to have as much control as possible over the theatre in which he worked. The conviction itself was also founded on the personal dislike that existed between Harris and Kemble, but Sheridan ought to have remembered that as far as Harris was concerned financial considerations played a much bigger part in his thinking and being than any purely emotional feelings. Consequently Kemble took his money and himself to Covent Garden, and left Sheridan gasping. The scene is described by James Boaden:

> The new allies invited Sheridan to witness their mutual felicity. When the wine had circulated freely, the proprietors of Covent Garden began to express their sentiments in a vein of the greatest cordiality – upon which Sheridan, with very bitter pleasantry, reproached them with their facility or their hypocrisy. 'Two fellows,' said he, 'that have absolutely hated each other deadly all their lives!'
> '*False*,' said Mr Harris (very whimsically), 'we have not hated each other these *six* weeks – have we, Kemble?' [42]

The jocular reply takes us right into the heart of the man. In the most amiable way, he had achieved a master-stroke of policy, and that gave him far more pleasure than anything else.

By this time, too, Harris had come to the opinion that Sheridan was, to use his own phrase, 'the Prince of Botherers' [43], and it is hardly surprising that a man of such careful habits should have felt a little contempt for a man of genius who, to a certain extent, threw his own livelihood away by sheer carelessness and procrastination. In an undated letter, Harris wrote about a plan put forward by Sheridan to erect two theatres, and showed his own impatience at its lack of realism:

> ... It is quite impossible Sheridan can seriously mean to erect *two* Theatres – whether small or large could not be of any consideration to us – if small, and shou'd be successful they would soon avoidably grow larger – but he must be well aware that the sum paid, or to be paid by Drury Lane, was merely a consideration to Cov. Garden for continuing the dormant Patent unexercis'd (except as a security to the Subscribers for rebuilding Drury Lane Theatre), and for which purpose (the prevention of more Theatres) it was reasonable that the Opera House should contribute its proportion and accordingly Taylor by deed (to which Sheridan and myself are parties) agreed to advance £5,000 –
>
> You must recollect that I had taken some ground, and had obtain'd his Majesty's consent for the erection of another Theatre, but being convinc'd that two Theatres, being under one direction, must infallibly ruin all the others, I desisted, and acquiesced in the above arrangement.
>
> I beg of you to consult with our good and able friends in Norfolk street – whether under the present circumstances it is expedient for me to protest formally against any plan so absurd as that of establishing three Playhouses when experience proves that London can hardly support two, in the Splendour that our Metropolis now expects. [44]

The letter is interesting partly because it shows his reasons for dismissing as absurd Sheridan's scheme for erecting two new theatres, and partly because he now explains his abandoning the notion of building a third theatre. In both cases he was guided by a desire for a profit on his investment, and by little else.

The contrast between Sheridan and Harris as principal proprietors and directors of the patent theatres is nowhere better seen than in their reaction to the destruction of their playhouses by fire. This happened at Covent Garden on 20 September 1808, when everything but the title-deeds and a few pantomime devices was lost. Harris's energy and Kemble's aristocratic friends soon brought about the rebuilding and the new theatre was opened to the public a year after the old one had been destroyed. When Drury Lane Theatre was burned down in February

1809, the banker, Thomas Hammersley, wrote to Sheridan saying

> Providence is very merciful to you in the great calamity that has befallen Drury Lane Theatre. It is of all opportunities that have ever happened to you the greatest; I have before talked to you of golden opportunities and your suffering them to escape, but this is a Diamond opportunity and if you let it pass by, I shall most lamentably conclude that you are under a state of judicial blindness, and that you are a man for ever lost both in this world and that which is to come. . . . Great good may be drawn out of much apparent evil, if you will only kiss the rod which *justly* corrects us [45].

I think we may guess what he means when we look at a report in *The Times*, 3 March 1809, that the Dukes of Devonshire, Bedford, and Norfolk, with Sheridan's other friends and associates, were to meet to try and alleviate his misfortunes; but Sheridan did not care for the idea of being publicly dependent on the great landlords. He valued his so-called independence, and preferred the notion of raising money by means of a lottery. He came to no firm resolution, and the immediate upsurge of sympathy that followed the fire gradually died away. At the end of May, he asked Samuel Whitbread to become a member of the committee for rebuilding Drury Lane Theatre, and some three years or so later, the new edifice was opened, but in the meantime, Sheridan had been shut out from any control in it. By sheer procrastination he had lost the readiest supply of money he had ever known, and it is not surprising he died in 1816 in rather miserable circumstances.

Harris lived for four years longer and in affluent conditions. From about 1795, his home was at Belmont, Uxbridge, and he collected about him a splendid display of some seventy pictures. He preserved these portraits of the leading actors and actresses of Covent Garden Theatre in a gallery that he had built for the purpose. He owned some others too: the painting by James Roberts of the screen scene in *The School for Scandal*, and the celebrated canvas by Hayman showing Garrick and Mrs Pritchard in *The Suspicious Husband*. He was a patron of Gainsborough Dupont, whose portraits of Lewis as Mercutio, Holman as Edgar, and some ten other players in their favourite roles, are now in the Garrick Club [46]. It seems to me typical of the man that in becoming a collector and commissioning paintings, he confined himself to the subjects he knew well.

Harris was obviously a man of limited gifts and imagination, but he was clear-sighted, energetic, and hard-working. John Opie's portrait of him shows a determined mouth and an intent gaze [47]. He looks good-humoured, and he certainly could be very charming and agreeable when necessary. Even Holcroft, who had complained so bitterly concerning *Seduction* and had been forced to make alterations in other plays against his better judgment, admitted that Harris behaved well sometimes. In fact, he wrote him a letter expressing his sense of obligation when Harris accepted a play in spite of their earlier disputes. Holcroft says, 'That you had conceived disadvantageous ideas of me, I knew; though I have no doubt, but I shall ultimately convince you, that, even supposing me to have been mistaken, my motives have been laudable. With me you were irritated; but you had the justice to forget the man, and promote the interests of the piece' [48]. On another occasion, when Harris called and criticized yet another of Holcroft's plays, the dramatist was sufficiently impressed to say, 'his ideas, though crude, have awakened reflection' [49]. In other words Harris knew what he wanted in the theatre, and his attitude to his authors was dictated by their success or failure in their vocation. The same criterion applied to the players: he could be friendly or formidable as the need arose. Mrs Jordan, who could easily outpoint Sheridan, stated that though Harris was anxious to see her, she was not eager to meet him 'unprepared' [50].

W. T. Parke says he was of a suspicious temper [51], and Holcroft stresses his changeableness. These characteristics make a man feared rather than loved, and it is certain that some of his measures and attitudes at Covent Garden did not exactly earn him popularity. Yet since a theatre must pay its way if it is to pay its actors, there is something to be said for a principal proprietor who sees to it that his playhouse makes a profit. Without a Mrs Siddons or a Mrs Jordan in his company, he found means of attracting large audiences and was willing to spend as much as forty thousand pounds on attractive scenery. His theatre greatly increased in value and, in 1799, the *Monthly Mirror* [52] wrote: 'How the property has prospered during his management appears from the value which is now set upon it, viz. £120,000, just double the sum at which it was sold to Messrs Harris, Rutherford, Colman, and Powell.'

Harris was purposeful and decisive. In this respect, Boaden interestingly contrasts him with Sheridan:

In the contest with Drury Lane Theatre, Mr Harris had this great advantage, his attention was directed exclusively to his management; and as that vested in him absolutely for life, he had no check upon him for partners in the concern, and could always command the necessary funds to carry his designs, however expensive, into effect. The great difficulty at the other house, was to get Mr. Sheridan to determine what should be done. . . . With his force in tragedy, comedy, and opera he ought literally to have shut up the other theatre. He never made even a drawn battle of it. [53]

In other words, Harris's competence and single-mindedness and possession of capital were altogether more effective in providing his playhouse with day-to-day success than Sheridan's fitful efforts at Drury Lane. Harris made his theatre pay, something very few of his successors achieved, but, of course, he never brought to it the occasional glory that marked Sheridan's reign.

Notes

[1] G. Colman, *A True State of the Differences subsisting between the Proprietors of Covent Garden Theatre* (London, 1768), 11.
[2] ibid., 12.
[3] *A Letter from T. Harris, to G. Colman, on the Affairs of Covent Garden* (London, 1768), 3.
[4] *A True State*, 12–18.
[5] G. Colman, *T. Harris Dissected* (London, 1768), 34.
[6] *A True State*, 4.
[7] *T. Harris Dissected*, 16.
[8] *A Letter from T. Harris*, v.
[9] ibid., 1.
[10] *T. Harris Dissected*, 2.
[11] *The London Stage, 1660–1800*, Part 4, ed. G. W. Stone (Carbondale, Ill., 1962), 1348.
[12] T. Holcroft, *Seduction* (3rd ed., London, 1787), v-xi.
[13] British Theatre Museum MS.
[14] *A Statement of the Differences subsisting between the Proprietors and the Performers of the Theatre Royal, Covent-Garden* (London, 1800), 32.
[15] ibid., 25–30.
[16] ibid., 47.
[17] BM Add. MS. 42720, f. 120; *The Letters of R. B. Sheridan*, ed. C. Price (Oxford, Oxford U.P., 1966), iii, 29, n. 2.
[18] *A Statement*, 55
[19] ibid., 38–9.
[20] St Vincent Troubridge, *The Benefit System in the British Theatre* (Society for Theatre Research, London, 1967), 132–3, quoting Thomas Dibdin, *Reminiscences* (London, 1827), I, 362–4.
[21] *A Statement*, 67.
[22] Folger MS. Y.d.35.

[23] *The Farington Diary*, ed. J. Greig (Hutchinson, London, 1922–8, 8 vols.), I, 157.
[24] *Letters of Sheridan*, I, 85. Cf. the preface to the first edition of *The Rivals* (1775), vii.
[25] 'A Friend to Comedy' in the *Morning Chronicle*, 20 January 1775.
[26] *Letters of Sheridan*, I, 87.
[27] ibid., I, 120.
[28] ibid., I, 231.
[29] Widener Library MS. in an extra-illustrated set of Moore, *Life of Sheridan*, VI, 70.
[30] Public Record Office MS. L.C. 7/3.
[31] Public Record Office MS. C/107/64 and 65. A note by Winston in Folger MS. T. a. 59, states that on 30 July 1779, Sheridan and Harris were also in treaty for the Pantheon.
[32] Folger MS. W. b. 104, no. 14. Another note by Winston (British Museum press mark C. 120h) records that Ford and Linley, as part-proprietors of Drury Lane Theatre, had an audience with the King at Windsor Park and objected to Harris's proposals for a new theatre. The King replied that he understood that Harris meant to open it by virtue of a dormant patent, 'in which case it was not in his power to oppose the undertaking was he even inclined to do it'.
[33] Folger MS. W.b.104, no. 15.
[34] Ian Donaldson 'New Papers of Henry Holland and R. B. Sheridan', *Theatre Notebook* XVI (1962), 119–21.
[35] See *Letters of Sheridan*, II, 170–4.
[36] Egerton MS. 2134, f. 75. Cf. *Report from the Select Committee on Dramatic Literature* (1832), 241–3.
[37] *Letters of Sheridan*, I, 245, n. 2, 247, n. 3, and 248, n. 4.
[38] *The Later Correspondence of George III*, ed. A. Aspinall (Cambridge, Cambridge U.P., 1967), III, 306.
[39] *Letters of Sheridan*, I, 231.
[40] BM Add. MS. 42720, f. 5.
[41] W. Fraser Rae, *Sheridan* (London, 1896), II, 130.
[42] J. Boaden, *Memoirs of the Life of John Philip Kemble* (London, 1825), II, 381.
[43] British Theatre Museum MS., Harris to his son, Henry, c. 23 May 1810.
[44] British Theatre Museum MS., Harris to Barlow, 'Bellemonts, Friday'. The cover is dated '12 May', and since Harris did not live at Belmont, Uxbridge, until after 1795 (see the *True Briton*, 25 July 1795), the letter may belong to 1797.
[45] British Museum MS. (pressmark C 120h), 1808–9.
[46] John Hayes, 'Thomas Harris, Gainsborough Dupont and the Theatrical Gallery at Belmont', *Connoisseur*, CLXIX (1968), 221–7.
[47] It is reproduced in Mr Hayes' article, from the original owned by Mr Mark Longman.
[48] *Memoirs of Thomas Holcroft*, ed. Hazlitt (World's Classics, 1926), 132, 154, 257.

[49] ibid., 295.
[50] *Mrs Jordan and her Family*, ed. A. Aspinall (Arthur Barker, London, 1951), 206.
[51] *Musical Memoirs* (London, 1830), I, 107.
[52] VIII (1799), 123.
[53] Boaden, op. cit., I, 312.

7 ARNOLD HARE

George Frederick Cooke:
the Actor and the Man

What might be termed the 'received view' of George Frederick Cooke could hardly be more simple — that he was a potentially great actor ruined by alcoholism. There is, of course, a very great deal of truth in this, but it is also an over-simplification which suggests a stereotype, rather than the complex amalgam of paradoxes and contradictions that is the man himself.

His first — and until recently, only, full-length biographer was the American playwright William Dunlap, who knew Cooke during the last eighteen months before his death in the United States [1]. To him Cooke left such records and papers as he had with him, and they seem to have had some conversations on the understanding that Dunlap would write his life. On these the work was based, and it still remains a primary source.

But several matters need to be remembered. In the first place, Dunlap's perspective is not a well balanced one. Over a quarter of his book is devoted to the events of the last eighteen months of Cooke's life. During those last months Cooke's weaknesses had become more serious, and his lapses more frequent. The Cooke Dunlap knew was an exaggerated version. Moreover Cooke's memoranda and conversation had become selective. What he did not wish to recall, especially if it detracted from his view of himself, he ignored; and he had developed a habit of romancing and embellishing fact which Dunlap noted but did not adequately allow for. In fairness it should be added that since his book was written immediately after Cooke's death and first published in 1813 (Cooke had died in September 1812), Dunlap was hardly in a position to do so. Most of the evidence that would have enabled him to check Cooke's notes was on the other side of the Atlantic.

What is not a matter of fact, but must have derived from Dunlap himself, is the moralizing tone which he adopts when the opportunity arises. There is so strong an element of the drunkard's doom about his account from time to time that it is difficult to avoid the suspicion that some of these matters are being dwelt on for didactic purposes. And it was as true then as now, that the liveliest and most memorable anecdotes are those of the 'man bites dog' variety, so that Charles Mathews on the burning of the pound notes, or the scarifying evening at Mistress Byrn's, or Dibdin on the stone-throwing in Greek Street, are the stories that linger in the memory; even in the theatre the fact that audiences raved about his Richard III and Shylock tends to be less vividly recalled than Lord William Lennox's story of the night he was so drunk that he nearly cut off his finger with Shylock's knife. And the good tale may often be embellished in the telling.

In this attempt to see George Cooke in better perspective I propose briefly to outline his career, drawing attention mainly to those aspects where Dunlap is least adequate; to consider some of his qualities as an actor, drawing chiefly on contemporary material not available to Dunlap; and finally to attempt some consideration of the paradoxical character of the man himself. I have set down the detailed evidence and arguments relating to these elsewhere. Here, it will be understood, I can only summarize.

Cooke was born, possibly in 1756, but almost certainly not in Westminster as Dunlap supposes, but in one of the many barracks then in Dublin. His mother was a border girl from Berwick who had followed the drum; whether George was born within the bonds of wedlock is not clear, though it seems unlikely.

It was in Berwick that he was brought up, educated, and apprenticed as a printer; it was there too, from his reading and the occasional visits of the Edinburgh company, that he acquired the passion for the stage that first led him into amateur theatricals and later to a journey to London with his friend Colin Mitchell, both determined to seek their fortunes as professional players.

Cooke had his first opportunity quite quickly. We find him with one of Whitley and Herbert's companies in King's Lynn in 1774, already playing young leads, and even trying his voice in musical pieces. (This is two years earlier than the putative first professional performance at Brentford in 1776, of Dunlap's account.) Subsequently, for some eight years, he led a wandering and comparatively hand-to-mouth existence, mostly with small and unestablished companies, and when engagements were not to be had, returning for short periods to his trade as a printer. There are glimpses of him, sometimes tantalisingly brief, in Suffolk with Standen, at the Haymarket (out of season), the China-hall theatre in Rotherhithe, and in the Borough; a winter in Suffolk, and a frustrating spring in Canterbury, with only Macklin's encouragement to console him for the lack of opportunity in a company where all the best roles were bespoken. By 1781—2 he had become a leading actor in the Nottingham-Derby company (one of Whitley's, again, though now after his death), but it was not till he joined James Miller in Manchester in 1784 that he could be said to have begun to establish himself as a leading provincial player. From then till 1800 he was a leading member of the best provincial companies in the north and west, with two spells also in Dublin. We find him in Manchester, first with Miller and later with Banks and Ward, where he was always popular with the local audiences; in York and Hull with Tate Wilkinson; in Chester, Newcastle and Sheffield with Austen and Whitlock (there, according to Wilkinson, he was something of a 'matinee idol' and had all the young ladies swooning after him). In Dublin his first visit ended in the disaster that led him to enlist in the army, from which he was later rescued by friends in Portsmouth and Manchester; but his second spell there, from 1797 till 1800, produced the call to Covent Garden at the age of 44 that gave him his decade as a national figure, and the only rival, in certain roles, to John Philip Kemble.

From October 1800 to June 1810 he was a leading actor at Covent Garden, spending his summers in guest appearances all over the country, from Plymouth to Edinburgh, from Dublin to York, the 'Inimitable', or the 'Incomparable', Mr Cooke, as the playbills had it.

By now, of course, the indiscretions as well as the triumphs of his life were public. Transgressions had to be periodically apologised for at Covent Garden and elsewhere, though it is not without significance that even in the last year they were soon forgiven, and a reference to 'my old complaint' could be received with humorous tolerance as much as irritation. The climax of these came in the autumn of 1807, which he spent in detention for debt in Appleby. It appears that he had defaulted on an engagement in Manchester, for which he had received payment in advance and for the return of which the managers naturally sued. Typically, he had gone through the money. Only his old friend Rock was able to rescue him with an engagement for Glasgow and Edinburgh. It is to this period of enforced idleness that we owe the compilation of the Chronicle of his life, and another of the fragmentary journals of the kind that were Dunlap's chief source material.

His enforced absence from London had whetted the playgoers' appetite. He returned to Covent Garden in March 1808 to the 'greatest money house, one excepted' ever known in that theatre. But by now his strengths were less able to compensate for his weaknesses, and his flights to the brandy bottle were becoming more frequent. In 1810, during one of his extended alcoholic festivals in Liverpool and district, Cooper, the American actor and manager, persuaded him to sign a contract for a tour of the United States and managed to get him aboard ship and away before he could change his mind. The exigencies of the sea voyage brought him to New York dried out and sober, and his opening there as Richard III was a triumph, but within days the call of the bottle was affecting his performances. Those last eighteen months, which Dunlap chronicles often in much detail, were an amalgam of triumphs and follies, which not even Cooke's iron constitution could survive. On 26 September 1811 he died of dropsy in New York, pursued even into his grave by a series of indignities by turns comic and macabre [2].

Summarized in this way, it does sound like a rake's progress, which in some senses it is. And yet. . . . As late as 1810, meeting Cooke for the first time, Dunlap could write:

> I could not but admire his appearance as well as his manner, so opposite to the idea I had formed of him, in consequence of hearing the many anecdotes circulated among theatrical people, of his rudeness and intemperance.
>
> He looked older than men I had been used to seeing of his age, but vigorous and healthful. The neatness of his dress, his sober suit of grey, his powdered grey hairs, and suavity of address, gave no indication of the eccentric being, whose weaknesses had been the theme of the English fugitive publications. . . . [3]

And the portrait of him out of costume by Drummond, later engraved in the *European Magazine*, a portrait for which he sat in 1805–6, shows a gentleman well-set-up and healthy looking, with an alert and intelligent eye, and a touch of benevolence in the countenance. Even allowing for the painter's desire to flatter his sitter, this is not a likeness of unrelieved dissipation. (A comparison with the Cooper engraving, also out of costume, that prefaced the London edition of Dunlap, is instructive here.) Cooke was much too complex a character for any stereotype to apply.

Nor could he be typed as an actor. Certainly in his last years he concentrated, as much by public demand as by inclination, on those major roles which he did best. But the earlier part of his career, like that of any provincial actor of his day, bred versatility. During his 38 years as an actor we have records to date of 325 different roles which he played. Of these, 245 were played during his provincial career and not again after his translation to Covent Garden. Another 67 which he had played provincially became part of his London repertory; while during that last decade he added 13 new roles. In his final eighteen months in North America he rang the changes on only 21 of these 80.

Two selected seasons for which records are reasonably complete, from the beginning and end of his provincial career, not only show Cooke's progress in his profession, but illustrate the demands on a good country actor at this time.

At King's Lynn in 1774 Cooke was at the beginning of his career, a young man working like a beaver to learn his way around the repertory. During a thirteen-week season he performed on 34 playing nights. One of the King's Lynn fairs, the Mart, took place annually in February, and for obvious reasons the company opened its season then, for the first week playing every night but Sunday, and following with five nights in the second week. During that time Cooke played in either play or afterpiece each night; sometimes in both. On the opening night he played Young Marlow in Goldsmith's *She Stoops to Conquer*; the following night Jaffier in Otway's *Venice Preserv'd*. On the Wednesday he was not in the cast of *The Provok'd Husband*, but sang a cantata after Act IV, and afterwards played Henry, the young romantic hero of Dibdin's *The Deserter*, in the course of which − if they presented it uncut − he sang three songs and took part in a duet and a concerted piece. Thursday saw him as Sir George Hastings in Kelly's *A Word to the Wise*, and as Whittle, the old man fallen in love with the young widow, in Garrick's *The Irish Widow*. Friday brought him Jack Meggot, the young man-about-town in Hoadly's *The Suspicious Husband*, after which he played Paris in *The Judgment of Paris* (presumably Abraham Langford's entertainment, rather than Congreve's earlier masque). Finally, on the Saturday he played the young lover Lionel in Bickerstaffe's comic opera *Lionel and Clarissa*, in which again he may well have sung three songs and taken part in a like number of concerted pieces. An energetic and versatile week's work.

In the second week the only character to be repeated was Henry; he added Granville in Kelly's tragedy *Clementine*, Young Meadows in Bickerstaffe's comic opera *Love in a Village*, Lord Duke in Garrick's farce, *High Life Below Stairs*, Epicene in *The Macaroni*, and Lord Aimworth, the aristocrat in love with the Miller's daughter, in Bickerstaffe's *The Maid of the Mill*.

With the end of the fair, this initial burst of activity came to an end; the company advertised that in future they would play only three nights a week, and after three weeks of that settled down for the remaining eight weeks to performances on Tuesdays and Fridays only. During that time Cooke added to his repertory, among other things, Hamlet, Don Felix in Mrs Centlivre's *The Wonder*, Zanga the Moor in Dr Young's melodramatic blank-verse tragedy *The Revenge*, Lord Hastings in *Jane Shore*, Alexander in *The Rival Queens*, and Posthumus, Macbeth and King Lear (the latter for his benefit performance) [4]. Three months of notable activity for a young man, even allowing that standards of performance may not have been of the highest. (It is fair to recall here that Whitley the manager had a reputation among his contemporaries both for his eye to the finances and his determination to raise and maintain the standard of his companies.)

Twenty-three years later, in Dublin in 1797–8, the picture is a different one. Cooke is now an established leading actor in the company (it is his Shylock that opens the redecorated and rebuilt Crow Street Theatre part way through the season). The company normally performs six nights a week. During a six month season we have records for 140 playing days, so that allowing for holidays the calendar is virtually complete. Of these, Cooke performed on 72, about three times a week on average, and on only one occasion did he perform in an afterpiece (Midas); 17 of the main roles were repeated more than once. The most frequent of these were Stedfast in Colman the Younger's *The Heir at Law* (7) and Sir William Dorrillon in Mrs Inchbald's *Wives as they were and Maids as they Are* (5), both of which had been introduced in London in the previous season, as had Haswell in Mrs Inchbald's *Such Things Are* (4). Penruddock in Cumberland's *The Wheel of Fortune* (5) and Octavian in Colman's *The Mountaineers* (3) were only a year or two older. There was a good proportion of the standard tragic roles – Iago (5), Richard III (4), Shylock (3), Stukely (3), Zanga (3) – but comedy had a fair representation also – Joseph Surface (4), Moody in Garrick's *The Country Girl* (3), Sir George Touchwood in Mrs Cowley's *The Belle's Stratagem* (3), and Harmony in

Mrs Inchbald's *Everyone has his Fault* (3). He played twelve other roles during the season [5].

For neither season has any objective critical comment survived, it rarely does in the provincial press at this time. Most of the comments are obvious managerial puffs, which are worse than useless. The editor of the *Liverpool Chronicle* in 1806 strongly asserted his independence from managerial influence, and said that when his sons went to the theatre they paid for admission like anybody else and did not accept free seats to buy favourable comment. But as he added that he himself had never set foot in the theatre, it would be too much to expect comment of any value from him. The *Chester Chronicle* in 1785 printed a notice of Cooke's Hamlet that was critical of some detail but on the whole enthusiastic and impressed; this may have been independent comment or a clever publicity hand. It is not really until the London years that thoughtful critical judgment becomes available, and it is from these years, at the peak of his achievement, that we can begin to put together some kind of assessment as to how he appeared to his contemporaries, and how he affected them.

Cooke made his first appearance at Covent Garden on Friday, 31 October 1800, as Richard III. Ten days later he added Shylock, and then Sir Archy MacSarcasm, alternating these until the end of November. Iago and Macbeth were added, followed by Kitely and The Stranger, and later Sir Giles Overreach, and these eight were the material of that first season. In all he gave 67 performances, of which 23 were of Richard, 10 each of Shylock, Iago and Kitely, 7 of Macbeth, 5 of Sir Giles Overreach and 2 of The Stranger. He coupled Sir Archy with Shylock on five occasions. These, with the exception of The Stranger, and the addition of Stukely and Sir Pertinax MacSycophant, were to remain his great roles. It was on these that his London and North American reputation was based, these that the provincial audiences to whom he returned regularly each year during the summer demanded to see and hear. Falstaff, too, in both versions, he played with some popularity; Pierre in *Venice Preserv'd*; Glenalvon in *Douglas*. His Hamlet was a failure in London, his Lear not much of a success. He created a number of new roles in new plays, the best of which were probably Peregrine in Colman's *John Bull*, Lord Avondale in Morton's *The School of Reform*, and Lavensforth in Mrs Inchbald's *To Marry or Not to Marry*. But in his last decade he was primarily a classical actor in a limited number of roles, and it is on these that he must be judged [6].

His initial impact on London audiences was remarkable, and its commercial success may be judged from the fact that his first benefit was one of the most crowded houses ever witnessed at Covent Garden and brought him in the very large sum of £560, in addition to which Harris presented him with another £160 – the customary charges of the house. (Clearly Harris could afford it – later that year we find him buying additional land adjoining his house at Uxbridge out of the season's profits. He had the delicacy to name part of it Cooke's Field!) [7] The daily prints report the performance at some length as they appear, and in 1801 the *Morning Post* does a long series of retrospective articles on all the main roles. (These are distinct from Charles Lamb's well-known essay on his Richard III.) Periodicals, too, like the *Monthly Mirror*, add their contribution, so that during the first seasons we have a good deal of contemporary comment. As always there is disagreement on detail, and what seems a new revelation to one writer can be perverse and disagreeable to another. Here we can record only the briefest of samples of how some of his fellows saw him at that time.

In appearance

> Mr. Cooke appears to be between forty and fifty years of age. His figure is stout and of a proper height. His features are thoughtful, bold and marking, and calculated to give the expression of scorn, envy, hatred, brutal ferocity and overbearing pride with unrivalled force and effect. His voice, though the modulations of it are not always pleasing, is extremely articulate and powerful; equal, when exerted, to any pitch or variety of passion; and in a subdued key, his very *whisper* may be distinctly heard throughout the house. [8]

The *Morning Chronicle* noted the same characteristics, but was less impressed. Of Richard III:

> His voice is uncommonly harsh, and at times unmusical. It seems even in some of the notes to be cracked; but it is full of strength and articulate. He has the art, too, of sliding into a falsetto, which has pathos and impression. In several instances he used this talent with felicity, and marked the transitions with which this character is so pregnant, with good effect; but that fine art of modulation which gives harmony to declamation, and without which no candidate for so high a department of the drama can be justified in his claims, Mr. Cooke wants. The ear is incessantly offended by harsh violences, which a correct judgment could not commit, and which are not atoned for by occasional beauties. It is possible that in characters which demand less exertion – where the voice is more level – and in which he might make more use of his lower, and less of his upper tones, he may be a valuable acquisition

to the Theatre. He is certainly no common Ranter. He discriminates accurately and the volume of his voice makes his whisper audible. [9]

This characteristic of his voice, powerful but sometimes harsh and grating in the upper register, clear and penetrating and moving in the lower tones, seems to have been generally agreed. Attitudes to his interpretations varied widely with the individual. But they all agreed on his originality. *The Times* felt that

> His conception of the character had all the merit of originality, and his originality was, without presumption or fastidiousness, masterly and impressive. There did not occur from the beginning to the end a single instance of imitation. He evidently acted from his own feelings, and there was not a scene in which he was not rewarded by the plaudits of the audience. [10]

And as with many a great actor, the overall impact of his conception transcended any individual peculiarities. The *Monthly Mirror* assessed him as a man of

> active and capacious intellect, with a profound knowledge of the *science* of ACTING. He has read and thought for himself. He appears to have borrowed neither from contemporary nor deceased excellence. He sometimes passes over what have been usually conceived to be *great points* in the character; and he exalts other passages into importance which former *Richards* have not thought significant enough for particular notice. His object seems to have been to form a grand, characteristic, and consistent *whole* – and that whole is the result of deep thinking, and well directed study, judiciously adapted to his individual powers of action; for Mr. Cooke not only *thinks* originally, but he looks, speaks, and walks unlike any other man we ever saw. "*He is himself alone*" – he is, therefore, in some degree a *mannerist*; but his *settled habits* are not injurious to the characters he has hitherto played, or is likely to play, in Covent-Garden: and his talents are so uncommonly brilliant, that though we cannot be altogether blind to his defects, they are forgotten almost as soon as noticed. Admiration supersedes objection; and such are the insinuating effects of his acting, that the peculiarities, which rather offend at first, grow more pleasing by degrees, and, before the close of the performance, have lost nearly all their weight in the scale of criticism. [11]

His only rival was John Philip Kemble, at this time still at Drury Lane; and the merits of their respective Richards became matter for excited debate. A pamphlet of 1801 describing and comparing both their interpretations makes fascinating reading but is much too long and detailed for quotation here. Instead, perhaps John Genest may be allowed briefly to sum up his view of the contest.

> Of these two great actors, Kemble's countenance was the more noble and refined, but the muscles were not so flexible and subject to command as

Cooke's – Kemble's graceful and manly figure added great dignity to those picturesque attitudes which he delighted to study and to exhibit – his face denoted, in the most expressive manner, a man of superior mind and judgement – his voice was (latterly) feeble, but of great depth – this was his principal natural deficiency.

Cooke did not possess the elegant figure of Kemble, but his countenance beamed with great intelligence – his eyes were fiery, dark, and at times terribly expressive, particularly of the worst passions of our nature – his voice, tho' sharp, was powerful and of great compass, a pre-eminence over Kemble of which he skilfully availed himself – his attitudes were less picturesque than those of Kemble, but they were just, appropriate and natural – Kemble's fine face and figure placed him eminently above competition in such parts as Coriolanus, Hamlet, &c, but Cooke's figure for Richard the 3d was as good as Kemble's – his face better, his voice better, his habitual manner better, as being more quick, abrupt and impetuous, and his attitudes better, as having less the appearance of study – it is not therefore to be wondered at, that in that character he should excel Kemble. [12]

And indeed, after the initial battle, Kemble never played the role again while Cooke remained in London. All the characters in which Cooke excelled involved – either from a tragic or a comic viewpoint – hypocrisy, jealousy, the darker passions of human nature. Sir Walter Scott in Edinburgh in 1813, after watching Kemble once more going through a nightly run of his great parts, was driven to recall the now dead Cooke. Acknowledging Kemble's greatness, he yet felt the fault of too much study.

... sudden turns and natural bursts of passion are not his forte. I saw him play Sir Giles Overreach (the Richard III of middling life) last night; but he came not within a hundred miles of Cooke, whose terrible visage, and short, abrupt, and savage utterance, gave a reality almost to that extra-ordinary scene in which he boasts of his own successful villainy to a nobleman of worth and honour, of whose alliance he is ambitious. Cooke contrived somehow to impress upon the audience the idea of such a monster of enormity as had learned to pique himself even upon his own atrocious character. [13]

A shrewd and revealing analysis.

Again and again the reviewers draw attention to the intelligence of Cooke's conceptions, and the extracts which Dunlap reprints from his papers and memoranda bear witness to his wide reading and thoughtful study. His comments on plays, authors or other actors are shrewd and sensible. As late as January 1809 he was collating the 1685 folio and Steevens' edition of *Richard III* and marking his own copy. He was sensitive about poverty and misfortune in others, and generous both of money and effort in their behalf. When in Suffolk in 1779, out of a job and tramping to Norwich in a vain — as it turned out — attempt to join the company there, he met Edward Cape Everard, in similar case and with the added complication of a heavily pregnant wife. Cooke immediately invited them to accompany him to Norwich and offered to share his income, such as it was, with them. In 1802 he travelled specially from London to Bath to perform in aid of the Bath Theatrical Fund, and would accept neither fee nor travelling expenses. He was a good conversationalist and his manners could be charming. Even the snobbery of Macready succumbed. Of a supper party after the play when Cooke had been playing for the elder Macready, W. C. recorded 'Henry Hanmer, then a young man, subsequently a Colonel in the Guards, was quite charmed with his mild and agreeable manners and his interesting conversation' [14]. To be approved by a man who later became a Colonel in the Guards! What greater accolade could there be? Yet Charles Mathews' wife, who wrote of him at the height of his celebrity in London,

> ... he often visited us, and a more cautiously abstemious person could not be found. Indeed it was difficult to imagine that he could ever be otherwise than the grave dignified gentleman he appeared. . . .

also records behaviour by him at a summer party in America which was boorish and offensive in the extreme [15]. The bottle had circulated too freely and Cooke's natural manner was completely reversed. In drink he could be obstinate, proud, uncontrollable, and the reputation he gained by his acting was frittered away by his unreliability. Perhaps even more telling than the grand anecdotes, are the prompter's quiet manuscript entries on the Covent Garden playbills. As early as 11 April 1802,

> Cooke attempted to perform but was too inebriated to proceed beyond a few speeches. The remainder of the part was read by Mr. Claremont.

And on 22 October 1804, playing the Ghost to Kemble's Hamlet

> The Ghost was drunk and found so much difficulty in expressing his "mission" and in keeping himself above ground that the Pit "rose at him" indignantly, to which he replied with a motion of defiance whereupon a row ensued which for some time interrupted the progress of the Tragedy.

There are other such entries. Yet no man was more aware of his weakness and what results it would have. Again and again, after a bad bout, he would attempt to reform, and would keep another of the series of confessional journals which always petered out into failure. In one of them, in 1794, he records meeting in the Bull's Head at Fairfield

> ... a certain clergyman, who is said to be a man of literature and abilities; certain he writes A.M. after his name. He was dirty, drunk, and foolish. Some of the company, though they all professed a respect for him, seemed to use him as an object of their mirth. I could not help viewing him with pity; – not that sensation that approaches to contempt, but a real, sorrowful feeling, as I cannot to please myself otherwise express it. In viewing him I thought of others. Drunkenness is the next leveller to death; with this difference, that the former is always attended with shame and reproach, while the latter, being the certain lot of mortality, produces sympathy, and may be attended with honour. From the general temper of the world it is too probable, with respect to the gentleman I am writing of, that a long and faithful discharge of the duties of his office will be almost forgotten, while the hours of his frailty, or to speak stronger, the periods of his vice and folly, will be clearly remembered and distinctly related. I think and hope I shall never forget him. [16]

Cooke might have been writing of himself – as he was intelligent enough to know.

Only a deep analysis might have revealed some of the root causes of his illness, for illness it clearly was. He himself noted an inability to concentrate, or to face up to decisions, 'when affairs or business are a little embarrassed and unsettled', and it is possible to relate some of his bouts to problems in his private or public life, from which alcohol was an escape. And when it released his rational control over himself there was commonly revealed a need for self-assertion that may well have been a cover for a deep-seated sense of insecurity.

> Tell the Chichester people that George Frederick Cooke will not be dictated to by them; I that have acted before royalty will not stoop to a country audience.

> What! do you hiss me? – hiss George Frederick Cooke? you contemptible money-getters! you never again shall have the honour of hissing me! Farewell! I banish *you*!. ... There is not a brick in your dirty town but what is cemented by the blood of a negro! [17]

The irony is, of course, that each such outburst, like that one at Liverpool, had to be paid for afterwards with a grovelling apology to the audience he had spurned.

As to the causes of that insecurity, we can only speculate. Was it related to his obscure birth and lack of contact with his parents? Did the frustration of his early years contribute to it, when, conscious of his ability, he was for so long unable to make a way in his chosen profession? His need for, and lack of, a durable relationship with the opposite sex may also have contributed (there were at least five Mrs Cookes, with or without benefit of clergy); the rivalry with Kemble, and the sense which in the end he was to acknowledge, that overall Kemble was his superior; and certainly the overwork and exploitation of those touring summers in his last decade, when, night after night, with the minimum of rehearsal and after arduous and weary journeys, he was expected to give star performances backed by mediocre companies – all these may have been part of a complex psychological and physical problem that for him was too great to be coped with.

S. W. Ryley, who worked with him and knew him well, summed it up in his book *The Itinerant*, and Cooke read the judgment in Philadelphia in the last year of his life.

> In some characters he is as much superior to any actor of the present day as Garrick was to those of his time; but they are limited to such parts as suit his figure, which wants grace and proportion; when these can be dispensed with, he has no competitor. As a man in private life, he is the gentleman, the scholar, the friend, the life of every party, an enemy to scandal and detraction, and benevolent even to imprudence. Such is George Cooke in his sober hours; but when stimulated by the juice of the grape, he acts in diametrical opposition to all this. No two men, however different they may be, can be more at variance than George Cooke sober and George Cooke in a state of ebriety. At these times his interesting suavity of manners changes to brutal invective; the feelings of his nearest and dearest friends are sacrificed; his best benefactor wounded, either in his own person, or that of his tenderest connection, and the ears of delicacy assaulted by abuse of the grossest nature. Such are the unfortunate propensities of this singular man; unfortunate, I say; because he seems incapable of avoiding them, although they have a tendency to ruin his health, injure his property, and destroy his social connections. No one can more regret these failings than he does in his hours of sanity, or make more handsome apologies, and if at night he creates enemies, his conciliatory manners in the morning are sure to raise double the number of friends. [18]

That is the paradox – and the tragedy – of George Frederick Cooke.

Notes

[1] William Dunlap, *The Life of George Frederick Cooke*, 2 Vols. (London, 1815).

[2] See Don B. Wilmeth, 'The Posthumous Career of George Frederick Cooke', *Theatre Notebook*, XXIV, No. 2.

[3] Dunlap, op. cit., II, 178.

136   THE EIGHTEENTH-CENTURY ENGLISH STAGE

[4] Playbills in the British Museum (Burney Collection).

[5] Information on the Dublin season was gathered from copies of the *Freeman's Journal* and the *Hibernian Journal* in the National Library of Ireland, Dublin.

[6] This conclusion is drawn from the evidence of Covent Garden playbills in the British Museum.

[7] *Bath Chronicle*, 15 October 1801.

[8] *Monthly Mirror*, November 1800.

[9] *Morning Chronicle*, 1 November 1800.

[10] *The Times*, 1 November 1800.

[11] *Monthly Mirror*, November 1800.

[12] John Genest, *Some Account of the English Stage* (Bath, 1832), VIII, 194.

[13] J. Gibson Lockhart, *Life of Sir Walter Scott* (London and Edinburgh, 1837–8), II, 262–3.

[14] Sir F. Pollock, ed., *Reminiscences of W. C. Macready* (London, 1875), I, 66–7. E. C. Everard, *Memoirs of an Unfortunate Son of Thespis* (London, 1818), 91. *Bath Journal*, 7–14 June 1802.

[15] Mrs A. Mathews, *Memoirs of Charles Mathews* (London, 1838), I, 139.

[16] Dunlap, op. cit., I, 77–8.

[17] The first of these statements is recorded by Lord William Pitt Lennox in *Celebrities I have known* (London, 1876), and quoted in A. Hare, *The Georgian Theatre in Wessex* (Phoenix House, London, 1958), 216. The second is recorded in Mrs A. Mathews, *Anecdotes of Actors* (London, 1844), 99.

[18] S. W. Ryley, *The Itinerant* (London, 1808), quoted in Dunlap, op. cit., I, 49–51.

8 K. E. ROBINSON

Stephen Kemble's Management of the Theatre Royal, Newcastle upon Tyne

An anecdotal tendency in the biographers' approach to the life of Stephen Kemble symptomizes their view of his importance. He has come to be regarded as the comic figure of the Kemble family. Tradition has it that his birth 'synchronised with [his mother's] imaginary delivery of the Princess Elizabeth' after a performance as Anne Boleyn in 1758, and that his debut at Covent Garden came about not only through the agency of Sarah Siddons but because the management mistook the 'big' Stephen for the 'great' John Philip [1]. Stephen himself encouraged the tendency, describing himself in 'An address spoken prior to my performing Falstaff in Drury-Lane Theatre' as 'A Falstaff . . . by Nature made',

> No man in buckram he, – no stuffing gear,
> No feather bed, nor e'en a pillow-bear!
> But all good honest flesh, and blood, and bone,
> And weighing, more or less, some thirty stone! [2]

But his importance extends beyond such caricature; he made a significant contribution to provincial theatrical history. Although his Falstaff was, as Sheridan recognized [3], not limited to his self-caricature – contemporary critics felt that it achieved the optimum balance between comedy and gravity [4] – his real interest lay, as Roger Kemble's had, in management.

The *D.N.B.* is in error when it implies that Kemble's first taste of management came in Edinburgh [5]; his entry into management in fact occurred in 1791 when on 7 March he took over the recently erected Theatre Royal in Newcastle upon Tyne at an annual rent of £300 from his brother-in-law, Charles Edward Whitlock, paying him, according to *The Theatric Tourist*, £1,000 for his properties [6]. In true Kemble fashion, Elizabeth Kemble had in 1785 married a theatre manager –

Whitlock was at that time managing the Bigg Market Theatre in Newcastle [7] — and it was presumably through her that Stephen and Elizabeth were induced to leave the Haymarket where they had played since 1786. Elizabeth opened in Newcastle on 26 January as Ophelia to George F. Cooke's Hamlet, and Stephen followed five nights later as Freeport to his wife's Amelia in *The English Merchant*. Built in 1787 and opened 21 January 1788, the Theatre Royal had already seen two changes of management when Kemble assumed control. The first managers were Whitlock and Joseph Austin, the latter retiring at the end of the first season in favour of Joseph Munden (30 April 1788), who in turn sold out to Whitlock (3 September 1790), granting him sole possession [8]. Whitlock provided some continuity, then, but he did not offer the stability entailed in Stephen Kemble's fifteen years of direction. Newcastle became a base for the most important of his managerial activities.

On Kemble's succession as manager, the Newcastle theatre formed part of a Northern circuit including Chester, Lancaster and Sheffield. Since the course of his management in Newcastle is closely related to the nature and viability of the circuit which backed it, any discussion of this management must take account of the circuit. Kemble was evidently dissatisfied with the circuit as he inherited it and, retaining Newcastle as his centre of operations, he set out to restructure it soon after he became manager. On 2 November 1791 he took the Edinburgh and Glasgow theatres at a rent of £1,200 or £1,350 per annum [9], Edinburgh, Newcastle and Sheffield forming the core of his circuit for the next two years. As the *Newcastle Chronicle* realized, to obtain the Edinburgh theatre was doubtless to 'enable the manager, whose spirited exertions have always kept pace with the contingencies of his situation, to maintain a better company, and pay greater salaries, than any other connection out of London could support' (5 November 1791). But before this could be realized, the Newcastle and Edinburgh seasons had to be arranged so that they did not conflict. For part of the 1791–2 winter season their seasons overlapped, the Edinburgh theatre opening on 28 January and Newcastle not closing until 26 March 1792, and Kemble was put to the expense of maintaining two companies. But in the following winter season he altered the Newcastle season to begin more than two months earlier on 12 November and to run until 18 January so that he could open in Edinburgh on 21 January 1793. The company then returned to Newcastle to take benefits (6 May to

17 June) immediately before Race Week when Mrs Esten starred (24 to 29 June). In subsequent years the Newcastle season began early in October and ended in the middle of January, benefits being taken normally at the end of the season.

Kemble experienced great difficulty in attempting to establish himself in Edinburgh. His immediate reception seemed auspicious, the receipts for the first night totalling £115 and those for the first four nights amounting to more than £470, but his fortune was short-lived. He had taken the theatre from Jackson with whom he was soon in altercation. It appears that Jackson claimed a share in the management whilst Kemble believed that although Jackson retained an interest in the property he himself had sole managerial rights. The executors of Lord Dundas's half of the patent stepped in, and the Press announced that Kemble was to co-operate with Jackson, paying a rent of £500 per annum, who must either reciprocate or forfeit his rights [10]. This ultimatum appears to have had little effect, however, for in August 1792 Jackson's trustees let the theatre to Mrs Esten whom Kemble had originally out-manoeuvred to gain the theatre. Litigation ensued between Kemble and Mrs Esten, and Kemble removed to the New Theatre for the 1793 season. The immediate results were again encouraging, the receipts for the first night exceeding £180, but Mrs Esten, losing badly in the Theatre Royal, had performances suspended on the grounds that the New Theatre did not possess the royal patent [11]. The ban was lifted on 9 February and Kemble, despite only four hours notice, re-opened. For a time it seemed that he might finally be victorious in his battle with Mrs Esten. Some of his supporters felt that they had located a loop-hole in her case, claiming that neither theatre had authority since the original patent had not been ratified by Scottish law, but the Court of Session found against Kemble. An appeal was lodged with the House of Lords, and until a decision could be obtained the New Theatre remained open 'with amusements of various kinds' [12]. But if Mrs Esten had been successful in the legal proceedings, Kemble retained popular support. A petition was brought on his behalf 'for a new patent to be vested in those who are his most warm supporters', and his benefit of £160 on 11 April reflects his popularity. Mrs Esten's performance in Newcastle in June 1793 is, however, a symbol of their conciliation [13]. Her losses had been heavy and she had for a time been 'incapable of performing, being dangerously indisposed with a nervous fever, in consequence of her agitation of spirits', and in August 1793 Kemble effected a compromise with her. They took the Edinburgh theatre jointly for seven years from Jackson's trustees with the concurrence of the patentees, Kemble soon assuming sole possession [14]. He celebrated this final resolution of his Edinburgh problems with a grand opening to the 1794 season, John Philip Kemble playing Hamlet to Elizabeth Kemble's Ophelia with Charles Kemble as Laertes. He retained the Edinburgh theatre until 1800 [15].

Once the position in Edinburgh was unambivalent and the Edinburgh and Newcastle seasons had been accommodated to the demands of a single company, Kemble effected further changes to his circuit. John Edwin, with his wife a member of Kemble's company in the split season of 1792–3, complained publicly of the excessive distance and cost entailed in a circuit embracing Edinburgh, Newcastle and Sheffield. He claimed that in thirty-seven weeks he had covered, including the distance from London to Sheffield, 512 miles at his own expense [16]. Sensitive perhaps to such criticism, and no doubt aware of the financial advantages involved in a more tightly-knit circuit, Kemble began to place less importance upon Sheffield and to concentrate upon establishing theatres in Northumberland, between Edinburgh and Newcastle. In 1794 he staged a spectacular opening with *Lionel and Clarissa* and a comparatively brilliant cast of his newly built theatre in Berwick upon Tweed (11 August), appearing in Morpeth in June of the same year; and in 1796 he opened a theatre in Alnwick under the patronage of the Duke and Duchess of Northumberland, who were later to help him out of difficulties in Newcastle [17].

The next series of major changes did not occur until 1799 when Kemble acquired the Durham circuit and the new North Shields theatre from Cawdell. Kemble's success in Edinburgh declined towards the end of his term of management, and, playing more and more parts himself to bolster a weak company, he appears to have cast around for fresh circuits [18]. Cawdell's was ideal not only because it enabled him to further tighten his circuit, but because although it was reasonably successful it had not yet seen the sort of management that Kemble was to bring to it. As a circuit it had benefited from the enthusiasm which his management had generated in Newcastle, but it had not experienced visits from London stars, apart from the occasional appearance of Stephen and Elizabeth Kemble, or the scenic extravaganzas which Kemble had provided in Newcastle. In the 1799–1800 winter season

Kemble dove-tailed the Newcastle and North Shields playing nights to provide a basic five nights a week: Monday, Wednesday and Friday were played in Newcastle and Tuesday and Thursday in North Shields. And in the following autumn he introduced a season in Scarborough between the end of Assize Week (mid-August) and the start of the new season in December. Once he had retired from the Edinburgh theatre, he put his trust in an extremely confined circuit comprising basically Durham, Newcastle, Northallerton, North Shields, Scarborough, South Shields and Sunderland. The Scarborough season was relatively extended and Northallerton and Stockton were played, the latter in its Race Week, on the return journey to Newcastle. The Sunderland and South Shields seasons were designed to interlock in much the same way as the Newcastle and North Shields seasons. Thus in a fairly typical year, 1802, Kemble's company moved to Durham once it had completed its Newcastle and North Shields seasons (terminating 27 and 28 January respectively) and then to Sunderland and South Shields in April. It returned to Newcastle in early June for the Race Week, remaining until the end of July when there was a brief gap before Assize Week (terminating 21 August). Judging from similar years it seems that it would then have played in Scarborough in late August and September, opening for Stockton Races (Mrs Kemble appearing on 4 October), and returning to Newcastle for the new seasons beginning 25 October and 9 November in Newcastle and North Shields respectively.

This, then, constitutes the background to Stephen Kemble's management of the Newcastle Theatre Royal. His effectiveness is to a large extent dependent upon his relationship with Newcastle and its audience, and this relationship is implicit in his varying circuits. Generally speaking, the more cosmopolitan his circuit, the more vital his management is; his ultimate decline correlates with the self-imposed stricture of his final circuit. Equally, the successful implementation of a cosmopolital circuit requires a related cosmopolitan outlook. Kemble's activity in the early years of his career in Newcastle, establishing himself in the Edinburgh theatre, helped him to maintain a certain distance from his public. Whitlock and his partners may lay claim to having provided the foundations of Kemble's first flush of success. They had not only drawn together a reasonably balanced stock company, its backbone comprising the Whitlocks, George F. Cooke and Joseph Munden, but had attracted London stars (presumably through Elizabeth Whitlock). Mrs Siddons, for example, visited Newcastle in

1789 playing opposite Cooke, But the Kembles brought London experience and reputation. Whereas the Whitlocks, who were essentially Newcastle performers — Elizabeth Whitlock appeared briefly at Drury Lane in 1783–4 but the greater part of her stage experience was gained at the Bigg Market Theatre with her husband — had yet to achieve their American, as Cooke and Munden their London, fame, Stephen and Elizabeth Kemble had fifteen years of London experience between them. Newcastle reaction to the Kembles was very much in terms of this experience. The enthusiasm for their first performances was unbounded. The *Newcastle Chronicle* felt that it ought to 'congratulate the Newcastle audience on so charming an acquisition' as Mrs Kemble (29 January 1791), and there was soon a conviction that 'the present is ... the strongest company ever seen here, ... no theatre out of London can hold any competition with this respecting the aggregate stock of professional abilities' (*Chronicle*, 24 February 1792). The Newcastle audience quickly came to regard itself, that is, as in a position of great theatrical privilege. Kemble's zestful management was felt to entail an obligation upon his public. 'The liberality and assiduity of the manager', felt the *Newcastle Chronicle*, 'are certainly entitled to the utmost support and highest thanks' (24 November 1792).

Kemble worked hard to maintain this respect, helped much by his wife's reputation. It was not limited to his role as manager. In conversation with Thomas Bewick, it is said that he frequently expressed his pride in the altruism that was found in so many of the famous names of his profession [19], and his own unselfishness, manifest in his donations to the debtors of Newgate and to local charities, increased the regard of his audience. As a manager he maintained, despite often indifferent houses, a balanced company, and coupled it with a 'judicious arrangement of characters' [20]. Elizabeth Kemble's versatility, equally at home as Ophelia or Polly Peachum, Imoinda or Betty Blackberry (in *The Farmer*), must have been a great advantage. Moreover, Kemble made it a rule to build his stock company around competent but lesser known London performers. In addition to the Whitlocks and the Kembles themselves, Grist, Inchbald and Mrs Hall formed the core of the 1791–2 company, whilst in 1794–5 Wilson, who had made his debut in Newcastle alongside Incledon in the summer, stayed on to join Egan, also from Covent Garden. Family connections and the increasing respectability of the Newcastle stage also enabled Kemble to provide his audience with the excitement of watching the development of future stars. Henry Siddons, Sarah's son, who had made his first appearance on stage as Zanga in Kemble's benefit at Sheffield in October 1792, and Charles Kemble, Stephen's younger brother, both acted with the company from 1792 to 1794. But the thing that most caught the imagination of the Newcastle audience and prolonged their sense of privilege was the importation of a greater number of London stars. In the summer of 1791 and the 1791–2 winter season alone, Mr and Mrs Pope, Mrs Jordan, John Philip Kemble, Bowden, Mrs Siddons and Lee Lewis all made appearances.

Such a policy was, however, costly. It was reported, for example, that in 1791 Kemble offered Pope £300 per week to appear in Newcastle in season, and later in 1805 Master Betty, the Young Roscius, was guaranteed £50 per night and a free benefit [21]. Further, Kemble spared nothing on properties and theatre decorations, employing Whitmore both as actor and scene painter. Spurred by the success of a similar venture in Edinburgh, he advertised that on 11 December 1793 the 'Theatre will be decorated in the style of a Fête Champêtre. All the pillars will be adorned with roses, lilies, and other artificial flowers and interspersed with 500 variegated lamps so as to make the whole Theatre represent an enchanted grove' (*Chronicle*, 7 December 1793). The *Newcastle Chronicle* was quick to realize the implications of Kemble's plans, noting that 'the ensuing season, though it may not be the most lucrative to the Manager, the receipts in it will be the most abundant ever known' (12 November 1791). His attempts to meet his expenses were not always successful, but he always had his family to fall back upon for help. When Mr and Mrs Pope were engaged to appear in Race Week, 1791, Kemble advertised an increase in admission prices from Boxes: 3/–, Gallery: 2/–, Pit: 1/– to Boxes: 5/–, Gallery: 3/–, Pit. 2/–; but the proprietors vetoed the rise at the last moment and the opening performance (10 June) was cancelled. Two days later the Popes opened as Lord and Lady Townly in *The Provok'd Husband* at normal prices. Kemble had apparently calculated his expenses at the raised prices, and lost heavily even though the Popes forfeited their benefits. His plight worsened in the following Assize Week when Mrs Jordan started, but failed to complete, her engagement with him. John Philip Kemble played in Newcastle for six nights (plus his benefit) in December to offset 'the great disadvantage' suffered by his brother [22]. Thereafter London continued to provide stars but they appeared at ordinary prices, except in July 1802 when the proprietors allowed prices to be doubled for Mrs Billington's engagement, and in 1805 when the Young Roscius performed. Considering the legal and other expenses incurred by Kemble in his colonization of the Edinburgh theatre and the ambitious natuie of his Newcastle programme, it is quite possible that there might be some foundation to Edwin's exaggerated attack on the wages that he paid to his company; although Kemble himself claimed that until he took the Newcastle theatre 'no performer in it, not even Mr Munden, had more than a guinea and a half per week', whilst Edwin had received more than one pound per night [23]. But once the Newcastle and Edinburgh seasons had been rearranged and Kemble had begun to create his Northumberland circuit, conditions seem to have improved. In 1795 it was felt that the Newcastle company must be the highest paid in the provinces (*Chronicle*, 3 January).

The shift away from Sheffield and towards the Northumberland theatres had important results. With theatres closer together it was possible to make a more financially rewarding use of London stars, offering them performances in two or more theatres within the same short engagement without any risk of exhausting public interest. Thus when Kelly and Mrs Crouch visited Newcastle for Assize Week in 1794, they also played for four nights in Berwick. Moreover it was easier to raise prices in theatres outside Newcastle, so that for Mrs Siddons's appearance in May 1795 for five nights in Berwick, a theatre Kemble himself had had built, the prices were Boxes: 5/−, Gallery: 5/−, Pit: 3/−.

The final period of Kemble's management accentuates the tendencies that are found in his consolidation of the Edinburgh-Newcastle-Northumberland circuit. The closer circuit made it even more possible to assure the financial success of employing London stars. Charles Kemble, in Newcastle to perform in the Race Week in 1803, also played to audiences in North Shields, South Shields and Sunderland; and the Young Roscius not only played in Newcastle, but visited Sunderland, South Shields, Durham and Berwick. Although these theatres were somewhat smaller than the Newcastle theatre, the receipts for Master Betty's performances must have been encouraging to star and manager alike. His performance as Tancred in South Shields on 10 September realized £100, a quarter of those wanting admission being turned away, whilst his two nights in Berwick as Douglas and Achmet (in *Barbarossa*) on 11 and 12 September brought in £107 and £117 respectively. By using these performances at the smaller theatres to break up the Newcastle openings, Kemble was also able to engage stars to play a greater number of nights in Newcastle without his public's appetite becoming satiated. In contrast to the six nights previously played by a top rank London performer, the Young Roscius, again in his 1805 appearance, played for thirteen nights in Newcastle. Even allowing for Kemble's high expenses, the receipts, averaging over £145 per night (the benefit amounting to £213 9s.), must have been satisfying [24]. As for the ordinary company actors, even if they often had to walk from theatre to theatre, the new circuit promised better conditions of employment. Benefits, for example, were taken at North Shields and Newcastle and Sunderland and South Shields in the same seasons. Kemble generously took £5 for expenses – he estimated his Edinburgh expenses at £40 [25] – and halved the remainder of the receipts. Additionally, a greater number of theatres over a smaller area led to an increased number of employed weeks in the year.

The Durham circuit benefited much from Kemble's management. The quality of its stock company was shared with Newcastle; it received its first London stars, and it felt the same sense of privilege that Newcastle had in Kemble's earlier years. It did not go unnoticed, for example, that *Speed the Plough*, performed in benefit for the poor of North Shields, had been first performed at Covent Garden on 8 February 1800, only ten months previously. But if the circuit was tighter, it was also constricting. Kemble was no longer travelling out of the area to cater for a completely different and cosmopolitan audience, but tied to a smaller circuit, seems to have given way to local demands upon him. As early as 1795 he had made a parochial gesture and engaged Jack Scriven, a Newcastle grocer who doubled as actor and clog dancer, as a regular member of his company, and in the following year he announced that William Smith, Esq., an 'independent Gentleman' from Durham, would play Hamlet and Macheath 'For the benefit of the Lying-in Hospital and the Charity for the relief of poor married women lying-in at their own houses' (*Chronicle*, 22 October 1796). In the later years of his management he gave heavy billing to performances provided under his aegis by the officers of local army garrisons. Mrs Kemble, who played London summer seasons at the Haymarket until 1795, always seemed a London performer to her Newcastle audience and never quite lost her metropolitan aura, but Stephen Kemble, despite his successful appearances at Drury Lane in 1802 and the

London conviction that 'It is to be regretted that his associations in the country prevent him from accepting a permanent engagement in London' [26], had put down roots too strong for there to be any immediate fear that he would leave Newcastle. The North had assumed an importance for him at variance with the distance which he had cultivated as a necessity of good management when he first assumed control of the Newcastle theatre. There is something defiantly regional about his description of Master Pritchard as the 'Young Roscius of the North' (*Chronicle*, 1 March 1806).

If a local circuit made its own demands, they were less sophisticated. It may, that is, have required some capitulation to local taste, but it does not appear to have demanded quite such high standards as those expected by a more cosmopolitan audience. The declining company hissed off the stage in Edinburgh at the close of its final season in 1800 was not given the transfusion of new talent that it needed, and Kemble fell back more and more upon visiting performers and his own and his wife's performances to give body to his seasons. The case of Mr Saxoni exemplifies the lapse in quality. As late as 1799 Mr Saxoni, a tight-rope artist, had been parodied on the Newcastle stage by Mr Martinelli's 'automaton figure, as large as life; which for variety and activity on the rope will far exceed Signor Saxoni, or the little Devil' (*Courant*, 21 December), yet in 1804 Kemble employed him for two weeks at the start of the new season. A year later, Mr Riche, another tight-rope artist, performed, to underline the change, on the same night that Colonel Mundy, of the Tynemouth Garrison, played Macbeth. The decline is obvious. It did not escape the notice of Kemble's public.

In 1804 the proprietors felt some unease about Kemble's management and advertised the theatre to let. Kemble was saved by the intervention of the Duke of Northumberland who wrote to one of the proprietors, Christopher Blackett, asking him 'to assist my friend, Stephen Kemble, whom I really believe to be a reasonable and worthy man' [27]. This unease may have had something to do with the decoration of the theatre. When in 1797 the rent was reduced to £220 per annum at Kemble's asking, he undertook to redecorate; and shortly after the increase to £300 per annum in 1804 the theatre was again redecorated, but this time at the proprietors' expense [28]. If there is any connection between these rent changes and the decorations, it would appear that Kemble was guilty of allowing some deterioration. Moreover, although Kemble successfully prosecuted the libellous attacks of the *Tyne Mercury* [29], the silence of other formerly friendly newspapers is meaningful. If they reported a theatre performance, it was one in which there was a London visitor. Even the *Newcastle Chronicle* falls into this category; indeed its only defence of Kemble's management when it was under barrage from the *Tyne Mercury*, was to list the London performers who had appeared in Newcastle and to declare that 'the stage performances in London are not better decorated' (7 January 1804).

The movement towards a clustered circuit, then, finally determined Kemble's demise as a manager in Newcastle. It may even be that his choice of the Durham circuit was partly conditioned by the relative weakness of his stock company towards the end of his Edinburgh management. William Macready, who had just acquired the Manchester theatre at a reputed rent of £1,600 per annum, took over Newcastle from Kemble at an annual rent of £450, and Kemble went off to Covent Garden to perform Falstaff. If there is a decline in Kemble's career in Newcastle, his arrangements for the summer openings in 1806 partly redeemed him in the eyes of his public. Although he had failed in other ways, he had not lost the ability to bring in London performers. Emery appeared in Race Week, the Young Roscius in July at normal prices, and Munden played in Assize Week. The *Newcastle Chronicle* summed up:

> Mr. Kemble, tho' on the eve of resigning management, appears still indefatiguable to please the public, as if determined we should be obliged to confess that "the weary sun would make a golden set." (21 June 1806)

On 1 November Kemble took his last benefit in Newcastle; at £106 it was respectable, but, sadly, over £30 less than a benefit in 1802.

Notes

[1] *D.N.B.*, XXX (London, 1892), 381.
[2] *Odes, Lyrical Ballads and Poems on Various Occasions* (Edinburgh, 1809), 26.
[3] Sheridan invited Kemble to play Falstaff at Drury Lane in 1802. See *Newcastle Chronicle*, 2 October 1802. Hereafter cited as *Chronicle*.
[4] See *Morning Chronicle*, 8 October 1802.
[5] The *D.N.B.* accounts of the Kembles in general are often faulty. Other errors are corrected silently.

[6] Referred to in Harold Oswald, *The Theatres Royal in Newcastle upon Tyne* (Newcastle, Northumberland Press, 1936), 37. I am indebted to Oswald at several points. He had access to the account books of the theatre for Kemble's period of management, which are no longer extant.

[7] See ibid., 8.

[8] See ibid., 28 ff.

[9] See *Chronicle*, 5 November 1791, and *D.N.B.*, XXX, 382.

[10] See *Chronicle*, 4 February 1792; *Newcastle Advertiser*, 5 November 1791; *D.N.B.*, XXX, 382; *Chronicle*, 25 August 1792; and *Edinburgh Courant*, 16 August 1792.

[11] See *D.N.B.*, XXX, 382; *Chronicle*, 25 August 1792 and 28 January 1793.

[12] *Chronicle*, 16 February and 2 March 1793.

[13] See *Chronicle*, 9 March (which contains a copy of the petition) and 13 April 1793.

[14] See *Chronicle*, 16 February, 9 March and 31 August 1793.

[15] See *D.N.B.*, XXX, 382.

[16] See *To the Public* (Newcastle, 1793), a small pamphlet. Kemble replied in a pamphlet of the same title and date, and Edwin published a further pamphlet, again of the same title and date, replying to Kemble. Edwin's first estimate of 532 miles is corrected by Kemble, and the correction is accepted by Edwin in his second pamphlet.

[17] See Madelaine Hope Dodds, 'The Northern Stage', *Archaeologia Aeliana*, 3rd Series, IX (1914), 59 and John Sykes, *Local Records* (Newcastle, 1866), I, 372.

[18] See *D.N.B.*, XXX, 382. For further information on the Durham circuit (including North Shields) see Robert King, *North Shields Theatres* (Gateshead, Northumberland Press, 1948), particularly 44ff; John Sykes, *Local Records*, I, 359; Thomas Richmond, *The Local Records of Stockton and the Neighbourhood* (London, 1868), 100; and Madelaine Hope Dodds, op. cit., particularly 59ff.

[19] See Oswald, op. cit., 44.

[20] See *Chronicle*, 27 July and 7 December 1793; Kemble's reply to Edwin; and *Chronicle*, 4 March 1792.

[21] See *Chronicle*, 17 November 1791 and 14 September 1805.

[22] See *Chronicle*, 18 June and 17 December 1791; and Oswald, op cit., 48. John Philip Kemble had wished to appear in Assize Week at London prices, but he also had met with the proprietors' veto.

[23] See Kemble's reply to Edwin (note 16 above).

[24] See *Chronicle*, 6 July, 14 and 21 September 1805; and Oswald, op. cit., 55.

[25] See Edwin's and Kemble's pamphlets, and *Chronicle*, 21 March 1795.

[26] See *Morning Chronicle*, 8 October 1802.

[27] See *Chronicle*, 7 January 1804, and Oswald, op. cit., 43.

[28] See *Chronicle*, 25 November 1797, and 20 October 1798, and Oswald, op. cit., 37.

[29] The case Mitchell *vs.* Kemble was heard 4 August 1806. Mitchell, publisher of the *Tyne Mercury*, was ordered to make a public apology. See *Chronicle*, 9 August 1806.

9 DAVID ROSTRON

John Philip Kemble's 'King Lear' of 1795

Introduction

Even with the full panoply of modern audio-visual aids, the task of accurately recreating and assessing a recent stage production is awesomely daunting; any attempt to recapture the details of an eighteenth-century performance is thus predoomed to all sorts of failure. It might be compared to the pursuer's optimistic attempt to follow tracks left by his quarry in the shifting sands of the seashore, and I must therefore commence with an apology for the inadequacy of this account of John Philip Kemble's performance of *King Lear* on 20 November 1795. By drawing on his prompt book and on accounts in contemporary periodicals or memoirs, I shall attempt to set this individual appearance in the context of the actor's career, to glance at his adaptation of the text and his preliminary preparations for the production, to sketch some of the details of performance, and finally to comment upon Kemble as interpreter of the role of Lear.

In November 1795, Kemble was thirty-eight years of age and at the height of his physical powers. Since his arrival in the capital, twelve years earlier, he had risen to be undisputed ruler of the London tragic stage, and was now Sheridan's acting-manager at the new Drury Lane Theatre, first opened in April of the previous year. Since the overwhelming success of the glittering and almost operatic *Macbeth* with which he had opened the new theatre, his achievements had won him many other golden opinions: his own translation from the French of *Lodoiska*, his creation of the role of Penruddock in Cumberland's *The Wheel of Fortune*, his presentation of *The Roman Father* and of D'Egville's ballet of *Alexander the Great*, and his own first appearance as the Duke in *Measure for Measure*, had been acclaimed by critics and public alike.

Adaptation

In spite of the ever-increasing impediment of his squabbles with Sheridan about money for productions, Kemble was determined that the new Drury Lane should retain the dominance over Covent Garden which it had exerted since the days of Garrick. A new production of *King Lear* — one of Garrick's most lauded achievements — would doubtless help to enhance his theatre's reputation for careful and sumptuous presentation of Shakespeare's plays; moreover, the textual adaptation already prepared for his performances in 1792 and 1793 would serve once more.

For more than a century, all stage presentations of *King Lear* had taken as their starting-point Nahum Tate's sentimental 'improvement' of 1681, with its excision of the Fool, its addition of a love affair between Edgar and Cordelia, and its happy ending in which Lear survives to live in peaceful retirement with Kent and Gloster, having handed over his realm to the radiant Cordelia. In 1756, when Garrick had made a step towards the restoration of a more authentic text in the first three acts, he had not ventured to restore the Fool or to jettison the Edgar-Cordelia nonsense, and the last two acts had remained heavily 'Tatefied'. Dr Johnson's famous support for Cordelia's survival probably influenced the retention of the happy ending in the version produced by George Colman in 1768, and used at Covent Garden by the actors Pope and Ross for the next five years, but Colman succeeded in eliminating the love of Edgar and Cordelia, leaving the first four acts virtually as Shakespeare wrote them, apart from the continued absence of the Fool.

Kemble was an enthusiastic adapter of Shakespeare's plays, with a tendency to restore a more accurate text than had been the custom earlier in the century; however, his version of *Lear* retrogressively restores the heroic passion of Edgar for Cordelia, and is so heavily 'Tatefied' as to deserve the lambasting it received from John Genest:

> There could therefore be no good reason for Kemble to revive King Lear, unless it were with a view of going on with the good work which Garrick had begun — nothing however could be further from his intention than this . . . . Shakespeare or Tate it was all the same to him. [1]

Apart from the characteristic suppression of Edgar's final speech, so that Kemble himself could bring down the last curtain with Lear's 'Enjoy the present hour, nor fear the last' [2], this adaptation is far from typical of Kemble's work on Shakespeare's texts, remaining very deeply rooted in Tate, and therefore bastardized and sentimentalized.

Preparations

With the text prepared, Kemble was able to proceed to the very simple task of casting. Around him he had gathered an established company of experienced players who were now familiar with his methods and discipline, and who knew their habitual positionings, moves and 'business' from a long acquaintance with the stock roles which were so important a feature of the Patent House companies at that period. No play commanded a more stable cast than Kemble's 1795 *King Lear*, for the Gloster, Edmund, Kent, Albany, Edgar, Goneril and Cordelia had retained these roles in all Kemble's performances in 1788, 1792 and 1793. The veteran Packer (sixty-five years of age in 1795, and a member of the Drury Lane company since Garrick's time) played Gloster, while the somewhat overconfident Barrymore undertook Edmund. Kent was in the hands of one of the stalwarts of the company, the pleasant-voiced Irishman, James Aickin, his stock roles as Belarius, Brabantio, Cominius, Escalus, Exeter (in *Henry V*), Gonzalo and Duke Senior indicate his suitability for the loyal and ageing Kent. Albany was played by John Whitfield, whose other regular Shakespearean appearances were as Don Pedro in *Much Ado* and Norfolk in *Henry VIII*, and Richard Wroughton — the company's standard Bassanio, Claudio (in *Measure for Measure*), Buckingham (in *Henry VIII*) and Aufidius — possessed sufficient ardour to make Edgar the sympathetic *jeune premier* demanded by Tate's version. Mrs Cuyler as Goneril, and Sarah Siddons in the rather unsuitable role of the youthful Cordelia, completed the established cast of the play. As Cornwall, Kemble brought in his younger brother, Charles, while Dignum (who had played an Esquire in the performances of 1792 and 1793) appeared as Burgundy. The only real newcomer was therefore Mrs Maddocks, replacing Mrs Ward as Regan.

Such extensive service with the company goes a long way towards explaining why, even after the more disciplined approach of Garrick, eighteenth-century rehearsals were described in 1775 as 'little better than a *theatrical muster*, who are called together to be in readiness for the night's review, without little more preparation than their bare appearances' [3]. Once an actor was familiar with his lines and with the general blocking-in of his comparatively few moves, he could assume that the production would retain its major features unchanged over a long span of years. Whereas Professor Hugh Hunt assures us that 'The approach of a modern producer to a play ... is ephemeral', and reminds us 'I have produced *King Lear* three times at wide intervals and each time I have adopted a different approach – the one that seemed to be right at the time' [4] , Kemble seems to have arrived at a conception of a role or of a play, and then to have fixed it almost immutably for the rest of his career [5] . On 31 October 1815, *The Times* praised him for this consistency:

> It is the necessary consequence of having maturely studied a given part, and arrived at a high degree of excellence in performing it, that the portrait, once finished, admits no novelty which is not a defect.

Consequently, rehearsals for revivals of familiar plays could safely be reduced to a few runs-through of the established highlights. C. B. Hogan's discovery [6] of Powell's notes as prompter at Drury Lane after 1794 reveals the astonishing fact that Kemble mounted the first performance of *The Wheel of Fortune* after only nine rehearsals of about one hour each, and that his first appearance in *Measure for Measure* was preceded by only two rehearsals. Actors therefore tended to rehearse on their own, without attempting much homogeneity of style and effect, and relied heavily on stock attitudes and gestures. Corporate rehearsals tended to concern themselves with entrances, exits, and the disposition of a few moves and tableaux. Kemble, at least, was scrupulous about attending the small number of rehearsals he *did* call, and we may safely assume that he was less cavalier in attitude than James Quin, who requested twenty-two rehearsals before his first appearance as Lear, but who, 'being at that time young and dissipated, attended only two of them' [7] . Unfortunately, Powell's notes supply no details about the preparations for the 1795 *King Lear*, but it seems unlikely, with so experienced a company, that Kemble would need to call many.

Among other preparatory considerations, it is probable that some of the scenery for the production was newly painted. Stock scenery was as common at this time as stock roles, movements and gestures, and Tate Wilkinson refers to one scene used from 1747 to 1790 in *The Fop's Fortune* and elsewhere as 'my very old acquaintance' [8] , but we know that Kemble had collected at his new theatre a distinguished company of scenic artists and machinists. As Sybil Rosenfeld and E. Croft-Murray have shown [9] , the 1795–6 season at Drury Lane utilized scenery created by Greenwood, Capon, Demaria, Marinari, Buzaglo, Malton, Edwards and Grieve, but this is one area in which the footsteps are obliterated in the sand, and all we know is that the fifteen different scene locations specified in Kemble's text [10] would provide ample opportunity for the display of the talents of such outstanding designers as Greenwood and Capon, and for the raising and lowering of scenery from the elaborate system of fly-galleries which was such an innovation in the 1794 Drury Lane.

Production

About other elements in the production, there is, on the contrary, a gratifying host of detail. The Garrick Club in London has kindly permitted an examination of the study and preparation copy [11], heavily marked for stage business, which relates to this production of 20 November 1795. Turning its pages, one is impressed by the meticulous attention devoted by Kemble to the minutiae of production: all calls are carefully noted, as are the hand properties to be borne by actors on their entrances, and there are several stage 'maps' indicating the detailed planning of some of the major scenes. For example, I.ii opens with Lear seated on a throne (presumably raised on a platform), in the dominant downstage centre position. He is surrounded by a Court of twenty-six subjects, and an undefined number of Guards who line the back of a formally arranged and balanced tableau. Later in his career, Kemble almost invariably used twelve Guards, Soldiers, or Lictors in all his Shakespearean productions [12]; perhaps the difficulties of managing Drury Lane for the financially irresponsible Sheridan caused him to leave the number unspecified on this occasion [13]. His map for the discovery of Lear's Court in 1795 was:

P.S.	Throne	O.P.
	Lear	
Kent		Gloster
2 Gent[s]. with Map		2 Gent[s]. with Crown
Albany		Goneril
Cornwall		Regan
Burgundy		Cordelia
Physician &		
Three Knights		Four Ladies & Aranthe
Capt. of Guard		Two Pages
Herald		Oswald
	Guards	

Other similarly symmetrical maps were supplied, for example, for the scene in front of Gloster's Castle in II.ii, for the arrival of Lear and Cordelia as Prisoners in V.iii, and for the final curtain.

Kemble also showed care in handling the withdrawal from the stage of the large number of characters in mass scenes [14], but the most interesting production notes refer to moves and stage business. I.ii, for example, was heavily annotated. On Lear's, 'Give me the map', during his division of the kingdom, 'The two Gents. who hold the Map *P.S.* advance a little and unroll it', in front of Lear, who remains on his throne throughout the flattering speeches of Goneril and Regan. While Cordelia whispers her unhappy aside, 'Now comes my trial. . .', the King shows his preference for his youngest daughter by an affectionate move down to her level: 'While Cordelia is speaking, Lear descends from the Throne, and walks to the front of the Stage supported by Kent *P.S.* and Gloster *O.P.*' After Cordelia's refusal to indulge in sycophantic flattery, Lear then 'Turns from her' on his line, 'hold thee as a stranger/Both to my blood and favour', and impressively advances on Albany and Cornwall to invest them with the power he has just denied to her:

> Lear goes up to them, beckoning the two Gents. that hold the Crown towards him, who thereupon walk down to his right hand, and kneel when presently he parts his coronet betwixt Albany and Cornwall.

With Lear now dominating the very centre of the stage, Kent kneels to plead with him, rising to his feet as the King's anger increases. Nicholas Rowe's 1709 edition of Shakespeare (possibly drawing upon Betterton's stage business), directs Lear to lay his hand on his sword on, 'Ha, traitor!', and Kemble followed this, but also took the King's anger a stage further:

> As Lear draws his sword, he is withheld by Albany *P.S.* and Gloster *O.P.*

On the final word ('Away!') of his banishment of Kent,

> Lear turns from him, and beckoning towards the Centre of the Stage, Gloster, Goneril, Regan, Albany, and Cornwall, confers with them till Kent is gone,

sternly ignoring Kent's farewell words to himself and to Cordelia.

Another carefully documented series of moves and business occurs on Lear's arrival at Goneril's Palace. After the King's acceptance of the disguised Kent into his service, Oswald enters from P.S. singing 'Tol de rol' and displaying his impertinence in dress, manner, movement and song:

> Oswald with his Hat on, trips impudently by the King, humming a Tune;
> when Lear speaks to him, he just turns, smiles in his Face, and capers out
> finishing the rest of his Tune.

This was an established stage convention by 1795, for Tom Davies says that Oswald 'generally enters the stage in a careless, disengaged manner, humming a tune, as if on purpose to give umbrage to the King' [15]. Kent and the Second Knight are sent after 'the clodpole', and the regrouping as he is haled back brings Lear to the centre of the stage while Kent manhandles Oswald face to face with the King before moving into further attack, probably with a staff, to drive the Steward offstage at a smart pace, accompanied by loud cries from the terrified coward.

Oswald is also much involved in a later succession of antics during the putting of Kent in the stocks before Gloster's Castle. Kemble worked out this byplay in some detail, but also perhaps with a little distaste for the dissipation of tragic dignity by the comic business of the Steward. Oswald first emerges from the Castle Gates (P.S.) and indicates his alarm at Kent's drawn sword in the quarrel by 'getting round to avoid Kent from *P.S.* to *O.P.*' Saved by the arrival of Cornwall, Regan and their guard,

> Oswald runs, crying out for Fear of Kent across the Stage to *P.S.*; the
> Captain of the Guard stops Kent *O.P.* and then retires a little.

Until Kent is securely in the stocks, Oswald cravenly keeps as far from him as possible, with Regan, Cornwall, Gloster and Edmund in between them; at the end of the scene, with Kent at his mercy, and everyone else retired into the Castle,

> Oswald commonly remains on the Stage to indulge in a few cowardly
> Anticks with Kent, and then follows the rest into the Castle.

Is it possible to detect here the stately John Philip's dislike for some comic business 'commonly' followed? 'Indulge' has a disapproving ring, and, in his 1809 production of *Lear* [16], Kemble's alteration of phrasing for this byplay, to 'indulge in a few vapouring Anticks with Kent', seems to convey distaste for a piece of frivolity which would be unlikely to appeal to a man who prided himself on scholarship and who was described as 'as *merry* as a funeral, and as *lively* as an elephant' [17] when playing comedy himself.

There was no danger of frivolity in the last scene of the play, from which I shall select a final example of Kemble's assiduous planning of complex movements. It is set in a Prison, with Lear in chains asleep upon a truss of straw, with his head in Cordelia's lap — another long-established stage convention. On Cordelia's ominous line from Tate, 'a sudden gloom o'erwhelms me, and the image/Of death o'erspreads the place,' the Captain of the Guard enters with drawn sword from P.S. and moves across O.P. He is accompanied by another Officer 'who remains *P.S.*, his Sword drawn', and two Ruffians with cords. 'Ruffians' is an interesting word. Tate's version ranks them as 'Officers'; in his *printed* text for the 1795 production, Kemble demoted them to 'Soldiers', but he subsequently decided that even this was too high a status for such villains, for he scored out 'Soldiers' each time it occurred, replacing it by 'Ruffians' in manuscript. This change (which would, presumably, affect their costume also) seems to have taken place during preparation or rehearsals, because some of the original *manuscript* notes on this scene mention 'Soldiers' and have been altered by Kemble; by 1809, the *printed* text used 'Ruffians' throughout. Another slight change (in manuscript in 1795, and in print in 1809) was the reduction in number from four to two Ruffians.

Lear has a nightmare about the recent battle in which his allies are defeated, and

> While Lear is talking in his Sleep the Soldiers take off his Chains, and raise him from the Straw; — Cordelia starts up speechless with Terror.

On the Officer's command, 'Make ready your cords',

> The two Ruffians
> 4 Soldiers prepare their cords, seize Lear, and are
> beginning to bind him

when Cordelia distracts them by running O.P. to the Captain of the Guard with the request that she be despatched before her father. The Captain agrees, and so

> The two Ruffians
> Two of the Soldiers quit Lear, and, seizing Cordelia, are
> preparing to bind her

when Lear, with his melodramatic Tatean line, 'Off, hell-hounds!',

> breaks free from the two Soldiers who held him, snatches
>   Ruffians
> the Sword of the Officer *P.S.* and kills the two Soldiers
> who are binding Cordelia; the Captain goes *P.S.*

This dismal situation is then saved by the punctual arrival of the heroic Edgar, with Albany, a Physician, Knights and Soldiers. Kemble's initial confusion at this point in planning the 1795 production is evident from the number of second thoughts in his manuscript directions:

> Cordelia meets Edgar in the middle of the Stage. – Lear
> leans exhausted on his Sword. Albany remains *P.S.* ~~First-Knight~~
>   Captain of the Guard goes to the Officer
> ~~goes over to Lear *O.P.* The Officer turns to the two Soldiers.~~ *P.S.*
>   and the Physician
> Lear's Knights range immediately behind Albany, Edgar, Cordelia,
>   Soldiers
> and Lear; and behind them Albany's ~~Guards~~. The ~~Officer and two
> Soldiers stand~~ *P.S.2 E.*

P.S. Enter	Edgar. Albany. Physician. Knights. ~~Guards~~. Soldiers.

P.S.	Albany, Edgar – Cordelia, Lear	*O.P.* 1st Row
P.S.	3rd Knight, 2nd Knight, 1st Knight, Physician Officer	*O.P.* 2nd Row
P.S.	Captain of the Guard Two Soldiers Soldiers *P.S.* Albany's ~~Guards~~	*O.P.* 3rd Row

These complicated examples provide ample proof of Kemble's forethought in production, and of a detailed planning most unusual in the period. However, it must be admitted that, with the exception of Oswald's byplay, such scrupulous notes are confined almost entirely to the scenes in which Kemble himself was to appear. The opening conversation between Kent, Gloster and Edmund; Gloster's scenes with Edmund in the second and third acts; Edgar's soliloquy, 'I heard myself proclaim'd'; and the first three scenes of the fourth act – in which Lear does not appear – contain few manuscript comments apart from directions about entry and exit. Kemble as producer always tended to be more expansive in his notes when Kemble the actor was directly involved, as may be deduced, for example, from the absence of manuscript notes on Mark Antony's great speech in the Forum (delivered by Charles Kemble) in the 1812 prompt book of *Julius Caesar* in the Garrick Club [18]. By the end of his career, this laissez-faire attitude was growing old-fashioned, and there was some justice in Hazlitt's comment that Kemble 'minds only the conduct of his own person, and leaves the piece to shift for itself '. [19]

One way in which Kemble drew attention to his own person was by the strategic placing of trumpet calls and other musical additives. Later in his career, he was to be even more notorious than Garrick for marking his every appearance with some musical display [20] , but in the 1795 *Lear* he successfully used music to underline both Lear's fondness for regal display and his subsequent fall from power. A Flourish of Trumpets at the end of the first scene prepares for the discovery of the Court, from which the King departs — after his quarrel with Cordelia — to the sound of Drums and Trumpets. Regal splendour still surrounds Lear after his division of the kingdom, his arrival at Goneril's Palace being heralded by Trumpets and Drums; by the end of the scene, however, his growing isolation is marked by a quiet departure after the curse on Goneril. The increasing power of Regan and her husband becomes evident in II.ii, in which Cornwall's arrival is preceded by a Flourish of Trumpets followed by a processional entry of the Captain of the Guard, Cornwall, Regan, a Page, two Ladies and an unspecified number of Attendants; this outward sign of almost majestic sway is completed by Guards who flank the Castle gates. The King's last attempt to retain his kingly embellishments, when he arrives before Gloster's Castle to find Kent in the stocks, is marked by Trumpets and Drums, which Kemble denied him thereafter. For the rest of the play, military music occurs in the battle scenes and in Edgar's duel with Edmund, and the pathos of the recognition scene between Lear and Cordelia is heightened by the 'Soft Musick' which may be deduced from the text. Even at the final happy curtain, with Lear's status re-established, Kemble sensitively resisted the temptation for a resonant climax, marking the old King's chastened state by the absence of any orchestral tribute. In 1809, he unnecessarily introduced a Flourish of Drums and Trumpets at this point.

If music played an important role in directing attention to the movement of power from Lear to his daughters, one startling lighting effect at the end of III.i (on the Heath) dramatically underlined the King's subjection to the elements. Kemble noted

> As Lear is going off, the Thunder cracks, and a Flash of Lightning strikes him full in the face.

Surprisingly, the press for November 1795 seems to have made no comment on this coup. The direction does not appear in the 1809 prompt book — which contains many references to the raising and lowering of the lamps at appropriate moments of light and darkness -- and it is possible that Kemble in fact discarded this difficult effect during the rehearsal period before his 1795 appearance. The absence of lighting directions in the earlier prompt book leaves us with another teasing uncertainty about the production: was there a separate cue-sheet for lighting, or were the directions accidentally omitted from the prompt copy, or were there indeed no variations in intensity of lighting throughout the performance? It seems unlikely that Kemble would have been insensitive enough to permit this, and we are perhaps entitled to assume that the lighting was varied in 1795 in a very similar manner to that which is indicated in so detailed a manner in the 1809 prompt book.

A little more detail is available about some of the properties. For example, Lear marked his divesting of the cares of kingship by assuming a non-regal hat and staff from I.iii onwards. Kemble used these properties to indicate extreme emotional anguish, for at the start of the 'Hear, Nature, hear' curse he noted, 'Lear throws away his Hat and Staff' (which were tidily collected by the First Knight at the end of the scene). In II.iv, on the discovery of the stocked Kent and of the unhelpful attitude of Regan and Cornwall, Kemble again conveyed the rising tension in Lear's mind and his abandonment of self-control by actions with the hat and staff: at 'Oh, Heav'ns!/If you do love old men', he 'Drops his Staff', and at 'My naked head exposed to th'merciless air', he 'Tears off his Hat', and throws it to the ground, from which it is retrieved by Kent.

In the final scene of the fourth act, Lear appeared with new properties: Gloster is prevented from hurling himself over the 'cliff' by the arrival of Lear, 'a Coronet of Flowers on his Head, Wreaths and Garlands about him, and a Sceptre of Straw in his hand'. By 1808, Kemble was wearing a large straw-fashioned crown in the fourth act, which unfortunately provoked considerable mirth in his audiences [21]; in this attire, he was, of course, following Garrick, who had brought fame to the straw regalia used by Lear in this scene, but whose appearance had caused tears rather than laughter among his spectators.

Interpretation

And so we reach the crucial matter of Kemble's interpretation of the role of Lear. We have seen that he expended great effort on the preparations for production, but how successful was he in promoting a sympathetic response in his audience, and in coming to terms with the titanic character of Lear? What was the response which he sought to arouse?

His adoption of a basically 'Tatefied' text would seem to indicate that he agreed with the somewhat sentimental view of Lear current in the eighteenth century. Even the sturdy commonsense of Johnson objected that the blinding of Gloster 'seems an act too horrid to be endured in dramatic exhibition' and that the death of Cordelia is 'contrary to the natural ideas of justice'; Kemble suppressed them both, for he was very much a man of his time and would doubtless have agreed with the sentiments expressed by *The Times* at the opening of the 1785–6 season (19 September):

> In dramatic pieces, exhibited in this school [of the people], one indispensable rule should exist, and every deviation from it should be discountenanced. Virtue should always be commended and rewarded, in spight of the injuries of fortune.

This over-simplification of the complexity of life extended to his conception of the role of Lear, in which he seems to have seen two important elements. First, the character of the King was shown to be composed of two contrasting ingredients, so that he was on the one hand 'a touchingly pathetic old man, and, at the same time, "every inch a King" ' [22] . This description is confirmed by Thomas Dutton, who claimed in 1801 that Kemble

> gave a masterly portraiture of the old, feeble, broken-hearted monarch, assuming all the decrepitude of a man, who, as he himself tells us, is turned of fourscore. His plaintive tones bespoke a heart oppressed with woe, and even in his assumption of madness, there was a kind of solemnity, mixed with the wildness of frenzy, perfectly congenial with the nature and complexion of *Lear*'s despair. [23]

In May 1808, *The Universal Magazine* was also speaking of 'a perfect semblance of palsied decrepitude' which nevertheless was so judiciously discriminated 'as to preserve kingly dignity with it'. His make-up was an important element in this creation of an old yet majestic man, for, in Lear, his countenance 'in grandeur approached the most awful impersonation of Michael Angelo' [24] .

Kemble was outstanding in his ability to communicate the age and the dignity of Lear. On his first appearance in the role, in 1788, he had been criticized for being too young in manner, movement and emotion to carry utter conviction; thereafter, he concentrated on conveying Lear's bodily senility: his toes were introverted to produce an unsteady gait, his movements were inelastic, his hand quivered, his voice trembled, his whole frame seemed to totter, as the actor drew on that masterly control of his physical powers which was such a feature of his death scenes as King John, Coriolanus and Richard III. The prompt book indicates that twice in IV. iv, while wearing his straw regalia, Kemble brought Lear's condition to a state of collapse: on 'Pull, pull off my boots', he 'Faints, and is supported by Edgar', while at 'Oh! I am cut to the brains', he 'Falls flat to the ground' from which he is raised by the Knights. Unfortunately, as Boaden admitted, Kemble's Lear was so frail that he lacked emotional force:

> He was too elaborately aged, and quenched with infirmity the insane fire of the injured father. (*Kemble*, I, 379)

The regality of Lear came naturally to an actor famous for his dignity and commanding presence; the qualities of pride and aristocratic assurance which had made his Coriolanus the wonder of the age, and which strengthened his Wolsey, brought to his Lear the stateliness and dominance appropriate to the old autocrat.

But there is more to Lear than a dignified old age. What else did Kemble discover within his character? The second major element in his interpretation was the developing contrast between the Lear of the earlier scenes and the more pathetic man of the central and final sections of the play. Many of Lear's horrific experiences stem directly from his own injustice, foolishness and 'blindness', but Kemble's conception saw him

> commencing as a tranquil, venerable monarch, made shortly after justifiably angry by the conduct of Cordelia; growing more and more seriously violent, as his vexations increased; and at last losing his wits from the overwhelming pressure of his sorrows. [25]

It sounds from this description as if Kemble's view of Lear's descent into madness was a fairly superficial one, taking Lear at his own valuation as 'more sinned against than sinning', and depicting him as almost entirely blameless. This was characteristic of Kemble, who could never bring himself to accept the flawed nature of many Shakespearean protagonists, and who had a curiously literal approach to the text: his Othello was genuinely 'one not easily jealous' and his Iago was sincerely 'honest'; his Richard III was a gentleman, and his Macbeth was filled with 'blameless ambition' so that even at his worst moments 'his original sense of right and justice still holds possession' and 'his early principles of virtue are not extinct in him' [26].

It was also characteristic of Kemble that he did not seem to appreciate that there is a development within Lear's insanity, leading to 'reason in madness'. This growth in perception of the world and in self-knowledge was a notable omission by Kemble, who delivered all his speeches on the heath with an almost monotonous affectation of madness which militated against the achievement of any subtle complexity in the interpretation. This absence of subtlety came partly from Kemble's fondness for reducing his roles to the expression of one dominating characteristic uncluttered by internal divisions or uncertainties, partly from his over-studious approach, and partly from his own physical limitations.

To deal briefly with each of these in turn. As *The Lady's Magazine* for September 1817 perceptively remarked on his retirement:

> The range of characters in which Mr. Kemble more particularly shone, and was superior to every other actor, were those which consisted in the development of some one solitary sentiment or exclusive passion.

Now, none of Shakespeare's major tragic roles may be accurately confined in this way, and Kemble's efforts to reduce and oversimplify these interpretations ignored the psychological complexity which a twentieth-century audience has learned to expect. His Duke in *Measure for Measure* and his Prospero were simple vessels of dignity and rectitude, in Hamlet 'he too uniformly sustained throughout the whole part the same melancholy mood' [27], and as Macbeth he 'was unequal to "the tug and war" of the passions which assail him, ... and maintained his ground too steadily' [28]. The single-minded Coriolanus lay just within the scope of such a technique – though there was some simplification and falsification even there – but the complexity of Lear's emotional, spiritual and mental progress lay far outside it. As Leigh Hunt acidly remarked of the scenes on the heath (*Examiner*, 22 May 1808): 'He is always stiff, always precise, and he will never, as long as he lives, be able to act anything mad, unless it be a melancholy mad statue.'

Kemble's second handicap was his careful and intellectual manner of preparation. On stage, his technique was described by Boaden as of 'the academic or critical style of acting' (*Kemble*, I, 175), and Leigh Hunt complained that 'there was much of the pedagogue in him' [29]. He was so precise, and so aware of the 'effects' he intended to make, that he was often unable to sink himself within the emotional experience of his role, thus offending against the main principle of acting which had long ago been enunciated by Aaron Hill:

> To act a passion well, the actor must never attempt its imitation, 'till his fancy has conceived so strong an image, or idea of it, as to move the same impressive springs within his mind, which form that passion, when 'tis undesigned and natural. (*Works*, IV, 355)

That Kemble was unable to reach this state in his portrayal of Lear is proved by his complaint to the actor Fawcett that he was distracted by the extraneous noises of the spectators, and that

> in Lear an audience quite unsettled him; the noise of the box-doors caught his ear, and routed all his meditated effects; and he found it absolutely impossible to do that at night, which he had thrown out during the rehearsal in the morning. [30]

His concern with the externals of technique and characterization, his tendency towards a frigid dignity on the stage, and his reluctance to feel himself at all transformed into the character he represented, meant that

> all he did appeared the result of study, and hence his performances seldom, if ever, transported you into an idea that you were witnessing a real scene. [31]

His bodily weakness was another restraint. Lear is one of the most taxing roles ever written, requiring the physical strength of a man not only at the height of his powers, but also in peak condition. Although he never lost the ability to exercise a strict control over his muscles at certain high points of action, Kemble was constantly dogged by illness and weakness which forced him to husband his resources for the great climaxes of each role; frequently, he felt able only to 'walk through' a performance, making what Leigh Hunt called 'that frigid reservation of himself for particular passages' [32], in which he would then blaze forth with unexpected spirit. In addition, his reactions were sometimes dulled by the opium which he took to quench his recurrent cough. Lear's scenes on the heath form a tightly-knit series of climaxes, whose intensity Kemble was unable to sustain; for example, *The Morning Post* (25 January 1788) complained that 'a want of bodily powers' obliged him 'to sink into softness, when the text obviously required the most choleric effusions of rage'.

Presumably, Kemble's dry, asthmatic voice – his weakest technical instrument, and one which was always liable to let him down – was partly responsible for his inability to communicate the depths of Lear's passion. He quite openly admitted that he normally cut 'O what a rogue and peasant slave' in *Hamlet* because his asthma left him with insufficient breath for it [33], and Boaden records that Macbeth's address to the Witches ('I conjure you by that which you profess') was drastically cut to the mere two and a half lines it occupies in Kemble's version because the actor's weak voice could make nothing of the speech [34]. It was mainly this infirmity which marred the mad scenes in *Lear* for Leigh Hunt, who claimed in the *Examiner*, 22 May 1808, that 'Blow winds and crack your cheeks' was delivered with 'a gloomy carelessness', and that, a little later in the play, 'the grave actor went through his gentle speeches with the dull calmness of a schoolboy'. Even allowing for Hunt's habitual, though perceptive, bias against Kemble, this remains a damning indictment.

Clearly, even though Garrick's friends were said to hail Kemble's Lear with delight [35], the interpretation fell far short of his predecessor's. It was, nonetheless, the greatest Lear of its age, an honourable and conscientious performance in a meticulously prepared production. On the whole, the central sections of the play failed, but there were several memorably successful moments. It was characteristic of Kemble to embed such highlights in his interpretation, for he tended to isolate certain climactic moments at which to unleash his powers, even if the overall dynamics of the performance suffered thereby; it was Macready who said of him that 'like a Rembrandt picture, his performances were remarkable for most brilliant effects, worked out with wonderful skill on a sombre ground' [36], and I shall conclude by attempting to describe two of Kemble's greatest moments in the play – the curse on Goneril and the conversation with Edgar disguised as Poor Tom.

The curse was probably the supreme moment of Kemble's performance, and throughout his career the tributes to it rang out with a remarkable degree of unanimity. At first, he listened with apparent acquiescence to Albany's excuse of ignorance about Goneril's conduct, then paused for a moment, with his eye fixed on the ground, as if winding himself up for some great solemnity; he then with one rapid glance at his daughter, rushed to the front of the stage, dropped on his knees, and with his hands strongly clasped, and his eyes straining upwards, began the imprecation. His first words, 'Hear, Nature, hear, dear Goddess, hear!' were slow and firm,

followed by 'an encreasing fervour and rapidity', which mounted to 'an almost breathless agitation.' 'As he spoke of Goneril his voice grew loud, inarticulate and hurried', then

> when he touched upon his own wrongs, and prayed that she might feel
> 'How sharper than a serpent's tooth it is
> To have a thankless child.'
> he seemed overwhelmed by a father's feelings; his strength failed, his head drooped, his eye wandered, and his voice sank and quivered, and faded, till it became almost inaudible

as he fell into 'the suffocation of the conclusive words' [37]. Even the most inveterately harsh of Kemble's major critics admitted to being moved in this fine passage [38].

Throughout the curse, the actor's vocal control was outstanding; carefully husbanding his weakest resource, Kemble avoided the temptation to bellow in a roaring declamation, and instead

> was not loud but deep, and apparently so full of rooted anguish, that not so much his lips as his heart uttered the horrid prayer. (*Monthly Mirror*, October 1810)

At the end of the speech, as Albany, Goneril and their attendants withdrew into the Palace, the prompt book indicates that 'Kent and the Physician raise Lear from his Knees, and bear him away'.

Another great scene was III. iii, on the Heath, with the Hovel situated O.P.U.E. Kent's courage, and his solicitude for his master, were much in evidence in the production notes, especially at the first appearance of Edgar in the guise of Poor Tom:

> Kent is leading Lear to the Hovel; when Edgar [dressed in a blanket] cries out, he starts back a little; and, upon his rushing out, stands with his sword drawn between him and Lear.

It is also Kent who restrains Lear from tearing off his clothes, and who supports the King when he swoons at 'To have a thousand with red-hot spits come hissing in upon them'.

Throughout the scene, however, the main emphasis was placed on the attraction which Lear feels for Edgar, which was expressed by

Kemble getting behind Edgar and marching after him as Poor Tom perambulated about the stage during his song, 'Be thy mouth or black or white'. The finest moment of the scene came when the King's powerful identification with the 'philosopher' made 'Lear and Edgar sit down upon the ground together' close to the footlights, as Kemble's notes indicate. In 1795, Edgar was played by the hard-working but essentially undistinguished Richard Wroughton; after 1795, when he was replaced by Charles Kemble, this colloquy between genuine and assumed madness became another of the highlights of the performance. W. Robson remembered that each was

> stimulated by the fine acting of the other to play up to his best! The one depicting poor outraged Nature, deprived of the jewel reason; the other, with an equally fine touch, showing that though he played the part of a mad-man, the madness was but assumed. [39]

When Gloster tried to dismiss Poor Tom, Kemble's notes show that he sought to give a graphic depiction of the King's unwillingness to be parted from his new friend:

> Edgar starts up, and passes by Lear, who, catching hold on his Blanket, is dragg'd a little way on the ground after him. [40]

Clearly, whatever the limitations of his conception of the role, there were certain moments at which Kemble was able to communicate more of the pathos of Lear's experiences than the 'old man tottering about the stage with a walking stick' seen by Charles Lamb.

Conclusion

Even at second or third hand, the high level of achievement in these crowning moments still communicates something of the intermittent power of Kemble's Lear. It seems likely, however, that they were the peaks of a not altogether satisfactory performance. Garrick's interpretation — perhaps the greatest Lear yet witnessed on the stage — had created a sense of grandeur and terror; he had emphasized the strugglings of parental affection, and then, in a series of swift transitions from one passion to another, he had 'faithfully represented all the passions of the soul' [41] so that the audience saw 'the elementary conflict re-imaged in his distracted looks' [42], in a way which lay beyond Kemble's scope. His portrayal was terrifying, and yet fraught with pathos; he possessed a warmth which Kemble — correct, classical, artificial, and self-consciously dignified [43] — could only rarely attain. By comparison with the sweep of Garrick's performance and the depth of its sensitive understanding, Kemble's was too cold, superficial and pedestrian. As Thomas Dutton said of all Kemble's acting:

> The *heart* is not touched — it is the *understanding* solely that Mr. KEMBLE appeals to. He is cold, as the lamp that lights the funeral vault. [44]

Kemble somewhat sentimentalized the King, glossing over his undoubted faults, and his interpretation lost impetus and conviction in most of the soul-searing scenes on the Heath which had been such a triumph for Garrick. Kemble worked hard at his production of *King Lear* on 20 November 1795, assiduously marshalling his forces in a clear-cut and unfussy series of dispositions, but his own performance, though containing some moments of imagination and pathos, seems to have been erratic, and the role of Lear essentially beyond his powers. Unfortunately, a meticulously prepared prompt book is not sufficient recipe for success in so gigantic and passion-torn a role as Lear.

Notes

[1] John Genest, *Some Account of the English Stage* (Bath, 1832), VIII, 131–2. Cf. Thomas Campbell (*The Life of Mrs. Siddons* (London, 1834), II, 122–3), who calls it 'that vicious edition of his'.

[2] Kemble showed a great fondness for granting himself a good curtain line. The third act of his version of *Coriolanus* concludes with the defiant line, 'There is a world elsewhere!' The Stratford prompt book of his *Hamlet* (probably 1807) shows that he scored out Horatio's final speech even from his own adaptation to bring down the curtain on 'The rest is silence'. The Folger prompt copy of the 1816 *Othello* reveals that the play ended with the hero's 'Oh! Desdemona!'

[3] W. Cooke, *The Elements of Dramatic Criticism* (London, 1775), 195.

[4] H. Hunt, *Old Vic Prefaces* (London, Routledge & Kegan Paul, 1954), ix–x.

[5] A comparison of the 1807 and 1811 prompt copies of *The Winter's Tale* (Garrick Club), or of the 1795 prompt book of *King Lear* (Garrick Club) with the 1809 prompt book in the Harvard Theatre Collection, shows the remarkable identity between productions at different periods of Kemble's career.

[6] C. B. Hogan, 'An Eighteenth Century Prompter's Notes', *Theatre Notebook*, X (1956).

[7] T. Davies, *Dramatic Miscellanies* (London, 1784), II, 278.

[8] Tate Wilkinson, *Memoirs of his Own Life* (York, 1790), IV, 91.

[9] S. Rosenfeld and E. Croft-Murray, 'A Checklist of Scene-Painters Working in Great Britain and Ireland in the 18th Century', *Theatre Notebook*, XIX and XX (1965–6).

[10] I.i   An Antechamber in King Lear's Palace
     I.ii   A Room of State in the Palace
     I.iii The Court before the Duke of Albany's Palace
     II.i   The Earl of Gloster's Castle
     II.ii & iv Before the Earl of Gloster's Castle
     II.iii A Forest
     III.i A desert Heath
     III.ii A Room in Gloster's Castle (presumably as II.i)
     III.iii Another part of the Heath
     IV.i   An Apartment in the Earl of Gloster's Castle (presumably as II.i & III.ii)
     IV.ii The open Country
     IV.iii Goneril's Palace
     IV.iv Another Part of the Country
     V.i   A Chamber
     V.ii   A Valley near the Field of Battle
     V.iii The Field of Battle
     V.iv   The Duke of Albany's Tent

[11] *Shakspeare's King Lear: As Altered by N. Tate, Newly Revised by J. P. Kemble; and acted by Their Majesties' Servants, at the Theatre Royal, Drury Lane.* (N.d., but interleaves marked 1794.) I am grateful to the Library Committee of the Garrick Club for permission to examine this text.

[12] For example, in *Coriolanus* 1806, *Henry IV, Part II c.* 1807, *The Winter's Tale* 1807 and 1811, *Henry IV, Part I* 1808, *Cymbeline* 1810 (where there are 12 British and 12 Roman soldiers), *Henry V* 1811, *Measure for Measure* 1811, *Julius Caesar* 1812.

[13] At Covent Garden, later in his career, Kemble's Order of the Ovation in *Coriolanus* utilized about 240 participants (see J. C. Young, *A Memoir of C. M. Young* (London, 1871), I, 62, and the list in Kemble's own hand at the front of the Folger prompt book for the 1806 Covent Garden production). At Drury Lane, however, Sheridan's meanness seems to have caused Kemble to rely on a very small number of supers for this set-piece, and on a 'mob' numbering no more than twenty (see *Thespian Magazine*, April 1793 and *The Times*, 9 February 1789).

[14] For example, on Lear's exit in I.ii, after Cordelia has thrown herself at her father's feet, the King sweeps offstage P.S. to the sound of music, and with a very clear disposition of the exit order of his entourage:
                    Trumpets and Drums
                         Lear.
                         Gloster & Burgundy.
                         Cornwall & Regan.
                         Albany & Goneril.
                         Oswald.

2 Pages.
4 Ladies & Aranthe.
2 Gents. *with Map.*
2 Gents. *with Crown.*
Captain of the Guard.
Herald.
Physician.
3 Knights.
Guards.

[15] T. Davies, op. cit., II, 273.
[16] I am indebted to the Harvard Theatre Collection for the most generous loan of a microfilm of this prompt book.
[17] J. Bannister in W. Oxberry, *Dramatic Biography* (London, 1825), I, 120.
[18] See D. Rostron, 'John Philip Kemble's *Coriolanus* and *Julius Caesar*', *Theatre Notebook*, XXIII (1968).
[19] In *The Examiner*, 1 December 1816.
[20] See *Black Dwarf*, IV, no. 3 (March 1820), and K. A. Burnim, *David Garrick, Director* (Pittsburgh, U. of Pittsburgh Press, 1961), 19.
[21] *Monthly Mirror*, June 1808.
[22] Campbell, op. cit., II, 118.
[23] T. Dutton, *Dramatic Censor* (London, 1801), II, 71–2.
[24] J. Boaden, *Memoirs of the Life of J. P. Kemble* (London, 1825), I, 379. (Hereafter cited as *Kemble*.)
[25] E. Mangin, *Piozziana* (London, 1833), 165.
[26] The quotations are from Kemble's own *Essay on Macbeth and Richard III* (London, 1817), 168–70.
[27] J. Galt, *The Lives of the Players* (London, 1831), II, 256.
[28] Hazlitt writing in *The Times*, 25 June 1817.
[29] Quoted from Leigh Hunt's *Autobiography* in W. Archer and R. W. Lowe (eds), *Dramatic Essays of Leigh Hunt* (London, 1894), xxiii.
[30] J. Boaden, *Memoirs of Mrs. Siddons* (London, 1827), II, 276.
[31] W. Oxberry, *Famous Actors* (London, 1894), 107.
[32] *The Examiner*, 5 February 1815.
[33] W. B. Wood, *Personal Recollections* (New York, 1840), 202.
[34] *Kemble*, I, 417.
[35] ibid., I, 379.
[36] W. C. Macready, *Reminiscences*, ed. Pollock (London, 1875), I, 150.
[37] Of these six quotations, the first, fourth and fifth are from *The Times*, 15 October 1810, the second and sixth from Boaden's *Kemble*, I, 378–9, the third from the *Monthly Mirror* of October 1810.
[38] See Archer and Lowe, op. cit., 225.
[39] W. Robson, *The Old Play-Goer* (London, 1846), 44.
[40] Garrick, at this point, had fallen asleep and been carried off-stage by Gloster and Kent (see Burnim, op. cit., 148).
[41] T. Davies, op. cit., II, 320.
[42] F. Gentleman, *Dramatic Censor* (London, 1770), I, 370.

[43] Mrs Siddons, speaking to the dramatist Reynolds, perceptively pinpointed one of the contrasts between herself and Kemble: 'My brother John in his most impetuous bursts is always careful to avoid any discomposure of his dress or deportment, but in the whirlwind of passion I lose all thought of such matters.' (Quoted in W. C. Macready, op. cit., I, 149.)

[44]   T. Dutton, *Monthly Theatrical Reporter*, December, 1814, 85.

Landscape in English Scenery in the Eighteenth Century

It is noticeable that Inigo Jones designed for the masques a number of rural scenes with and without villages and thatched cottages, and that this penchant of his introduces a unique note into baroque scene design. Italian designers such as the Parigis displayed their mountains, their deserts and their groves but they were far from the pastoral vein exploited by Jones. There was warrant sufficient for Jones's landscapes in Serlio's satiric scene of trees and country dwellings, which he based on Vitruvius's recommendation that such scenes should be composed of trees, rocks, hills, mountains, and some rustic huts [1]; the licence necessary to castigate vice could only come from the mouths of rustics who had no respect for rank. Jones's country settings were more natural and therefore more English in tone than those of his predecessors and contemporaries abroad, as his sketches of forests and his pastoral settings for *Chloridia, Florimène*, and *Salmacida Spolia*, with their back shutters of tranquil cornfields in open country, bear witness. This sense of nature Jones achieved within the formality and symmetry inherent in the wing and shutter system.

The sophisticated theatre of the Restoration concentrated on public or private interiors, and laid-out parks and gardens. If there were landscapes, as in the operatic *Tempest*, they were of the familiar baroque type of three-perspective cypress alleys and a rockbound sea shore. However, we must bear in mind that two Restoration scene painters, Isaac Fuller and Thomas Stevenson, were landscape artists, though it is doubtful whether they had the opportunity of using these talents in their scenery for the dramatic operas.

The type of baroque landscape in vogue with Italian scenographers was seen in Aaron Hill's production of Handel's *Rinaldo* in 1711. A prospect of steep mountains rose from the front of the stage to the full height of the most backward part of the theatre. In it were shown rocks, caves and waterfalls. Real water was used for the cascade and was employed again for *Clotilda*, when 'by reason of the Hot Weather, the Waterfall will play the best part of the Opera' [2]. No wonder the *Spectator* [3] mocked at 'real Cascades in artificial Land-skips', and sensibly remarked that 'Scenes which are designed as the Representations of Nature, should be filled with Resemblances, and not with the Things themselves'.

Strangely enough it was the pantomime that brought back the rustic scene. Or on reflection not so strangely, since there is a parallel between neo-classical use of it for the satiric play, performed after the ardours of tragedy, and that of the knockabout fun of the harlequinade after the legends of gods and goddesses. The rustic setting was again suitable for a degree of licence after the more serious preoccupations of the main dramatic offering. Rich employed as his scene painter George Lambert, a young landscape painter who was influenced by the style of Wootton. It is significant that he chose, instead of the customary decorative artist, an easel painter of country scenes. Lambert started work at Lincoln's Inn Fields in 1726–7, and worked there and at Covent Garden until 1761. In 1727 he painted a farmyard scene depicting open country with cornfields for the grotesque part of *The Rape of Proserpine*; and in the serious part of the same pantomime, the first of many scenes of a volcano in eruption. In the farmyard scene Rich performed a famous trick. An egg on a dunghill grew larger and larger until it cracked open, and a tiny Harlequin emerged who proceeded to grow to adult height [4] – 'a masterpiece in dumb show' [5]. When another version of the pantomime, as *Harlequin Sorcerer*, was given at Covent Garden in 1752, the farmhouse scene, which was an excellent setting for pantomime tricks, was retained. It was Lambert again who painted it, and also the back part of the farmhouse with a shed which is the only design of his we have. Various tricks were again contrived, as for instance the conversion of a mound into a washing tub and stand, probably by means of a flap device [6].

By this time Lambert was a well-known landscape artist. Though one cannot be sure how far his scenic style derived from his easel pictures, there must have been some resemblance. Lambert was a tranquil painter, who studied trees with loving care and produced views seen in a quiet but luminous light. He was an obvious lover of the English countryside, and one imagines that he may have carried these qualities into his stage work.

Covent Garden established a landscape tradition with Nicholas Dall, another painter of the countryside, who overlapped with Lambert and with John Inigo Richards, who was Lambert's pupil. We have little information about Dall's work in the theatre. As an artist he was influenced by Richard Wilson, and his paintings of parks are serene and rich in light. We know that Dall and Richards were sent to Stratford in 1761 and Dall to Windsor in 1768–9 to make sketches on the spot for two afterpieces. This is evidence of the growing attention to realistic representation.

Gray's *Elegy* was published in 1750, and its glorification of the humble life of peasant and shepherd made a deep impression and heralded the romantic love of country scenes in literature and in art. Such a stage scene was one by Richards for *The Maid of the Mill* (pl. 1), which is typically English in feeling. We know that Richards also painted a country church, and a hedge and gate with a farm cart and hayrick, which must have been similar in kind. He also designed exotic scenes. When he came to illustrate Asiatic views for *The Choice of Harlequin, or The Indian Chief* in 1782, he copied drawings by Tilly Kettle, and for the dramatic opera *Ramah Droog*, drawings of India by Thomas Daniell, both of whom had worked in the East. We have a sketch for a scene in the latter which shows an English fort on a mount in what purports to be an Indian setting. Apart from a few exotic trees it has little local colour, and is as placid as any English landscape. This water-colour, incidentally, can be compared with the engraving on the score, and is so close as to prove that the score engravings of the 1790s were authentic records of the scenery.

Woods were regular stock scenes, often cut to reveal prospects behind. Roger Pickering in 1755 mentions views of the country among the usual stock scenery [7], and in a well-known passage in *The Case of the Stage in Ireland* (Dublin, 1758), rural prospects of groves, forests, and deserts are included in a list of scenes necessary for theatres [8]. Both the Covent Garden inventory of 1744 and the Crow Street inventory of 1776 refer to 'long woods' (central perspective scenes which stretched back to the full length of the stage), and both mention the popular waterfalls. In addition Covent Garden possessed a short wood and a village.

A boost was given to landscape art in the theatre by the coming into use of act drops. These could resemble easel pictures, since they were painted on one plane. Some painters chose as their subjects classical ruins, but others depicted pure views. One of the earliest was for *Harlequin Sorcerer* (1753) by Lambert: 'a scene drops and gives us a prospect of ruinous rugged cliffs, with two trees hanging over them beautifully executed'. Drury Lane followed suit in the same year with a drop in *The Genii* 'containing a rural prospect which exceeds any landskip yet shown on the stage... the reapers enter, the scene rises and leaves them in the field' [9]. Garrick required a landscape curtain for *Cymon* in 1766, and this was probably re-used for *Alfred* in 1773, as the prompt book specifies 'Drop Landskip after Acts I and II'. Robert Carver's famous Dublin drop was said to depict a storm on a coast with the sea dashing against the rocks. Edward Dayes considered it 'the finest painting that ever decorated a theatre' [10].

Carver, an Irish scene painter who worked for Garrick in the 1770s, displayed a scene of the waterfall at Powerscourt for *A Trip to the Dargle* at Smock Alley in 1762, and in 1772 Bamford and Jolly supplied for *Harlequin in Ireland* at Smock Alley a set of local landscapes which included views of Killarney, O'Sullivan's Cascade, Turk Mountain, and the mountains of Glena, thus preceding by six years De Loutherbourg's famous *Wonders of Derbyshire*. The pleasures of recognition were being catered for outside London, and the scenes must have been to some extent realistic since spectators would have known the originals.

It was De Loutherbourg, an Alsation brought over from Paris by Garrick, who established England's lead in romantic scenery. He transferred to the stage the influence of Salvator Rosa and Gaspard Poussin. In contrast to the quiet pastoralism of his predecessors, he depicted, both in his pictures and his scenery, mountain grandeur and wild torrents under dramatic and even lurid light, to create effects of the sublime and the picturesque. The scene from his first pantomime, *A Christmas Tale* (pl. 2), well illustrates the breakaway from the calm domestic scenery of Richards. With its forbidding mountains, distant view of a romantic ruined castle perched on a crag, and its broken foreground of rocks, it is quite unlike anything that we know had gone before. Though it has not yet departed from a central perspective, it is less symmetrical than was customary. De Loutherbourg proceeded to break up the rigid perspectives and formal settings inherited from the neo-classical and baroque stages into dispersed, free-standing pieces irregularly placed: he also increased the use of groundrows. By abandoning formality he was able to represent the picturesque. A wizard at perspective, he broke up the back flat into several pieces and then brought them into a new perspective whole. For *Omai* he is said to have employed as many as forty-two separate entities to build up a scene of a frozen ocean [11].

The key piece in De Loutherbourg's landscape revolution was *The Wonders of Derbyshire* of 1779. Here he discovered the picturesque, the rugged, and the sublime in the hills and dales of that county, and not in any distant country. He brought to the audience's attention the fact that in England could be found the qualities which so appealed to the romantic imagination. The tone was set by an act drop of mountains and waterfalls which Angelo described as 'most beautifully executed exhibiting a terrific appearance'. Of the whole pantomime he says, 'never were such romantic and picturesque paintings exhibited in that theatre before' [12]. Eleven of the twelve scenes were localized, the exception being the final transformation. Further romantic effects were obtained by showing scenes at different times of day. Thus, we have leadmines and landscape at daybreak, Matlock at sunset, and Dovedale by moonlight. The critic of the *London Magazine* carped a little about details of authenticity; after praising Buxton Wells and Poole's Hole for their exactitude, he goes on,

> The view of Castleton ... is given with great truth and taste, that of the entrance is too much beautified and illumined.... If the short view of the road between the rocks was designed for Middleton Dale, it was an imperfect one. [13]

This is evidence of how carefully scenery was regarded for realistic accuracy of presentation. De Loutherbourg had spent some time making sketches in Derbyshire for this piece, the first based on views of the countryside. The mounting doubtless benefited from De Loutherbourg's lighting reforms, which enabled him to create subtle gradations of tints and atmosphere by means of transparencies and coloured silks placed in front of the lamps.

De Loutherbourg did not confine himself to English scenes, but designed a Greek setting for *Electra*, an early example of an Egyptian one for *Sethona*, and a Spanish background for *Robinson Crusoe*. His outstanding work in exotic style was for the pantomime *Omai* at Covent Garden in 1785. Based on Captain Cook's South Sea voyages, the scenery was taken from drawings and prints by John Webber and William Hodges, who had accompanied Cook on his expedition. The team of painters who executed these was Richards, Carver and Hodgins. Again the designer varied the lighting to show a royal burial ground by moonlight and Otaheite by sunset.

De Loutherbourg was fascinated by transitions of light, and experimented with them in his model theatre, the Eidophusikon. Here he used the Argand lamp for the first time, which gave a much more brilliant light than candles and oil lamps. He placed a batten of lamps above the proscenium behind slips of stained glass and thus tinted the scenes from above and in front, enabling him to show the gradual change from the cool light of dawn to the warmth of the morning in one scene, whereas before such contrasts had necessitated a change of setting. He also changed the scenes with noon over Tangier, sunset over Naples, and moonrise in the Mediterranean. Gauze was certainly used by him for mists. He also depicted moving clouds by means of raising diagonally on revolving cylinders frames covered with painted linen twenty times the size of the stage. This type of sky panorama is illustrated in Bamber Gascoigne's *World Theatre* from an Italian water-colour in Stockholm dated about 1750. This picture also gives a hint as to how De Loutherbourg may have contrived his illusion of vast perspectives with miles of distance in so little a space by placing scenes on a succession of groundrows.

In the sale of De Loutherbourg's effects there are listed forty-nine rural scenes, twenty-three rural and architectural scenes and thirty-six cloud and water scenes [14]. His influence was widespread and, as many of his settings were copied in the provincial theatres, the taste for romantic landscape was widely disseminated. The vogue for the picturesque thus created was exploited by William Gilpin in his series of picturesque tours from 1782 onwards.

One of the painters who executed many of De Loutherbourg's scenes was Thomas Greenwood the elder, who became Drury Lane's chief resident painter on the death of French in 1776. He too painted landscapes, as well as the more conventional infernal regions, enchanted gardens and palaces. Unlike Lambert, Dall and De Loutherbourg, he was not well known as an easel painter of landscapes, and seems to have concentrated on the profession of scene painting. We have four illustrated scores of his scenes for dramatic operas. All are landscapes with buildings, and they give a good idea of his placid, expansive style.

The Siege of Belgrade might count as a camp scene were it not for the broad flow of the Danube painted on the backcloth, and the distant view of a fortress and town with its' oriental flavour of minarets. His view of the Bay of Naples from the quay, with Vesuvius in the distance (for *The Pirates*), was taken from designs made on the spot by the composer Stephen Storace. At Kemble's new Drury Lane in 1794, Greenwood provided a scene of a moated castle in the spacious and tranquil setting of a park for Storace's *Lodoiska*, and for another Storace comic opera, *The Haunted Tower*, he painted an open landscape with the tower on the stage right balanced by a small building with a cupola on the stage left. But Greenwood also realized some more romantic scenes as, for instance, for *The Witch of the Lakes* at Sadler's Wells in 1788, which included a rocky glen by moonlight, a cataract, the lakes of Cumberland and Fingal's Cave, which he took from descriptions by Pennant and others, thus forestalling the nineteenth-century habit of quoting authorities. Just before he died he was working on scenery for Monk Lewis's *Castle Spectre* which was completed by his son. Gothic melodrama, with its attendant gloom and apparatus of spectres and apparitions, was hardly suited to sober, realistic English views. Rather it was the romantic spirit which triumphed in the last year of the century in the well-known scene for *Pizarro* of craggy mountains and tempestuous torrents, which may have been from a sketch by De Loutherbourg. Only the palm trees, sign manual of the exotic, indicated its Peruvian setting.

The two streams of landscape scene painting in the eighteenth century both contributed something novel to the theatre. The quiet pastoral scenes were hardly paralleled in Europe, and had moved nearer realism than those of contemporary settings abroad. As early as 1764, Brandes was struck on his visit to England by the 'realistic productions of actual scenes' in contradistinction to 'gaudy Opera decorations' [15]. But it was the wild romantic scenes that put England in the lead. For the first time Italian and French scenographers followed English taste in scene design and did not lead it, and for this we are indebted to the influence of De Loutherbourg.

Notes

[1] Cf. Barnard Hewitt, ed. *The Renaissance Stage* (Miami, U. of Miami Press, 1958), 32.

[2] Quoted in *The London Stage 1660–1800*, ed. Emmett L. Avery (Carbondale, Ill., 1960), Part 2, 249.

[3] No. 5, 6 March 1711.

[4] Cf. César de Saussure, *A Foreign View of England in the Reigns of George I and George II* (London, 1902), 274–5.

[5] From John Jackson's account in his *History of the Scottish Stage* (Edinburgh, 1793), 365–8.

[6] Cf. G. W. Stone, ed., *The London Stage 1660–1800* (Carbondale, Ill., 1962), Part 4, cxlix, which quotes *Have At Ye All; or The Drury Lane Journal*.

[7] *Reflections upon Theatrical Expression in Tragedy* (London, 1755), 59.

[8] The passage is on p. 35.

[9] *London Magazine*, June 1779, p. 31.

[10] Edward Dayes, *Works* (London, 1805), 323.

[11] 'Historical Sketch of the Rise and Progress of Scene-Painting in England', *Library of Fine Arts*, May 1831, 328.

[12] H. Angelo, *Reminiscences* (London, 1828), II, 248.

[13] January 1779, 31.

[14] *A Catalogue of Drawings of James Philip De Loutherbourg*, sold by Peter Coxe, 18 June 1812. The catalogue is in the Victoria and Albert Library. (I owe this reference to Dr Joppien.)

[15] J. A. Kelly, *German Visitors to English Theatres in the Eighteenth Century* (Princeton, N.J., Princeton U.P., 1936), 99–100.

11 GRAHAM BARLOW

Sir James Thornhill
and the Theatre Royal, Drury Lane, 1705

In recent years the work of Sir James Thornhill has been attracting a new interest. It has received considerable attention from art historians in their endeavour to place Thornhill in his rightful niche in the history of English painting since he has, up till now, stood in the shadow of his son-in-law, Hogarth. They also indicate, at the same time, how strongly he was influenced by his masters, Verrio and Laguerre, whom he superseded as Historical Painter to the Crown during a wave of cultural nationalism. The paintings that have been the especial study of the historians are, however, those large-scale historical and decorative works to be seen, for example, in the dome of St Paul's Cathedral, or on the walls and ceilings of great houses, such as Hampton Court Palace, Greenwich Hospital or Blenheim. Almost completely neglected are James Thornhill's designs for the theatre, and yet one can hardly recall a major work of his which does not have about it something highly theatrical. Indeed his characteristic method, learned from Verrio and Laguerre, of grouping his characters either in an architectural or landscape setting, and then enclosing his decoration within an architectural frame so closely resembling a proscenium arch, makes the hunting down of works designed specifically for the theatre extremely difficult. All his major works, for which he was honoured with a knighthood and the distinction of Sergeant Painter, were undertaken after his theatrical debut at the age of 29, for his first known commission was to design the settings for Thomas Clayton's opera, *Arsinoë, Queen of Cyprus*, at the Theatre Royal, Drury Lane, in January 1705.

Thornhill's designs for this opera are not all lost like so many other early designs for Drury Lane and, though they are not artistically dazzling, they are of some considerable importance since, as far as I know, we have no other evidence to tell of theatrical practices, in terms of actual designs of the period, as opposed to book-plates such as those for the opera *Ariadne* [1], which was performed at the new Drury Lane in 1674. Unfortunately however, unlike Webb, Thornhill has not left us any ground plans for his productions. Had he done so, we would know perhaps a little more than we do about the physical conditions of the Theatre Royal at the beginning of the eighteenth century — the theatre Colley Cibber attributes to Christopher Wren [2].

Initially my interest was not entirely concerned with Drury Lane but with Thornhill and his second theatrical venture which was at Hampton Court Palace in 1718. My thought was that if it were possible to discover the staging conditions with which Thornhill provided Colley Cibber and the King's Company of Comedians for their seven plays in the Great Hall [3], one might be able to suggest that similar conditions existed at Drury Lane. In much the same way one tries to deduce the methods of the King's Men who, before the Civil War, played their repertoire in the Globe, Blackfriars and the Cockpit-in-Court as well as in the Great Hall in Hampton Court. The likelihood that conditions were similar is stimulated by the wording of the advertisements found in the *Daily Courant* during late September and October 1718, for the performances at Drury Lane. From the *Daily Courant* No. 5298, Tuesday, 14 October 1718, we have this advertisement:

> This present Tuesday, being the 14th of October, will be presented *Love for Money; or, The Boarding School* as it was acted yesterday before His Majesty at Hampton Court. With several entertainments of dancing proper to the play by Mr. Thurmond, Mr. Topham, Mrs. Bicknell, Mrs. Teno, Miss Smith and Miss Lindar.

Furthermore, apart from one performance in 1731, again by the Drury Lane Company, the seven plays in 1718 were the last chapter in the dramatic records of command performances at Hampton Court. The last words regarding Thornhill's theatre in the Great Hall are to be found at the end of the century, when we are told,

> The stage, nevertheless, continued to block up the hall till the year 1798 when James Wyatt, then Surveyor General of the Board of Works, obtained of George III permission to remove it which was accordingly done and the hall restored to its original form and beauty as we see it now. [4]

Throughout the whole examination of this problem, I have been repeatedly drawn back to the fact that there are two major problems when organizing the material, the first one of attribution, the second of scale (particularly when trying to arrange 'The 1st Great flat Scene' (pl. 9) and the 'State Bedroom' (pl. 8) designs into the Hampton Court stage). Moreover, I have gained increasingly the impression that all these drawings are associated with the one production, that is, *Arsinoë*, and therefore that all provide information regarding the theatre of Drury Lane in 1705, rather than that in the Great Hall of Hampton Court in 1718.

All my suggestions regarding Drury Lane are, at the moment, based entirely upon Thornhill's drawings and contemporary observations; I have not, as yet, entered upon any textual analysis of the plays performed at Drury Lane, nor have I pursued the changes wrought upon Drury Lane after 1747.

If, as I shall try to show, all of these drawings are related to the 1705 production of *Arsinoë* at the Theatre Royal, Drury Lane, then the most important sketch is that of the proscenium arch from Thornhill's *Sketchbook* (recto 46) (pl. 7), for it reintroduces the controversial problem of the design of that playhouse. What I am suggesting is that Thornhill has given us a key to partially solving the riddle which surrounds the acceptance of one of four designs for a playhouse attributed to Sir Christopher Wren, or to Webb. The probability arises that the All Souls drawing (Vol. IV, 81) (pl. 11) is, with modification, the more likely plan for the Theatre Royal than that currently accepted (Vol. II, 81) (pl. 10).

I should like first to examine those sketches which we definitely know to be designs for *Arsinoë*, considering them as designs in a state of flux, how they relate to one another, how they work technically and how they relate to the text; second, I should like to trace the manner in which they arise out of the very rough sketches in the *Sketchbook*, and how the finished designs emerge from the sketched scene; and third, to show how these finished designs take their place in the proscenium arch drawn in the *Sketchbook*. In conclusion, we can consider that proscenium in relation to the Wren groundplan and contemporary observations on the building. All the works illustrated here are generally accepted as the work of James Thornhill. Their precise dates are not all known and are partially conjecture, and not all sketches are definitely accepted as designs for *Arsinoë*. The designs are drawn from the collections in the British Museum, Victoria and Albert Museum, and the Art Institute of Chicago.

The works from the *Sketchbook* are difficult to date because the binding did not take into account the date of execution, and only four drawings have dates upon them. Further, some pages are obviously trimmed. The only authority who hazards attribution is W. R. Osman in an unpublished thesis on the work of James Thornhill [5], and he is supported by E. Croft-Murray, Keeper of Prints and Drawings at the British Museum and an authority on English decorative painting [6].

There are three rough sketches of full sets in the Print Room of the Victoria and Albert Museum. They are definitely labelled *Arsinoë*; they show Act and Scene numbers and sometimes give additional information. The fourth gives the Act and Scene, that is, Act II scene i, but not the name of the opera.

The finished sketch, which I shall call '13 Pots', 'The 1st Great flat Scene' (pl. 9), the *Sketchbook* sketch for the same set, and the 'State Bedroom' (pl. 8) are not placed, although Mayhew [7] and Southern [8] link 'The 1st Great flat Scene' with the 'State Bedroom' and attribute these to the Hampton Court Theatre in 1718. If one accepts temporarily that they are all from *Arsinoë*, these drawings appear to me to be three different stages in Thornhill's progress towards the finished design for the production at the Theatre Royal, Drury Lane. I shall begin with scenes which are more carefully worked up but not completely resolved. I should point out that the text is ordered according to the continental system of scene numbering, whereas Thornhill adopts a numbering consistent with the scene changes.

First amongst this group is a garden, Act I scene i (pl. 3). This scene does duty also for scenes ii, iii, iv and v. The drawing appears to have on the prompt side, wings I and II, tall trimmed hedges or rusticated stone with sculptured fountains. Both wings have archways; both develop into trees linking with cloud borders, the darker tone indicating the top of hedgery which is in perspective. The individual shapes of the flats is penned in, as are the sky borders: the rough stage acting area is also indicated. Although the flats are painted to give the impression of a third dimension there is a line at the base and the top of the flat to indicate its two-dimensional structure. An interesting point is that the base line suggests an oblique system for the grooves (i.e. they do not run 'on and off', but are angled). This is the only design in which such a technique is suggested. Thornhill may have been influenced on this occasion by his knowledge of Andrea Pozzo's work *Prospettiva de Pittori ed Architetti* (1692–1700), for it is likely that he was in the company of John James before he worked with him at Greenwich and before James published his translation of Pozzo's work in 1707. Wing III is difficult to define clearly; it seems to be heavily profiled, describing trees and their boughs rising from behind a balustrade terminating in a pedestal with ornamental urns. The top of this wing grows into a cloud border as do the others.

All the wings and borders have pencil lines underneath, clearly indicating the relationship between the border and the wing. This pencil line is sketched in in a gentle curve, arching over the stage. Wing III on the O.P. is designed symmetrically with wing III on the P.S. But wings I and II O.P. are of a different design to the wings on P.S. I and II, depicting balustrades at their foot upon which stand tall sculptured figures, and behind them grow trees to meet the cloud borders. This suggests an early stage in the designing, for it is difficult to know whether Thornhill is offering two possible designs in the same sketch or not. Later we shall see that in other plans he gives the same design to both sides of the stage. Each wing also seems to have an arch either cut into it or painted on. The wings on this side appear more three-dimensional, or more Serlian, but on the other hand, are more loosely carried out. The scene is lit from stage right, as are all the sketches, and it is indicated in the notes to be 'by moon light'.

Beyond these flats, moving upstage, is an almost symmetrically designed garden with a fountain at the centre in the middle distance, and beyond a classical piece of architecture around which are trees, and beyond that a great range of hills move off into the distance, in style reminiscent of Poussin, a painter whose work Thornhill admired. The drawing and shading seem to indicate a step linking the wings P.S. and O.P. III. James Laver [9] draws attention to these steps, and seem to think them real. Alternatively, we could imagine them as painted on the shutter, and Thornhill employs them in order to move off the stage and onto the shutter into the middle distance more effectively. But a certain weight may be added to Laver's suggestion in that the steps appear in all full-stage scenes. The problem which I cannot answer now, as to whether or not the steps were a permanent feature or related to the shutter system, depends upon the manner in which the stage was built.

There are several interesting technical points to note. First, there is a dotted line running vertically through the steps at the base up the centre of the lawn, garden and sky, all this suggesting a shutter scene. Secondly, as the vertical line is up the whole back scene it is not likely to be a relieve scene, although it would not be difficult to make it one. Thirdly, there is a pencil arch shape over this back scene which might give the impression that there was not a set of wings in position III. For at the O.P. side it relates to the wing O.P. III but, and here lies the problem, on the prompt side it appears well on stage, suggesting that it is an arch set upstage of wing P.S. III on which there is painted a part of the total landscape which then marries with the pattern of the scene. But I would imagine that this pencilled arch gives Thornhill a rough guide to the composition of the set as a whole. We shall see that all the scenes terminate in this arch over the stage. I should mention further the pencil lines from the downstage corners of the sketch which go to the pencilled arch in the shutter. I interpret these lines as Thornhill's attempt in the composition to relate the trees and landscape to a dominating feature such as a large elliptical arch downstage.

Whether the scene was ultimately symmetrical or not we do not know, but clearly it need not have been if Thornhill worked through the permutations allowed, if wings of other scenes were used in conjunction with this, or again if these were specifically kept for this scene and not used again. We shall see the possibility of this in Act II scene iii and the unplaced sketch '13 Pots'. The bed seems to be a practical piece of furniture.

The next scene (pl. 4) is Act I scene iii, entitled 'Room of State'. This scene does duty for Act I scenes ix, x, xi, as well as Act III scenes i and ii. This 'Room of State', or 'The Queen's Apartment' as it is called in the text, necessitates the removal of scene i completely, and in its place are set on the P.S. three wings showing an interior, a Room of State and Arsinoë on another couch. Wings, designed in perspective, show deeply arched and recessed alcoves with, on the on-stage side, coupled pilasters supporting a heavy cornice, and above an arched coffered soffit. Before the pilasters stand pedestals with standing figures upon them once again. But this treatment does give a broken and more interesting profile to the flats. On this occasion the wings are more definitely set in the 'on and off' position. All borders appear to be heavy drapes or arches in place of the cloud and tree borders.

With regard to the O.P. side we appear to have a problem. This could be one long flat wall, but I think not. It is the artist's impression of the real State Room which he then adapts to theatrical form on the P.S. side, and it is fairly normal to start on the left of the page and alter on the way across as alternative possibilities occur to the artist. This is an interesting point to remember, when we recall the frontispiece to the text of *Ariadne*, indicating, as it does, two such walls. The back scene here gives us several problems which I believe are resolved by a consideration of the more finished sketch, a 'State Bedroom' (pl. 8), which could serve as a 'Room of State', with a bed painted and a couch supplied further downstage. It seems that in the sketch Thornhill has been carried away and indulged himself; 'statues and bustoes', vases, alcoves and niches appear in profusion. The design is overburdened with these objects and yet they are not central. What is central is an empty alcove housing nothing. But this alcove is framed by an arch, the supports of which are organized to relate to the wings downstage. The step at the foot of the back scene which we have previously observed is also shown. But I will return to this scene later to suggest that the finished 'State Bedroom' sketch, attributed to Hampton Court, is in fact the back shutter for *Arsinoë*, Act I scene iii.

The next scene (pl. 5), Act II scene i, described as 'A Great Hall looking out on a Garden', serves also for scenes ii, iii, iv, and possibly scenes v and vi. This is not labelled for *Arsinoë*, but such a scene would answer the direction of place in the text. In this design the three wings O.P. and P.S. are clearly indicated as columns, supporting a heavy vaulted ceiling, each border's edge becoming the coffered soffit of an elliptical arch and so measuring off the bays of the chamber, until we find, upon moving upstage, the arch gives onto a well-regulated garden, an ornamental pond, a river, and on the far bank poplars and a distant mountain range, all painted on a shutter. Again we find a vertical line, heavily inked at the centre of the base, which we take to indicate the join of the shutter. This whole design seems quite established in Thornhill's mind for both sides are symmetrical on this occasion. There is also downstage a heavy swag of material, which could possibly be the same as the border used in a previous scene, adding a touch of colour.

We now move on to Act II scene iii, 'Arsinoë in a fine Garden' (pl. 6), which in the text is Act II scenes viii, ix, and x. What happens in the scene change is that the tree wings replace the columns and the sky borders replace the vaulting. The new back shutter shows a new garden, 'with ships, haven, etc., and a distance'. There is, as ever, a mark struck on the horizon almost centre; there are also the pencilled lines suggesting the under-drawing for wings and the arch form of the cloud borders. Possibly at one time Thornhill thought of having poplars on the shutters in this scene as well as in the previous garden scene, then thought better of it, and broke the monotony by changing to rounder forms. On the other hand, the shutter used for Act II scene i might have been modified to do duty for Act II scene iii also.

If the finished sketch, '13 Pots' [10], has any place in *Arsinoë*, it could have been Act II scene vii for a little comic bawdy scene coming between the palace hall and the garden scene. This design shows only two wings before the shutter. All the other sets have three wings and then a shutter, thus suggesting that there was a shutter at the mid-stage position. This design does seem, however, to have a different proportion when compared with the others. The basic scenic method would therefore seem to be three sets of grooves each side of the stage for the wings. The grooves are set 'on and off' stage, and there is a shutter system beyond the third set of wings. There is possibly also a second shutter system upstage of the second set of wings. Each series of wings and shutters has its own set of borders. All this one would of course expect to find, though I would have expected, considering the depth of the stage, another set of grooves. One could possibly interpret Colley Cibber's remark [11] — 'That where the Doors of Entrance now are, there formerly stood two additional Side-Wings, in front to a full Set of Scenes, which had then almost a double Effect in their Loftiness and Magnificence' — to mean that the 'additional Interposition of those Stage-Boxes' causes the first set of wings to be removed in favour of the new entrance doors, thus leaving the three sets of grooves which Thornhill employs, but until I have completed the reconstruction of the set I cannot be sure. The possibility that there were further shutters upstage of the main shutter in order to create a more spectacular relieve scene should not be ruled out, for there is ample depth to accommodate such scenes.

We do not have the designs for four other scenes in *Arsinoë* but we might reduce this lack to two, if we doubled some of the scenes. We do not have Dorisbe's apartment nor a prison scene. One suggestion is that for these and maybe for the others, Drury Lane's stock was employed. Returning now to the sketch for the 'State Bedroom' (pl. 8), I would like to suggest that this drawing is Thornhill's final design for the Act I scene iii shutter. My reasons for this are two. First, if we accept this scene as a shutter, it is far too large to be operated at Hampton Court, where the width of the hall is only 40 ft. For, if we read the scale of '17 ft. 6 ins.' indicated on the side of the drawing, then the illegible 2? ft at the foot of the drawing would be 21 ft, which would require an operating width of at least 42 ft. For this scene to work at Hampton Court it would have to have been tumbled, which would have been an interesting early example of this technique of changing scenes. But more important are the elements of the composition of this drawing. Clearly this drawing, while it contains all the elements of the back scene in Act I scene iii, is also a refinement. The design is simpler in terms of architectural embellishment, while retaining the alcove for the bed, the alcoves for the statues of Apollo and Diana, and also the pilasters which link with the columns in the foreground in a more simplified form. These columns link, in turn, in perspective with wings and borders of a similar design in grooves further downstage towards the proscenium. At the same time Thornhill has achieved more successfully a much greater impression of depth. This is aided again by the appearance of the step up into the bed area, which might relate to the step on the stage. One further design feature which links this design with those of *Arsinoë* is that of the method Thornhill adopts of using the elliptical arch which diminishes, in perspective, to the more round-headed arch centre back. This relates the design to Drury Lane therefore, and gives us a measured drawing for the same, though it may be a back shutter measuring overall 21 ft by 20 ft.

If we turn our attention now to 'The 1st Great flat Scene' (pl. 9), we have before us another scale drawing. Richard Southern in *Changeable Scenery* [12] does not attribute it to any particular play, but describes an elaborate process for changing this decoration and considers it as an upstage shutter. If this were so, and Richard Southern argues convincingly for the shutter method of changing such a scene, then on the grounds of size alone this design could not be employed at Hampton Court. On the other hand, if it were tumbled then perhaps it could be, but I find several other points of disagreement with Richard Southern on this design, principally regarding the measurement of the drawing, but also as regards its structure and function. These differences suggest to me that this design was for the proscenium arch of Drury Lane and was used during the entertainment of singing and dancing before and after the opera *Arsinoë*. The subject matter has little to do with this opera, but is a typically Thornhill piece of decoration, employing architecture, sculpture, classical iconography, and, to crown it all, a deity in glory in the heavens, all features to figure in his later works. But I would argue that this is an early work in that here, more than anywhere else, his sources are barely concealed. In this instance

Thornhill has taken and reorganized a design from the pattern book of Daniel Marot [13]. The transformation is quite simple. Marot's design employs the same architectural structure but renders the stone in a rusticated manner, for, before it, Marot shows Neptune reigning in his horses as they plough through turbulent waves. It is the figure of the giant Neptune that fills Marot's central alcove which Thornhill replaces with Atlas, rather uncomfortably placed, bearing the world and surmounted by Peace supported by the regal emblems of the lion and unicorn. Neptune's horses are now managed by Venus who moves through the heavens over the clouds. Thornhill supplies the drapes and putti to do the stage management. He frames the whole design in such an unimaginative manner that one wonders why it is there. It was not included in his first thoughts, to which he keeps fairly faithfully, as is evidenced by the early pencil sketch [14]. But surely this stone arch is part of the scenery as opposed to the outer archway which similarly frames the whole piece. It is only penned in around the columns leaving the rest of the frame, still apparent, in pencil. I suggest that this outer arch with its supporting columns is the proscenium arch of Drury Lane in 1705. I accept Southern's interpretation of the scale line but apply it differently. Southern, I believe, measures from the base of the column, whereas I measure from the base of what I have described as the scenery. And, further, Southern does not accept the outer stone work as shutter but as part of a semi-permanent structure.

If, however, we apply the scale to the drawing then we find that the distance between the bases at the foot of the columns is 26 ft, and if we measure the vertical height at the centre of the sketch we find the figure is 31 ft. If we now turn to the pen and ink sketch of a proscenium arch to be found in the *Sketchbook* (pl. 7), we find that these same measurements occur, 26 ft at the base of what appears to be a column, and 31 ft to the underside of an elliptical arch. Presuming now that the 'State Bedroom' is a design for *Arsinoë* at Drury Lane, it can be shown that the ellipse of the main archway in this sketch is similar to that of 'The 1st Great flat Scene', and therefore to the outer archway on that same drawing. Thus I suggest that we have, admittedly very roughly drawn, an elevation with some vital measurements indicated upon it, of the Theatre Royal, Drury Lane. My impression is strengthened by the embellishment of what appears to be a royal coat of arms.

Before passing on to consider the implications of this rough sketch there are two further observations to consider when comparing this drawing and 'The 1st Great flat Scene'. First, both have round columns supporting the arch. The pen and ink sketch is drawn inaccurately with regard to the ordering of column, capital and entablature, but perhaps we should take this drawing as no more than the loosest of indications made by Thornhill for his own information, to be corrected later, when he develops the scale drawing. And this is done on 'The 1st Great flat Scene', for there we see the entablature correctly supported and carried out in some detail. Of still greater significance is the second point of similarity, that is that in both drawings the entablature appears to move in a graceful curve. In the drawing from the *Sketchbook* the cornice line curves as it moves from what I have described as the proscenium arch towards the auditorium, embracing the forestage. Overall, there is indicated a dome, the highest point of which is 40 ft above the stage. It is disappointing that there is no indication as to the stage door and boxes, probably because they did not affect Thornhill's design, but we are told that the whole breadth is '54 ft. 8'.

A site plan for Drury Lane at the time of the reconstruction after the fire of 25 January 1672 gives the width of the theatre as 60 ft. This had remained constant since the first building in 1663. If we accept Edward Langhans' [15] measurement of Wren's longitudinal section (pl. 10), in which he states that the walls approximate to 2 ft 9 ins thick then, by addition, we arrive at an overall breadth of 60 ft 2 ins, which figure only needs the correction of a rendering of plaster to satisfy the 60 ft overall requirement.

The real implication behind my suggestion is, that if we accept Cibber's word for Wren's authorship of Drury Lane, we should look for a plan that takes into account Thornhill's proscenium arch. The drawing that has generally been accepted, not without reservations, has been that suggested by Hamilton Bell [16] in 1913, namely Wren's section entitled 'Playhouse' (All Souls, Vol. II, 81) (pl. 10). But this drawing fails to show, in section, the proscenium drawn by Thornhill. If we continue to be guided by Cibber and upon his authority still accept Wren as the architect of the Theatre Royal, then I suggest that the All Souls plan, section and elevation, Vol. IV, 81 (pl. 11) comes in many ways closer to our requirements, for this drawing helps to answer many of the outstanding questions that the other plan fails to satisfy. Several points in its favour are that this drawing suggests a proscenium opening of approximately 26 ft, that is the distance between the bases of the columns in Thornhill's 'The 1st Great flat Scene', and has a curving arrangement for entrance doors and side boxes as well as a breadth of approximately 54 ft. Moreover, the length of the plan measures approximately 139 ft, which would allow for the purchase and addition to the building of the 28 ft of Vinegar Yard to the original 112 ft.

The section on this page reveals, all in pencil, the auditorium arrangements, the realization of the pencilled boxes on the plan, and the suggestion of the roof area. Then, in pencil, in the top left corner, there is a sketch of what looks like the proscenium arch of this planned theatre. Inside the archway is scrubbed the impression of a setting but the archway itself looks very much like the elliptical arch and columns in the Thornhill drawing. Two other points of similarity are the curving side doors and boxes and, of course, the suggestion of a dome overall. There are, therefore, a considerable number of features that bring together the Thornhill proscenium arch and the Wren plan and elevation.

Could it be possible that we now have the plan for the proscenium arch of the Theatre Royal, Drury Lane, of 1674 as well as the plans for the 1663 theatre possibly built by Webb and so heavily influenced by Inigo Jones, which we see here in the process of being redesigned by Wren after the fire? We are told by Hotson [17] that it was the back stage area that was most severely damaged, but I wonder if the fire actually destroyed the fundamentally classical structure of a basically circular drum into which a proscenium arch is cut and surmounted by a dome. This is the kind of structure one would expect from a close scrutiny of all these drawings, a building which, in style, reveals its dependence upon influences stretching back via Inigo Jones to Palladio, Serlio and Vitruvius. John Dryden mentions that it was only 'half destroyed by Fire' [18]. Hotson [19] tells us that the wind was south-westerly, which would mean that the fire was being blown away from the building. And, incidentally, the only part of this plan that is finished in ink is the auditorium.

If then we called this plan the Theatre Royal, Drury Lane or the Playhouse, how does it measure up to the comments of its contemporaries? How different is it from what I shall call Bell's drawing? First, there is the question of this domed ceiling over the house which is suggested by both Wren's plan and Thornhill's sketch, and yet does not appear on Bell's section. His drawing shows a flat, if slanting, ceiling, and above it a straightforward mansard roof.

To support my speculation I offer three corroborating pieces of evidence which suggest that the dome, or part of it, existed from 1664 until at least 1705 and possibly later. I shall take them in chronological order. First, there is the mention of a cupola in Samuel Pepys' *Diary*, when an entry for 1 May 1668 includes the comment, 'To the King's Playhouse, and there saw the *Surprisal*; and a disorder in the pit by its raining in from the cupola at top, it being a very foul day' [20]. This note, as I have mentioned, is dated 1668, that is, before the alterations caused by the fire. Second, there is to be taken into account the rather primitive drawing of the Theatre Royal to be seen on the extract from Ogilby and Morgan's map of 1681–2 (pl. 12). Here, however simple the portrayal, a dome clearly rises over the rooftop. Indeed the draughtsman has gone to some trouble to make this feature clear, for he has crosshatched the background. This would suggest that the dome was still there several years after the reconstruction of 1672–4. The final piece of evidence comes in the form of a song from the second volume of *Penkethman's Jests* published in 1721. The first verse tells us that

> Near famous Covent Garden,
> A Dome there stands on high;
> With a fa, la, la, la, la, etc.
> Where Kings are represented,
> And Queens in metre die,
> With a fa, la, la, la, la, etc. [21]

We could further hazard that apart from the motto 'Vivitur Ingenio' over the stage there was also written, 'That All the world are in effect but players', 'This apt as well as common saying', says the editor of Wilks' *Memoirs* in 1732, 'adorns with great propriety the roof of one of our Theatres' [22]. It will be remembered that Wilks was a member of the Drury Lane Company.

It is possible that in a subsequent alteration to the theatre the dome was left but its light, if it were glazed which has been suggested, was blocked by the hanging of a flat roof over the auditorium, while maintaining the existence of the original proscenium arch, but I cannot enter into that possibility now.

If we now accept Thornhill's proscenium arch as that of Drury Lane, then Bell's section does not show such an arch and all endeavours to reconstruct Bell's section have resulted in a flat, squared off entablature spanning the gap. But Bell himself had reservations regarding this point when considering the *Ariadne* engraving [23], suggesting that the arch in the drawing was scenic and two-dimensional. This notion I would support, since this arch is a painted valance and the artist has left out the elliptical arch surrounding the piece of scenery. My only suggestion is that he was working up a plate to be placed on a square page and thought his composition adequate. On the other hand the plan with the sketched proscenium arch does seem to echo Thornhill's drawing.

The highly controversial subject of entrance doors I cannot deal with here, but it seems to me that if we develop the suggestions offered by the section and thumbnail sketch on the Wren plan (pl.11), we could come to an interpretation of Colley Cibber's statement regarding the alterations effected by Wren in 1672 and Christopher Rich in 1696.

With regard to the auditorium, Wren's plan rather than Bell's section would appear to measure up to the observation of Henri Misson in 1698:

> The pit is an Amphitheatre, fill'd with Benches without Backboards, and adorn'd and covered with green cloth. . . . Farther up, against the wall, under the first Gallery, and just opposite to the Stage, rises another Amphitheatre. The Galleries, whereof there are only two rows, are fill'd with none but ordinary People, particularly the Upper One. [24]

Further, in *A Critical Review of Public Buildings*, 1734, the author states that 'the division in the middle was an absurdity'; the Wren plan, which shows a division in the pit, might provoke such criticism.

Such a division would seem to be an inheritance from the Court theatres where one finds this aisle leading from the stage to the royal dais which is shown on the drawing. Possibly one of the methods Garrick and Lacy adopted in order to increase the capacity of the house was to bridge this gap with benches, though the raised platform for the king and patron had probably been removed at a much earlier date.

I realize that these speculations are still in need of much more research before they can be accepted, and this paper is really a progress report. But I offer them to you for consideration, for they do help to shed some light, if only dimly, upon 'that plain built house' and 'mean ungilded stage', 'a bare convenience' [25], for which Dryden apologized upon the opening of the theatre in 1674.

Notes

[1] A. Nicoll, *The Development of the Theatre* (London, Harrap, 1949), 165, fig. 195.

[2] C. Cibber, *An Apology for the Life of Mr. Colley Cibber*, ed. R. W. Lowe (London, 1889), II, 82.

[3] ibid., II, 208–9.

[4] D. Lysons, *Lysons' Middlesex Parishes* (London, 1800), 67.

[5] W. R. Osman, 'A Study of the Work of Sir James Thornhill' (University of London Thesis, 1950).

[6] E. Croft-Murray, *Decorative Painting in England, 1537–1837* (London, Country Life, 1962).

[7] E. de N. Mayhew, *Sketches by Thornhill in the Victoria and Albert Museum* (London, H.M.S.O., 1967), 11.

[8] R. Southern, *Changeable Scenery* (London, Faber, 1952), 177.

[9] James Laver, 'Some Unknown Theatrical Designs by Thornhill', *Mimus und Logos* (Emsdetta, 1952).

[10] Victoria and Albert Museum, sketch D.29–1891.

[11] Cibber, op. cit., II, 85.

[12] Southern, op. cit., 177–82.

[13] Daniel Marot, *Das Ornamentwerk des D. Marot* (Berlin, 1892), 43.

[14] Thornhill *Sketchbook*, recto 50 (prints and drawings), BM 100240/1/201.6.8.

[15] E. A. Langhans, 'Wren's Restoration Playhouse', *Theatre Notebook*, XVIII, No. 3 (1964), 91.

[16] H. Bell, 'Contributions to the History of the English Playhouse', *The Architectural Record*, XXXII (1913), 359–68.

[17] L. Hotson, *The Commonwealth and Restoration Stage* (Harvard U.P., Cambridge, Mass., 1928), 253.

[18] J. Dryden, *The Prologues and Epilogues of John Dryden*, ed. W. Bradford Gardner (New York, Columbia U.P., 1951), 60.

[19] Hotson, op. cit., 253.

[20] H. McAfee, *Pepys on the Restoration Stage* (London, Oxford U.P., 1916), 300.

[21] *Penkethman's Jests* (London, 1721), II, 35.

[22] R. Wilks, *Memoirs of the Life of Robert Wilks* (London, 1732), 1.

[23] Nicoll, op. cit., 165, fig. 195.

[24] H. Misson, *Misson's Memoirs and Observations in His Travels ove; England*, trans. Mr Ozell (London, 1719), 219–20.

[25] Dryden, op. cit., 60.

Acknowledgements

I gratefully acknowledge permission to reproduce the illustrations, which has been granted by the Warden and Fellows of All Souls College, Oxford (plates 10 and 11); The Trustees of the British Museum (plates 7 and 12); The Victoria and Albert Museum (plates 3, 4, 5, 6 and 8); and the Art Institute of Chicago (plate 9).

Plates

1 John Inigo Richards's scene for *The Maid of the Mill*, 1768.

2 Philip James De Loutherbourg's scene for *A Christmas Tale*, 1773

3 Thornhill's 'Garden by Moonlight' (*Arsinoë*, Act I scene i).

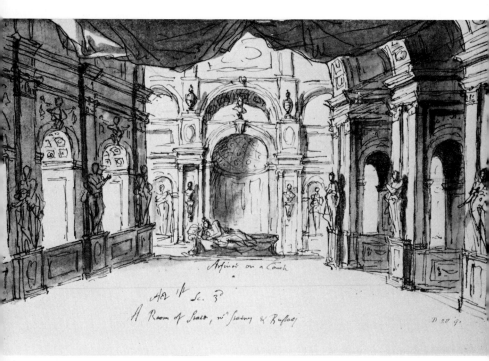

4 Thornhill's 'A Room of State' (*Arsinoë*, Act I scene iii).

5 Thornhill's 'A Great Hall looking out on a Garden' (*Arsinoë*, Act II scene i).

6 Thornhill's 'Arsinoë in a fine Garden' (*Arsinoë*, Act II scene iii).

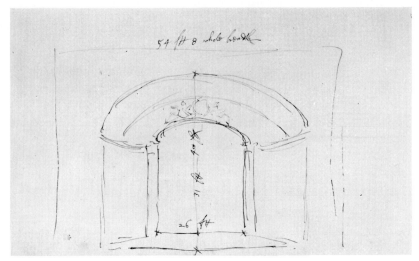

7 Thornhill's sketch for a proscenium arch (*Sketchbook*, recto 46).

8 Thornhill's 'A State Bedroom'.

9 Thornhill's 'The 1st Great flat Scene'.

10 Wren drawing from All Souls, Oxford, (Vol. II, 81), showing longitudinal section for a playhouse.

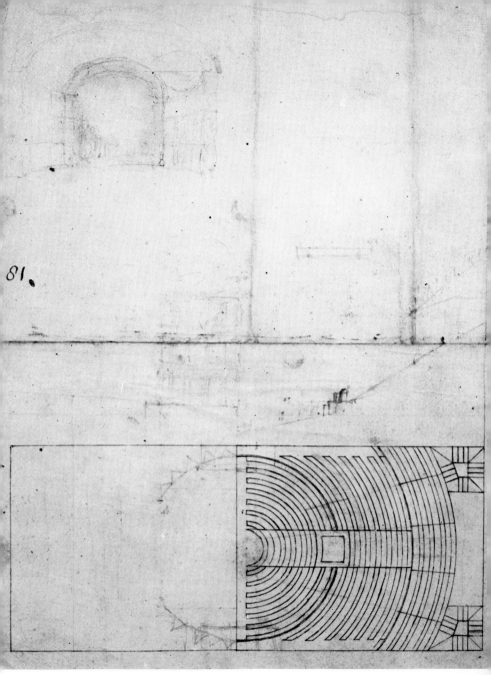

11 Wren drawing from All Souls, Oxford (Vol. IV, 81), for a playhouse
on the antique Roman model.

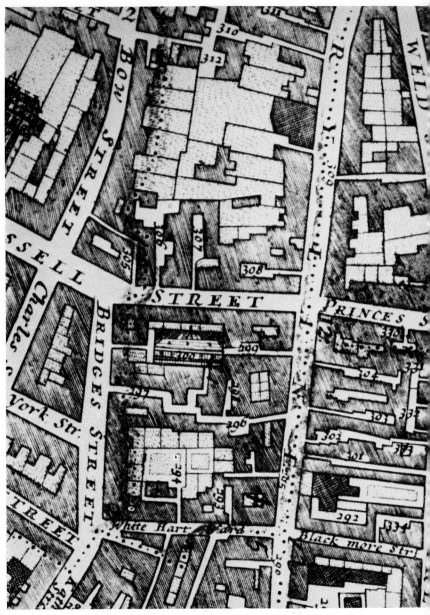

12 Extract from Ogilby and Morgan's map of 1681-2 showing Drury Lane Theatre.